It's Only
Slow Food
Until You
Try to Eat It

Also by Bill Heavey

If You Didn't Bring Jerky, What Did I Just Eat?:
Misadventures in Hunting, Fishing, and the Wilds of Suburbia

It's Only Slow Food Until You Try to Eat It

Misadventures of a Suburban
Hunter-Gatherer

Bill Heavey

Atlantic Monthly Press
New York

Published simultaneously in Canada
Printed in the United States of America

FIRST EDITION

ISBN-13: 978-0-8021-1955-1

Atlantic Monthly Press
an imprint of Grove/Atlantic, Inc.
841 Broadway
New York, NY 10003

Distributed by Publishers Group West

www.groveatlantic.com

13 14   10 9 8 7 6 5 4 3 2 1

For Michelle

Contents

Introduction:
How Hard Could it Be?

As the buck rises from its bed in the underbrush forty yards away, every cell in my body decides to attempt a jailbreak. I'm twenty-four feet up a tulip poplar in my hunting stand, where I've been concealed for the past four hours. I would very much like to come to my feet but my legs are shaking too hard. They aren't my legs anymore.

I'm drowning. I simply can't suck in air fast enough to keep up with my body's needs. And I haven't moved a muscle. Meanwhile, the small percentage of brain still under my control is grappling with the fact that I've been sitting as motionless as possible all afternoon, watching and waiting for a deer, *and this buck has been here the whole time.*

The interruption in muscle service shows no sign of letting up. I want to stand. I want to be able to pull back the string of my bow and be ready should the deer come my way. But first somebody needs to persuade my legs to stop auditioning for *A Chorus Line.*

I double down on my efforts to pull myself together, and it's the impossibility of this task, by which I realize that I'm now in an out-of-body state. The deer seems to exist in a tunnel, alone and apart from all other things. I distinctly note the nap of the deer's hair—how it lies in one direction along its back, the opposite direction at the juncture of chest and shoulder. The buck drops its antlered head almost to the ground and stretches its entire body. And then freezes. It becomes a lawn statue.

I'm certain that the buck will hear—as I can—the timpani of my heart or the way I'm gulping air like they won't be making more

1

anytime soon. I know that this is the fight-or-flight response, the body's response to a life-or-death situation. And it would make perfect sense were I some early hominid out picking berries who suddenly found himself face-to-face with a giant hyena. But I'm not. This deer poses no threat to me. It's not even aware of my existence. And if it were, *it* would be the one to run. But it doesn't. It just stands there.

Whence the physiological ruckus?

It's because I'm hunting this deer. I've come to these woods seeking its life. Not this particular one, but any legal deer to be found in this place. This is my third fall spent trying to kill one with a bow and arrow. I've never come this close before. That I might carry out the act has lit up more than just the fight-or-flight response. There's more to it than that. Because while I've never done this before, there is nevertheless something familiar about it. As if all along I've had this neural pathway, this hunter's hardwiring inside me, but had never hooked it up until this moment. In the days to come I will reexamine these feelings and conclude that I'm right, that this wiring is extant in all of us, but latent. Inactive in all but the few who choose to hunt large animals at close range. In the days to come, I will increasingly feel that I'm going down a path trod by others before me.

Think about it. "Anatomically modern" humans—people who look like us, minus smart phones—date back about 200,000 years. We'd like to think we're recent models, and although we are, evolutionarily speaking, that's still an awfully long time without an upgrade. For 95 percent of that time, all but the last 10,000 years, we lived in small groups of nomadic hunter-gatherers. And we survived, or didn't, by our abilities as hunters. Which means that everyone alive today—from the worst slob hunter to the most radical PETA activist—is the direct descendant of a long line of master hunters. Because if your ancestors hadn't excelled as hunters they wouldn't have been around long enough to pass their genes on to you.

Certainly no member of the Heavey clan has hunted for four generations, which is as far back as any of us remembers. When I was growing up, the thought of becoming a hunter crossed my mind about as often as becoming a Hindu. I came to hunting late—in my thirties—and by the most circuitous of routes. As a freelance writer, I wrote travel stories, features, and profiles. I had fished in summer camps as a boy and rediscovered fishing when some friends gave me a spinning rod for my twenty-first birthday. A story I wrote about fishing the rivers around D.C. ran in the *Washington Post Magazine*.

In the manner of freelancers everywhere, who are always in search of larger, more lucrative markets, I sent a copy to *Field & Stream*. It wasn't long before I was writing regularly about fishing for the country's oldest hook-and-bullet magazine. But fishing, the hook, was only half of what the magazine covered. If I wrote about hunting, the bullet, I could double my market. Only I didn't want to hunt with bullets. From what little I knew, it was not particularly difficult to wait in an elevated box overlooking a field of corn or soybeans for a deer to show itself and shoot it from 200 yards. This didn't appeal to me. But having to get close—say, within twenty-five yards—and using a bow and arrow, did. Not everyone thought this was a great idea. "How could you kill an innocent animal?" my mother asked one night over dinner. I pointed out that we were having veal. "That's different," she said.

Having no friends who hunted, I went at it solo, not the fastest way to learn. But I'm stubborn and have a high tolerance for failure. I kept at it. Almost in spite of myself, I learned a lot sitting like a monk in the woods in my climbing treestand. The most surprising thing I learned was that I actually liked hunting. I'd been afraid I'd find it boring. It wasn't. Not at all. There was a lot more to deer hunting than I'd thought. If you live in the suburbs and routinely arrive home to find deer chowing down on your expensive landscaping, killing a deer would seem about as easy as rolling down the window. After all, you can run at those deer screaming bloody murder and waving your arms, and all they do is amble off a ways, maybe into a neighbor's yard, and wait for you to go inside. At which point they return and resume eating. An animal that dumb couldn't be hard to hunt, right? Successfully, I mean. As a prey species, however, whitetails are experts at reading the intentions of potential predators. Those deer you just

3

chased know that you pose no real threat. If you did, you wouldn't be making all that noise. Real danger doesn't make a sound until it's too late.

What I loved about deer hunting was how it transforms you from an observer to a participant in the natural world. Clichéd as that sounds, it was true for me. When you're hunting, everything around you matters in a way it didn't before. The wind—which I'd never considered at all—suddenly becomes a matter of life and death. Deer apprehend the world primarily with their noses, just as we do with our eyes. A deer downwind of you will scent you—"bust you" is the hunter's term—and be gone before you ever see it. Period. On the other hand, if the deer is upwind of you, you're still in business. Unless, as often happens, the wind shifts.

Every sound also matters. The woods are a spiderweb, and when you enter, it's as a fly hitting that web. The animals throughout—seen and unseen—register your arrival and alert each other. Squirrels and birds are the loudest and most easily noticed by humans, but everything, including deer, know of your arrival. There's not much you can do about this. What you can do, once you have ratcheted your way up a tree, is sit quiet and still. Do this, and within fifteen or twenty minutes the woods will return to a baseline level of activity. The woods will absorb you. Sit still enough and a goldfinch will land on your chest, fluff and groom itself for a few seconds, and fly off, having mistaken you for a tree. Sitting motionless but present, alert to the wind on your skin and the intermittent patter of acorns falling, you may hear a sudden uptick in chatter among the birds and squirrels. Another fly has hit the web. Now you are one of the animals being alerted long before you see the intruder. It could be anything, including a deer.

I realized the very first time I hunted that I loved this state of state of consciousness, relaxed but aware. It was a kind of active meditation. There was something about it that was terribly compelling and grounding and exalted all at the same time. But entry into this world came at a price. You had to be hunting—I did, anyway—to achieve the transformation. "Hunting," incidentally, doesn't necessarily mean killing. You must, however, have the intention of killing if the opportunity presents itself. That's what makes it hunting.

This transforming intent is, of course, what has me so electrified at the moment.

The buck statue finally becomes animate again, wandering up the ridge to my right. This is good. At least the deer is upwind of me. My legs are still shaking hard but not as wildly. I'm able to stand. I reach and lift my bow from the hook that I screwed into the tree trunk to keep it handy. I do this in super slow motion, taking the better part of a minute. And then I watch, heartsick, as the buck, a five-pointer, wanders into the brush and disappears. I am devastated, but remain standing. Unless you have a good reason to move, you don't. I have no idea what the buck is up to, whether he's going off to feed somewhere far away or is rather cruising, sniffing the air for a doe in heat. It's November, the mating season, when the rush of hormones causes deer to let down their guard a little. It's not impossible that the buck will come back this way. As may other deer. Or no deer at all.

I don't know how long I stand there before there are footfalls in the leaves behind me. It's deer. It's definitely not squirrels, which move brusquely and are much louder than deer. By the cadence I know that these deer—I'm pretty sure it's more than one—are at ease. They're walking but have no pressing appointments. They're ambling along, maybe grazing as they amble. It's too late for me to turn around. Deer don't resolve detail particularly well but are uncanny at zeroing in on the slightest movement. So I freeze. Moments later, a doe, her tail sticking nearly straight out, something I've never seen before, passes almost directly beneath my stand. Following right behind her is the buck, its nose right under the doe's raised tail. He's actually trying to perform a sex act with the doe that was illegal in Virginia until 2003. This is something else I've never seen.

For the next half hour, the doe leads the buck in slow loops and figure eights all over the ridge. She must be right on the verge of being ready. My problem is that while they have come within range several times, I haven't had the angle for a shot. I've drawn, been ready to shoot, but let the bow down each time. A bowhunter's only ethical shot is when the deer is broadside or quartering slightly away. Only then is the heart-lung area unobstructed by heavy muscle and bone. You aim for a spot in the center of an area about the size of cantaloupe just behind the shoulder.

The light has started to fade as the doe turns again and circles back. I draw again. But this time, the doe turns broadside and the buck mirrors her movement. They are all of eight yards away. I aim, noting the burrs sticking to the buck's coat just below where I want my arrow to go. I shoot. A compound bow releases a solid thunk of stored energy at the shot. The doe startles reflexively but doesn't alter stride. The buck, his nose still right under her raised tail, doesn't react at all. He neither breaks stride nor lifts nor drops his head. The two keep going as if nothing has happened and are gone from sight in seconds. *You can't have missed him,* I wail silently. *Not at eight yards.* I can't have missed. It's not possible. But there's no other explanation. And then a slight rustling in the leaves from the direction they took. Then a single click, even fainter, yet distinct. Then silence. An image of a hoof striking stone arises in my mind. I don't move for an eternity, during which I hear no deer sounds at all. In a few minutes it will be dark dark. Too dark to register even the white bark of a sycamore tree. At last, in the utter silence, I lower my bow on a rope to the ground and quietly climb down.

Wearing the headlamp I carry in my pack, I find my arrow sticking out of the dirt at precisely the angle I shot, as if it has penetrated nothing more substantial than air. But as I pull the shaft from the ground, I feel that it's slick, then see the blood coating it. I look in the direction the deer walked and find a few feet away a dark medallion of blood on the leaves. Droplets on the leaves lead to another medallion ten feet farther on. Fifteen yards from where I shot it lies the buck. I touch his flank and see the entry wound on his left side. I roll the body over and see the exit wound on the other side. I made a perfect shot. The arrow passed through the deer as if through air. The buck never even knew he'd been shot. He was alive and dogging that doe until he felt weak, staggered—click!—and died. It is as clean a kill as you can hope to make.

Elation and euphoria are flooding me. I start to cry out, "Yes!" but my voice instantly sounds wrong here, a transgression, and I swallow the word before it escapes my lips. As if this joy must not be spoken aloud. I had wondered how it would feel to kill an innocent animal and now I know. It feels fantastic. It feels great. After hundreds of hours—learning to shoot a bow, to sit quietly in the woods, to read deer signs, and to accept failure—I've finally killed a buck. I have at last been validated, initiated into the ranks of successful hunters. It feels awesome, in both the modern and the archaic senses. I'm overwhelmed by the gravity of what has just happened and by the wonder and shock I feel at the fact that it *has* happened. I feel incredibly alive and vivid in this most mysterious and improbable of worlds. I kneel and stoke the buck's flank. I apologize for taking its life. I murmur, "Thank you," to the deer.

That night, I remove the tenderloins, the two prime strips of meat that lie along a deer's backbone. I rub them with garlic, olive oil, salt, and pepper. I broil them in the oven, open a bottle of wine, and slice a loaf of French bread. The meat, the whole meal, are fantastic. Venison is denser and more finely grained than beef. It has a different flavor. This must be what people speak of as the "gamy" taste. I like the gamy taste. It's something to enhance rather than disguise. The Indians used to speak of "making meat," a phrase I had once thought awkward and now find apt. To put on a plate and eat the cooked flesh of an animal you sought, killed, and brought home is a quietly powerful experience, one not easily described. It's unlike anything else I've ever done, and it's full of interlocking opposites: pride and humility, exhilaration and contrition. It's an experience that everyone ought to have at least once. Although when I try to imagine any of my friends doing this, I can't.

There was, I realized later, something subversive about what I had done. Food is energy. Energy is power. And in killing my own meat, I had taken back power from those who usually exercise it. Once I started adding up the people and entities I had ripped off, there seemed no end to them. No government inspector had stamped my deer. No chain of agribusinesses had raised the animal on a farm and transported it to a

7

feedlot. No feedlot hands had administered the hormones and antibi-otics that allow a cow to eat the diet of corn by-products and grains that fatten it up by 400 pounds in three or four months as it stands knee-deep in its own shit in a crowded pen. No one had loaded the deer onto a truck for the ride to the slaughterhouse or to the butcher. Not to mention the chain of wholesalers and buyers and distributors and truckers who did not handle it on the way to its final commercial destination—shrink-wrapped on a pure white Styrofoam tablet and bathed in the fluorescent light of the supermarket.

The subversiveness of my actions appealed to me. I'd cut out the middlemen, done an end run on the bureaucracy that decides what is fit to eat. I'd gone to the source.

At the same time, I wasn't out to take on Monsanto or ADM. I didn't want to change the world. I was, however, curious about whether the experiences I'd had hunting my own meat had corollaries in other kinds of food. Wild plants, for example. Or plants you grew yourself. A vegetable garden. I knew nothing of either of these. Actually, that wasn't quite true. I recalled being in the woods along the Potomac River with Paula Smith, a woman I'd met at Fletcher's Boathouse, a hangout for anglers along the river. We'd been out looking for shed antlers—every year bucks drop their antlers in the winter and grow a new set. We hadn't found any sheds, but when we had almost returned to the boathouse, Paula told me to hang on a moment. She waded into a bunch of low-growing greenery, produced a glove from the blue duffel bag she carried, put it on, and began tearing off handfuls of the plants and shoving them in a paper sack.

I walked over and picked one myself. Paula shouted at me but already my hand stung as if pricked by hundreds of needles. "You dumbass!" she hollered. "Why do you think they call 'em stinging nettles? Jesus, don't you know anything?"

I knew that my hand hurt a great deal. She explained that she was picking these for one of the Fletcher brothers who ran the boathouse and who liked to eat some stinging nettles each year as a "spring tonic." This was among the stranger things I'd ever heard. I asked who would be dumb enough to do intentionally to their tongue what I'd just done by accident to my hand.

"You dope. They don't sting once you cook 'em!" She went on to say that they were very nutritious and one of the first edible greens to appear in early spring. In the old days, the first fresh vegetables after a long winter were a big deal. "Ray's old school," she said, referring to the Fletcher brother in question. "So I bring him some. At least you won't grab 'em like that next time."

Paula lived in the house of Gordon Leisch, a retired fisheries biologist who liked to fish and whom I knew from the boathouse. He provided room and board in exchange for Paula's help renovating the place. As I got to know them, I realized that the two of them ate wild meat and fish almost exclusively. Gordon got two or three deer a year, either on his annual hunting trip to Nebraska with his son or from his brother, who lived farther out in Virginia. He also hunted wild turkey, waterfowl, and the occasional squirrel or rabbit. He and Paula fished the Chesapeake for rockfish, bluefish, spot, and perch in his seventeen-foot boat. I'd gone along with them a few times. They butchered the game and filleted the fish themselves, and stored it all in two big freezers.

Paula was about as eccentric as you could get and still be on the right side of crazy. What worried me occasionally was how well we got on with each other. We'd initially bonded over a shared love of finding dropped deer antlers. Deer antlers are like human fingerprints, no two alike. They've always fascinated *Homo sapiens,* which is why they figure in cave painting so prominently. To me, they're like distillations of the wild into bone sculptures that you can look for on the ground. I liked finding them. Paula, on the other hand, was obsessed with them. She loved them beyond reckoning.

It wasn't until another day when Paula and I were shed hunting in a small hunk of urban wasteland that I realized she knew more than just stinging nettles. It was a late spring day in a triangle of woods cut off from the rest of the world by major roads on each side. We nearly got run over just getting in. A tide line of litter thrown from car windows marked its outer edges. Two steps deeper in plunged you

9

into the dimness beneath the canopy of vine-choked trees. This was where people dumped bigger stuff—appliances, reclining chairs, mattresses, old kitchen cabinets, all the disposable trappings of modern life. It also happened to be the public land closest to Georgetown that the police didn't routinely check, so a fair number of homeless people who panhandled there made camps of tarps and plastic sheeting. We were here because it was also home to a herd of a dozen or so deer.

We saw the deer almost as soon as we entered. Accustomed to humans, they circled rather than fled, maintaining thirty yards and a protective screen of undergrowth between themselves and us. To me, this seemed odd. There were hungry people here and a ready supply of meat. But it was obvious that these deer were not hunted. My reverie was interrupted by Paula. "If you're a deer here, you eventually get hit by a car," Paula called back over her shoulder. "Why I usually don't find any decent fucking antlers in here. But deer're always here and you gotta look, know what I mean?" I followed Paula through the dense foliage.

Soon we were passing people who studiously avoided eye contact and all seemed to be wearing several coats even though it was anything but cold. Paula detoured around their camps, keeping a respectful distance. She had a nodding acquaintance with a few and was on a first-name basis with others. They evidently knew Paula and viewed her as a fundamentally different order of being from, say, me. I was just another outsider. Paula, on the other hand, was someone who understood the facts of their situation and didn't hold it against them. I wondered if she thought of me the same way these people thought of her. After all, I was from the world she had left long ago, the one in which people had careers, property, cars, and kids. Paula was a loner, owned almost nothing, and was a creature of the fringe.

Paula pressed on through the vines and bushes. I followed and we came out atop a rock ridge, where she removed her hat to wipe her brow. Her long black hair was cinched, per usual, into a tight ponytail, which she tucked down inside her shirt. "This place fills up this time of year. See, they throw the homeless out of the shelters on March first. It's like an explosion."

She kicked at some trash at her feet and shook her head. "Used to have a better class of homeless, you know? I'm not saying they were model citizens or anything, but they didn't just throw their trash everywhere like they do nowadays."

We descended toward a wet area. There were deer droppings everywhere, but that in itself didn't mean anything in terms of shed antlers; it just meant that deer liked to poop here. By her pace and general manner, I sensed that Paula had given up any serious shed hunting. "Show you something," she said over her shoulder. She tied the chin strap of the battered Tilley hat that was part of her uniform, lowered her head, and bashed her way through the underbrush. (Tilley hats are heavy canvas deals favored by yachty people. Paula would never spend the seventy-four dollars one cost new, but she had a knack for finding them along the river.) The vegetation opened up again and we were heading up a trickle of water that passed silently over sand and rocks. And then Paula was standing in an oval of sunlight, a tiny glade. At her feet was a patch of shin-high greens growing in a pool of clear water. With a kind of theatricality I'd never seen in her before, she bent from the waist, swept her arm down like a dancer, and snatched up a few sprigs of the plants. Then she popped them into her mouth. "Watercress," she announced. "Only place in D.C. it grows." She stopped, raised a finger, and amended her previous statement. "Only place it grows that I'll eat it, I mean." She snatched another handful. Almost without thinking about it, I followed suit. Aping things Paula did—things I would never consider doing on my own—has become natural to me over the years. "Nice, huh?" she asked. "Sorta nutty, little peppery. I fucking love the stuff."

The watercress exploded in my mouth. It was peppery and slightly bitter but rounded with a nuttiness that whetted a desire for more. It was crisp, crunchy, and succulent. But the astonishing thing wasn't exactly a taste, at least in the way I normally thought of tastes. There was something about the plant that I would have dismissed as New Age blather up until that moment. There was a distinct vitality to it. It tasted nothing like any watercress I'd ever eaten before. It tasted alive.

11

It was only much later that I would accept what the small amount of scientific work on wild edible plants has repeatedly demonstrated, which is that a wild plant is always more nutritious than its domesticated counterpart. Like helicopter parents, we supervise every aspect of a cultivated plant's life. We feed and water regularly. We weed out competing plants and protect it from pests. We do everything but enroll it in after-school enrichment courses. Then, as if determined to undermine our own efforts, we harvest them before they're ripe—before their nutritional peak—because they ship better at that stage. Wild plants, of necessity, are scrappier and tougher. They develop deeper, larger root systems. They are more efficient at absorbing nutrients and in turn produce highly concentrated phytonutrients, the very compounds that we eat plants to obtain—vitamins and minerals, plant phenols, and omega-3 fatty acids. Some of these phytonutrients are particularly bitter, the better to protect the plant from predators and pests. The most compelling argument for eating wild plants may have nothing to do with wildness at all. It's simply that a wild plant you pick today and eat tonight or tomorrow is far more fresh than what's available in stores. The average "fresh" green bean in a grocery store, for example, was picked sixteen days ago, during whith time it has lost 45 percent of its nutritional value.

As I say, I didn't realize any of this until much later. What I had had was a brief moment of illumination—*It's alive!*—before my mind snapped shut again. It shut because I suddenly realized that what we were doing was crazy. "Jesus Christ, Paula!" I sputtered. "This water's gotta be filthy. It's D.C. groundwater, runoff from God knows where. And there's deer shit and homeless people crapping everywhere." I was already imagining explaining to the emergency room doctor that my stomach was exploding because I'd decided it was a good idea to eat watercress growing in an inner-city park full of feces.

Paula shrugged but looked unconcerned. She chewed some more, swallowed, and wiped her hands on her jeans. "It does look nasty, okay? The stream over there"—she pointed to a slightly larger rivulet running parallel to this one, only a few feet lower—"is fucking sewage. But this is the seep from the ridge." She raised her chin to indicate the rock ridge we'd

12

just descended. "That water gets pushed through layers of sand before it comes up here. You know who used sand as a way to filter water? The fucking Greeks! Anyway, I've been eating off this patch for years and I've never gotten sick. But only right here. Okay, let's go. We don't get on the road by two-thirty, we'll spend all afternoon stuck in rush hour."

This book began when I set out to see how much of my own food I could get directly, with no middleman. In other words, by hunting, fishing, foraging, and growing a garden. I'm not the most likely guy to write a book about food. I can cook, but only a little and only when there's no way around it. When I was growing up my mother, an excellent cook, served our family three homemade meals a day. I had neither incentive nor interest in learning my way around the kitchen until I was out of college. And by then my father's cooking genes had taken over. It was all Dad could do to open a can of soup.

Nor am I a discerning eater. No one, for example, has ever accused me of having a sophisticated palate. When deciding whether something in my refrigerator has become hazardous, I'll trust anyone else's nose, including that of my daughter, Emma, over mine. I used to buy the least expensive olive oil on the shelf because I can't taste the difference and because, like my father before me, I'm cheap. I stopped only when my significant other made me upgrade.

Like pretty much everyone who grew up in the 1960s in the suburbs, I ate what my mother brought home from the supermarket. When she would stop at a roadside stand advertising "local produce," my sister and I greeted the chance to eat seasonally with irritation. After all, they had the same stuff—and more of it—at Giant, which had the additional benefits of being air-conditioned and free of mosquitoes. And the notion that certain foods were "seasonal" was clearly ridiculous. Giant had any fruit or vegetable you wanted whenever you wanted it. And whenever you shucked Giant's corn—the only help I remember ever giving my mother in the kitchen—you weren't going to be surprised by some big fat worm inside.

Looking back, it wasn't that I felt cut off from the rhythms and cycles of the natural world: I wasn't even aware that there was a natural world to be cut off *from*. Sure, I knew nature's broad strokes—that geese flew south in the winter and back north in spring to have their babies, that farmers planted in the spring and harvested in the summer and fall. But all that stuff, however real, existed apart from me and seemed to be doing just fine without any input from me. And vice versa. I now think of the world I grew up in and the natural world as two parallel universes. And it wasn't until I began hunting and fishing that I realized that the one which I—like most Americans—was born into is by far the stranger and less likely of the two.

There's one more thing that should disqualify me from writing this book. I've always thought there was something vaguely pathetic about people who were obsessed with food. It was like they didn't have enough to do.

Nevertheless, my tasty and subversive experiences with deer and watercress led me to wonder how much of my own food I could get, not just locally, but by my own hand. How far, I wondered, could I get trying to close the distance between me and what I ate? It wasn't a new idea, of course. Countless people have written versions of the same thing. They'd vowed to eat only food grown within a short distance of home or turned a quarter-acre yard into an intensively cultivated garden. I had actually tried to read some of these books. But I always hit a wall. The author would go on for ten pages about how an unexpected encounter with rhubarb changed his life. (Yeah, I did do the same thing with watercress. But give me a break. Mine was pretty short.) This was when I would drop the book and fantasize about tying these people to telephone poles and force-feeding them Cheetos.

And maybe the focus of my book really was different than that of the books I'd read. They dealt with cultivated plant and animals, however painstakingly raised. I was interested in wild ones. They were inner-focused, seeking an enhanced sense of domesticity. I was headed the other way, in search of the most direct connection with nature I could find. (True, I was planning a garden, but I thought of that more as an insurance policy than anything else.) They were cooked. I was raw. Except for the Cheetos, of course.

14

While I knew a bit about fishing and hunting, it would be hard to find someone who knew less about gardening, let alone foraging. Fortunately, I was okay with this. Ignorance and incompetence are my forte. When I began writing for *Field & Stream,* it was obvious that the "expert" end of the spectrum was overrepresented. The masthead was loaded with writers who could tie a fly out of tinfoil and dryer lint and then catch the wiliest of trout on it, men who could shoot a running chipmunk at 200 yards. The "doofus" end, though, was wide open. This was where I planted my flag. My core principles were that enthusiasm trumped skill and that hunting and fishing were way too much fun to be dominated by experts. Initially, the editors were surprised that my bumblings elicited a "Hey, I'm just like that, too!" response from the readership. I wasn't. Failure is a far more universal experience than success.

An attempt to "eat wild" (a term I'd seen in some foodie magazine at a doctor's office) seemed to connote things radical, adventurous, and not for the faint of heart. These are, not coincidentally, the qualities a good stunt requires. And yet, if you gave the notion any thought—and it was my hope that people wouldn't—"eating wild" was anything but radical. For most of our history, eating wild was what people did. It was the norm. Except, of course, that it wasn't called "eating wild." It went by a simpler, more humble term: "eating."

I was also drawn to the idea that, as with hunting, I must have come from a long line of people who had a knack for finding wild edible plants. I had to possess some innate ability and I hoped to access it. Although, once again, no one in my immediate family had done anything even remotely agricultural. We were a twentieth-century suburban family. We never grew anything but grass.

Despite this, I decided to go for it. I reasoned that the foraging instinct couldn't be very far from the hunting one. Wild plants grew all over the place, after all, and what was vegetable gardening but throwing some seeds in the dirt and hitting them with some Miracle-Gro and water now and then?

In other words, how hard could it be?

Chapter One:
Blood, Guts, and Other Signs of Spring

Fletcher's Boathouse sits in a tiny cove along the Potomac, two miles north of Georgetown and about fifteen minutes from my house in Arlington. Long before the time John Smith passed through here during his 1608 exploration of the river, the Powhatan Indians had a seasonal fish camp there. The boathouse itself has been there since the 1850s, and was in the hands of the Fletcher family until recently. The government bought out brothers Joe and Ray Fletcher a few years ago. There was never much money in the business and none of the Fletcher children wanted to run it. It doesn't really matter who owns it. The cove is one of those places where the earth concentrates its power. For centuries it has exerted a magnetic pull on river rats, fishermen, odd ducks, outlaws, and misfits of all descriptions. It is well inside the Beltway, but if you point your car down the steep curve of road that bores into the blackness of the tunnel beneath the C&O Canal—perpetually dripping water and so cramped you can easily touch the rocks on either side out your windows—you emerge in a different world. Marks painted on the boathouse rental counter delineate the crests of past floods. There are no truly permanent structures down on the floodplain. Even the cinder-block office has a provisional air about it. Down here, the river always gets the last word.

White perch season is a big deal in these parts because you really don't want to eat any fish that spends its entire life in the Potomac, unless you're curious about undergoing a sex change or are experiencing a decreased will to live. It's not that "the nation's river" lacks fish.

There are plenty of fish here: largemouth and smallmouth bass, catfish, walleye, sunfish, and crappie, to name but a few. The real problem is that forty years after the Clean Water Act, the D.C. section of the Potomac is so loaded with pollutants—everything from raw sewage, PCBs, and agricultural runoff to heavy metals, lethal bacteria, and birth control hormones—that you could probably improve the water quality by peeing in it. For years, a sign put up by the District Department of the Environment on the boathouse dock's light pole warned of the river's health hazards. Owing to high levels of bacteria, it forbade swimming. It warned that fish from these waters contained PCBs and other chemical contaminants, and banned the eating of carp, catfish, and eels outright; it recommended that "healty adults" limit their intake of largemouth bass to no more than half a pound per month, and limit sunfish or "other fish" to no more than half a pound per week. It didn't give details of what would befall those exceeding the limit, but sudden swelling of the hands and feet, dissolution of internal organs, and enlarged nipples all seemed likely. At the bottom of the sign there was a phone number listed for further information. Call and you got a recording saying it was no longer in service. If you live in the D.C. metropolitan area, you know that this is pretty much par for the course for municipal agencies in the District. The only exception is the city's parking enforcement operation. That functions flawlessly.

White perch, however, are one of the few species that are in, but not of, the river. For the past 10,000 years or so a few kinds of fish that spend nearly all their lives in salt water prove that they either have never read Thomas Wolfe or have decided that he's full of it. Prompted by a springtime urge to reproduce, these fish—including perch, herring, and shad—leave the salt water in which they spend the majority of their lives and go home again, to the Potomac River waters of their birth. No one knows for sure what triggers their migration, why the fish insist on returning to the very same pools and riffles in which they were hatched, or how they manage this trick. Whatever it is—a certain slant of the light, a scent in the water measurable in parts per billion, a magic water temperature—they all make the journey more or less at the same time, usually in late March and early April. And they are highly motivated little fellas. They fight river currents, expose themselves to commercial and recreational anglers, and generally get beat all to hell to get where they want to go. If you happen to be an angler in the D.C. area after safely edible fish, the spring run has got your name written on it.

There was a time when the Potomac's spring migrations of fish were of such size and duration as to seem incomprehensible to us now. There was a time when the river was said to run alternately silver with shad and black with herring. I asked Gordon, who grew up fishing the river and is in his seventies, if this ever really happened. Normally a soft-spoken man, he said, "Hell, yes, it happened! I saw it every year growing up. Water black with herring, silver with shad. What we've done to this river is criminal. There's no ther word for it." These days both fish have been depleted to the point that it's no longer legal for recreational anglers to catch them. Commercial fishermen, who take many times more fish and are the ones directly responsible for destroying the fishery, are, naturally, still allowed to catch them. They have better lobbyists. That leaves perch, which Paula and Gordon also pursue. There are two kinds. Yellow perch are great eating, but, for reasons known only to themselves, seldom migrate farther than certain deep holes near Occoquan, twenty-five miles short of D.C. Luckily white perch come all the way up, and are the sweetest-tasting fish in the river. Their run, which once lasted for months, has dwindled to where an angler counts himself lucky to get into them a few days each season. Some years, the perch hardly show up at all. The dismal state of the fishery is belied by the appearance of the Potomac, which—at least visually—remains a wild and scenic river. There are parts of it where you see no buildings or wires and you can feel how it must have been a century ago. It's only when you develop an interest in what lives below the surface that you realize how much has been lost and how little is being done to restore it. It's a subject best not to plumb too deeply if you are prone to cynicism.

Because the perch run was my shot at catching, reasonably close to home, fish that I could eat safely, I'd been pounding the river's perch holes for weeks. Nothing. I made an offer of each unsuccessful outing to the fish gods, proof of my humility and worthiness. I went out in company and alone. (I preferred company, since I figured pretty much anyone taking me out knew the river better than I did.) I'd gone on rising water and falling, warming temperatures and cooling. I'd yet to bring home enough perch for a single dinner.

A river looks like a pretty uniform thing until you try to fish it. Beneath, especially near the boathouse, the river's topography is as varied as the mountains of Afghanistan. Fishermen will tell you that 80 percent of the fish are found in 20 percent of the water. Around Fletcher's, the split is more like 90/10. Moving your line as little as two feet can spell the difference between catching and not catching fish. Learning where the holes are and when they're most productive can take a lifetime. If I had to live off perch I'd starve before I amassed anything close to that kind of knowledge.

Although she hadn't spent her entire life on the Potomac as had some of the other boathouse denizens, Paula Smith was adept at both sussing out productive holes on her own and somehow convincing—or possibly coercing—longtime Fletcher's regulars into telling her about others. She had been showing me holes and telling me their names: Boiling Rock, the White Sign, Walkers Point, Hens and Chickens, and Dixie Landing. This last one got its name decades ago from a boathouse employee who liked to row downstream to Georgetown, tie up, and go to Dixie Liquors, a store at the D.C. end of Key Bridge. Usually too drunk to make it all the way back upriver, he would beach the boat and sleep it off at the same place each time. I guess Dixie Landing sounded more picturesque than Drunk Beach.

By all accounts, Paula just showed up at Fletcher's one day, one more bit of flotsam deposited by the spring floods. She was unemployed, and looked as if she might have spent a few days sleeping outside. She dressed like a man: blue jeans rolled up at the cuff, an oversize heavy shirt with her hair tucked down the back, a battered Tilley hat on her head. She was more than a little unconventional and

19

there were some who thought she was flat-out crazy. But she impressed the regulars with her knowledge of fish and deer and her general woods sense. She hung out, seeming to live on cigarettes, coffee, and air. After a while she began lobbying for a job working the dock, the lowest rung at the boathouse. Joe Fletcher didn't want to hire her. He pointed out that she was too small to manhandle boats and anchors. Besides, the last thing they needed was a nutcase on the payroll. But Paula is a powerful presence under normal circumstances, and especially so when she wants something. Eventually Ray Fletcher, the softer-hearted of the two brothers, gave her a chance. In short order Paula showed herself to be the most conscientious, hardest-working employee the boathouse had ever had, running the dock like a general and scrubbing the inside of the rental boats free of every speck of fish blood, bait, and sand. Paula's haphazard appearance belies her exacting standards of cleanliness and her ability to focus for long stretches on meticulous tasks. According to Danny Ward, the only non-Fletcher to make a career of working at the boathouse, "She was the only employee we've ever had that I had to tell to work less hard."

I was desperate to get on some perch but so far that spring Mother Nature had been like the doorman of some trendy club, granting entry to the guy beside me and the one behind, but not to me. Paula had been passing on boathouse scuttlebutt, tantalizing reports of anglers who had gotten into good runs of fish at one spot or another, only to return the next day and totally blank. Rowing back to the boathouse after another perchless day—a wonderful workout for those seldom-used back muscles, especially when you are bucking a stiff northwest breeze and an outgoing tide—I had imagined how it would feel to get into a good school of perch, to have even a few hours of the kind of fishing Gordon says was routine when he was a boy growing up along the Potomac seventy years ago.

That night Paula called, saying the next day was looking like the best shot so far. "If they're ever gonna come thick, it oughta be to-morrow, honey," she said. "River's falling, and they like that. Water temperature's pushing fifty degrees, and they like that, too. I'm not saying we'll get into 'em, because they're fish, you know what I mean? But the fuckers've gotta be somewhere around by now." She said that Gordon couldn't make it, because of a doctor's appointment, but that he'd meet us down at the boathouse later.

The next morning we met at Fletcher's, where we ran into Dickie Tehaan as he was loading his rods into a rowboat. Dickie is a minor legend among boathouse regulars, both for his fishing skill and for the bucktail jigs he ties by the score. These are known around the boathouse as "Dickie jigs," and are as generic a term among river rats as "Kleenex" is among the general population. A fair number of the best perch anglers use nothing else, claiming Dickie jigs outfish even live bloodworms. Dickie won't sell them, but he gives them away to people he likes. When he suggested that the three of us go in his boat, he didn't need to ask twice. "If Dickie's not catching 'em, they ain't in the river," Paula said, as Dickie pulled toward a hole on the Virginia shoreline. Sharing a boat with Dickie filled me with confidence. Fishing at its highest levels is no different from other "sports." What separates Tiger Woods or Roger Federer from the rest of the crowd is more about mind-set than muscle. What sets Dickie apart from other anglers is more than the ability to detect the slightest bump of a fish mouthing a jig and the reflexes to set the hook instantly. It's something intangible. It's fishing juju. It's sorcery.

Somehow he finds where the fish want to be on a given day. Somehow, the barbed bucktail that he selects—which may be heavier or lighter, bigger or smaller, and in colors from white and yellow to orange and purple—is the one the fish are hungry for. Experience is essential, of course, and Dickie has that in spades. He grew up in a house five minutes' walk from the boathouse and with the river as his chief playmate. He once passed up a promotion at nearby Sibley Hospital, where he works in the parking and maintenance division, for fear it would cut into his fishing. But experience alone fails to account for it. There are other guys with similar river pedigrees. The thing about Dickie is that he has the river in his blood. He feels things others don't. Although he's a little older than I am, there's an innocence about him that is childlike

21

and suggests that he may be attuned to frequencies most of us shut out as we grew up. He doesn't belong in a place like D.C. He's not a striver. He is without pretense. Whatever he is, Paula's right about one thing. If Dickie's not catching 'em, they ain't in the river.

We reached the hole Dickie wanted, dropped the rock anchor in about thirty feet of water, and made sure it held. Then we started fishing. We each had a two-ounce lead weight at the end of our lines and two Dickie jigs tied just above. Once the weight hit bottom, you reeled the slack out of your line; pumped your rod slightly, to lift the sinker up a few inches; and then let it fall. This motion animated the jigs, which darted around like disoriented minnows, an easy meal. The deer hair the lures are made of is hollow, and what looks lifeless in your hand billows and pulses in the water. Fish most often strike as the lure is falling, so the trick is to keep the line tight enough on the fall to detect a strike but not so tight that you impede the jig's action. And then, like the old joke about the obsessive-compulsive who endlessly follows the shampoo tube's "lather, rinse, repeat" instructions, you jig the lure again and again and again. You jig until Dickie decides to move or you get a strike or Jesus comes back.

Today, however, was payday. Within three pumps of the rod, I felt the electric pulse of a fish, set the hook, and reeled up a good-sized white perch. "Yeah, baby!" crowed Paula. "That'll work! Throw him in the basket!" I unhooked the fish and slid it into the basket tied over the side. The basket was made of wire, with a spring-loaded lid that only opened inward, so you could put fish in but they couldn't get out. Dickie had a perch on before I got my rig back in the water, and Paula was right behind him with a double, a fish on each jig. We exchanged wide-eyed looks, fully aware that this was exactly what we'd been praying for and also scared that we'd queer our luck if we spoke of it. (The baseball pitcher who wears the same socks every game as long as he's winning has nothing on the fisherman when it comes to superstition.) A giddy feeling, a kind of perch madness, washed over us. We were jacked on fish. Our senses sharpened, time slowed, and the world shrank to the wand in your hand and the sensations it telegraphed.

Moments after our jigs touched bottom, something bumped them almost every time. We kept happily reeling fish up, swinging them aboard, and sliding them into the basket. At a certain point I realized that I was thirsty and—during the five seconds it took my jig to fall through the thirty feet of water to the bottom—I would resolve to stop after the next fish long enough to open my water bottle and take a swig. But every time I forgot until the jig was once again falling, at which point I again resolved to drink after the next fish.

We were careful not to advertise our success. The last thing we wanted was company. When a guy in what had once been white coveralls motored past in a skiff, we dropped our rod tips and studied the scenery as if it were of far greater interest than the fishing.

After three hours, the basket was nearly full and weighed almost more than I could lift. We'd also filled the cooler we'd brought our sandwiches in. Dickie wasn't ready to stop, though. He produced a stringer—a length of nylon cord with a steel pin on one end and a metal eye on the other for tethering fish. You pass the pin through the fish's gills, out its mouth, and through the ring. We began adding fish to the stringer. Although we were all catching fish steadily, Dickie was catching more than Paula and me put together. It was like being in a documentary film about fishing voodoo. I was fishing the same two white Dickie jigs above the same two-ounce sinker that Dickie himself was fishing. I had memorized and was imitating his fishing cadence—how often he popped the sinker, how high, how low he dipped his rod tip as he followed the lure back down. I'd even asked to change positions in the boat with him a few times on the off chance that the spot he was fishing—a full three or four feet away—was relevant. It wasn't. He outfished me two or three to one no matter where he went in the boat. It was maddening. And Dickie's unaffected humility made it all the more provocative. It would have been easier if he'd been trash-talking. That I could absorb and dish out in return. Who was he to be so definitively favored by whatever deity controlled fishing luck? Damn it all, I was a good person, too. In some ways. "Dickie," I finally blurted out, alarmed that my mock outrage sounded much less mock when spoken than it had in my head. "What the hell are you doing that I'm not?" He shrugged, embarrassed, reddening slightly. "I don't know," he finally said sheepishly. "Maybe it's just that I've been doing it longer." Paula, whose back was to us during this exchange, was silent for a few moments. Then she said, "It's feel. He can feel when a fucking perch *looks* at his line."

Finally, at noon, Dickie said that he needed to get to work and was happy to donate his share of the catch to us. We hoisted the fish basket and stringer back over the side, pulled the anchor, and headed in.

My wish to find out what it was like when the planets aligned, perch-wise, had been answered. When we pulled up to the dock the boat looked as if it had been filled with silver ingots. The floor of the boat was shining with sunlight refracted by innumerable fish scales. I felt like a general returning to a victory parade. By this time, Gordon had arrived. A smile lit up his face as he caught sight of what was in the boat. "About damn time somebody brought in a haul like that," he said by way of a greeting.

Gordon had come prepared: four fillet knives, a bucket to throw guts in, newspaper to cover the picnic table, a cooler full of ice. Half an hour later, the three of us were wordlessly absorbed in converting all the recently swimming fish to a school of boneless fillets. It looked like the bedroom scene from *Macbeth*. We were up to our wrists in gore, guts, blood, and slime. God help you if your nose itched. When my phone rang in my pocket, I never even considered answering. Bent over my board with my blood-slick hands and a long fillet knife, I found myself dazed at the carnage I'd wrought. Dark entrails and red viscera oozed up through gills under the pressure of my blade. Fine-grained yellow roe seeped from the vent on each female's underside. Each male seemed ready to burst with unexpressed white milt. And every last fish wore the same expression of vacant, stunned amazement at no longer being among the living. The soap that could absolve me of the smell permeating my hands, clothes, and soul had not been and would never be milled.

The other thing was that my fingers had gone numb. I scraped my cutting board clear of guts and scales with the edge of the blade and reached for another frozen perch. Paula and Gordon were adamant that cold fish are firm fish, and that firm fish are easier to clean. So all hundred or so of ours were buried in coolers filled with ice. No doubt they were right. But my fingers had lost all feeling. As a novice at the art of filleting, I couldn't help thinking that benumbed fingers, slick hands, and razor-sharp knives were a trifecta of amputation. If I had cut my hand, I wouldn't have felt it. And, my blood being the same red as that of the fish, I wouldn't have seen it. I'd have just kept merrily cutting away until I felt a vague lightheadedness, at which point I would have keeled over from loss of blood. Then, as everything faded to black, the final voice I heard on earth would have been Paula's, irritated as ever, barking, "What? You taking a break already?"

I said nothing of my concern. Paula and Gordon had each been at this a good many years, still had ten fingers apiece, and weren't complaining. Besides, I was determined to learn the skill of filleting. Learning to eat wild, I realized, involved more than just the acquisition and the eating. There was some important groundwork in between. Plenty of people can catch a fish. But filleting fish was a keystone in what I'd already come to think of as "separator knowledge," my name for those skills or information by which one group of human beings distinguishes itself from others. I first formulated this idea right after college while working part-time in an after-school care program. I was twenty-two years old and was considering, among other pipe dreams, a career in teaching. For some reason, I prided myself on the notion—completely untested—that I had a knack for connecting with kids. One day a six-year-old boy on the playground approached. He said, "Bill, do you watch *Dukes of Hazzard*?" referring to a then-popular TV show. Almost before I'd finished answering in the negative—I'd intended to follow up by asking what he liked about the show—he was already walking away. He was interested in conversing only with others who loved a television show about two good ol' boys and their extremely hot cousin, Daisy, as they evaded Boss Hogg, the corrupt Hazzard County commissioner, in an orange 1969 Dodge Charger R/T. If you did love that show, there was potential for a deep connection. If not, there wasn't. In much the same way, I could see that my world was becoming a place where you fall on one side or the other of knowing how to fillet a perch or fletch an arrow or follow a deer trail.

The filleting tutorial, per Gordon, went like this: First, you got a safe grip on the fish, because a dead perch could hurt you. Its dorsal fin has nine spiky spines that can inflict nasty little puncture wounds unless laid flat against the body. You then clamped the head to your cutting board with your off hand, dorsal fin toward you, and, starting just behind the gill, you sliced into the body of the fish until you reached the backbone. Without removing the blade, you turned it ninety degrees in the direction of the tail and cut along the backbone, severing the rib bones, all the while keeping the blade as close as possible to the spine. The closer to the spine, the more meat you got. To get the best knife angle on the spine, the one that yielded the most flesh, it was best to position your cutting hand below the level of the fish, which meant moving the fish to the edge of the working surface. Most of the meat on a fish is in the upper half—measured lengthwise—of its body. The lower half mostly holds organs and viscera. If you were doing it right, you'd notice a convex bend in your blade as you pressed down to fillet, conforming to the humped shape of the fish's body. Fillet knives are designed to be flexible for just this purpose, and that bend meant you were doing it correctly. After your blade exited at the tail, you flipped the fish and repeated the two cuts.

At this point you had two lengths of fish detached from the body, scales still on. The skeletal body and its contents went into the gut bucket—gently, as it was considered bad form to splash guts on your coworkers. Next you moved on to deboning and skinning. You laid the fish skin side down, looking and probing with your (numb) fingers for the ends of the severed rib bones. Then you slid your blade beneath them and cut them away. The last step was the greased pig contest of fish cleaning, removing the skin. The difficulty here arose from the fact that you'd already disposed of every part of the fish you could get a grip on. Paula solved this problem by pinning the skin to the board with the point of a second knife, but I had only one and had to manage as best I could with my fingers. I could find no good way to do this, and it was so frustrating I briefly considered using my teeth. If and when you somehow did get a grip, the counterintuitive trick, according to Gordon, was to move the fish rather than the knife. You pulled the fish against the blade. "You lose a lot more meat if you move the knife," he said. "Don't ask me why because I don't know. But the best way is to keep the knife in place and just sorta saw that skin back and forth a little while you pull."

After you'd deboned and skinned one fillet, you did the same with the other. And then, from a fish that came to the boat weighing three-quarters of a pound or so, you had two boneless slivers of alabaster flesh—either of which you could have swallowed in one large bite. And then you picked up another fish and did it all over again.

Fish cleaning required the full engagement of those parts of the brain governing small motor skills and personal safety. While this left a lot of mental real estate open, it didn't lead to much conversation. Except for Paula, of course, who is generally uncomfortable with silence in company, and thus kept up a running feud with the hornets that were invariably attracted to fish guts, and especially to those of the fish under one's knife at any given moment. I ignored the wasps, hoping they would return the favor. With Paula, it was war. While friendly and fearless toward animals normal humans fear—I'd seen her pick up a nasty-tempered three-foot brown water snake with perfect equanimity—she hated hornets. Any landing on her cutting board or hovering close enough got flattened by a deft slap with the back of her hand, followed by a gleeful, "Take that, motherfucker!"

For me, cleaning fish—a task both repetitive and exacting—induced a trancelike state. Time flattened out and the world shrank to the cut I was making at that moment. There was something simultaneously gross and pure, sacred and profane, about the task. The blood and slime were predictably repellent, of course. But the meat itself had a purity that at times seemed almost holy. It was immaculate, fine, and absolutely uniform in texture. It was amazingly clean stuff. I knew this about fish, of course. Everyone who has ever eaten fish knows it.

And yet it was as if I'd never understood how utterly the flesh of a fish differs from that of a mammal, with all of a mammal's veins, fat, and connective tissue. Fish made meat seem gross by comparison. In the same way I was struck by the dichotomy of the ultimate destination of these fish, and of eating itself. On the one hand, of course, it was the most natural thing in the world. We emerged from the womb sucking and continued the habit until the end. Stomachs, like Neil Young's rust, never slept. Our bodies required a continuous supply of other bodies, both animals and plants. It suddenly struck me as a disgusting little business, really, all this eating and excreting. It was a wonder we had any spiritual impulses at all.

Finally we could see the bottom of the cooler. We parceled out the last fish and piled the last fillets into the other cooler. Paula took the knives and cutting boards to hose them down behind the boathouse. I took the gut bucket and walked a hundred yards to the footbridge over the creek where it enters the cove. I hoisted it over the railing and dumped it. The water streaked red and the bones and skin swirled as they washed away and disappeared into the river. The first time Gordon had told me to go dump the gut bucket here, I thought it was a rare act of irresponsibility on his part. That was before he explained that fish guts nourished nearly every organism in the river. The fry of every fish ate them, as did a host of aquatic insects and microorganisms, all of which belonged in a healthy river. I'd since learned that one of the tricks biologists were using out west to repopulate salmon rivers was to "plant" carcasses of hatchery-raised salmon in them as food to nurture the few salmon fry that were born wild.

We divided up the fillets—we'd cleaned more than a hundred fish—and went our separate ways. It was still light out when I got home, but I felt as though I'd been awake for two days. Later I'd freeze the fish as Gordon had instructed. He and Paula caught fish when they were plentiful in order to eat them all year, and the process had turned them into zealots about freezing techniques. They packaged fish in meal-sized portions in pint ziplock bags. You put the fish into just enough salted water to cover them, squeezed the air from the bag, and wrote the species and date on the outside with a Sharpie. Bags were frozen in a cardboard box to achieve a brick shape, which made for space-efficient stackability. They were equally zealous about shelf life. Frozen fish less than six months old was treated as fresh. From six months to a year, the fish was still good but was usually combined with other ingredients and made into patties or—Paula's favorite—fish loaf. After twelve months, you bit the bullet and chucked it. But I would deal with freezing tomorrow. For the moment, I stowed my rods and tackle, threw more ice into the cooler, and stripped naked at the top of the basement stairs. I threw my clothes down and headed for the hottest shower I could stand, trying in vain to scour the fish smell from every pore. The last thing I wanted was perch for dinner. I had a glass of wine and spaghetti with some microwaved Newman's Own Five Cheese Sauce. Within half an hour I was asleep.

It was nearly a week later before I got around to preparing some of my own perch for dinner. The delay in cooking my catch had been that I wasn't the only one who was going to be eating it. My daughter Emma, who lives half the time with me and half the time with Jane, her mother and my ex-wife, would be dining as well. And Emma, ten years old at the time, could be something of a tough sell when presented with new foods. I needed the time to ponder my approach.

Either baking or broiling was the healthy choice, of course, but frying seemed the way to go with a girl who routinely begged to be taken to McDonald's. Frying it would be. I thawed some fillets and patted them dry. It was easy identifying the ones I'd filleted. Mine were the ones that looked as if they'd been hacked to death in a knife fight. I shook them all up in a bag with cornmeal, paprika, onion powder, salt, and pepper. I poured canola oil into my biggest skillet and stuck a candy thermometer in it, waiting until the thermometer read 370 degrees. I knew this was the magic temperature from having observed Joe Fletcher at the boathouse's annual fish fry. He'd have twenty gallons of oil on a propane burner that sounded like a fighter jet taking off. No fish went in until the oil hit 370. You certainly couldn't argue with the results. There had never been a bit of leftover fish at the event. The skillet was sending out little searing droplets of oil when I laid the fillets in. When they were the right shade of brown, I tonged them out onto paper towels. I mixed up my own version of tartar sauce, an ever-changing ratio of mayonnaise to ketchup with lemon juice and minced sweet pickle. Somewhere I'd read that James Beard said that Americans would eat anything if it was the right shade of orange. This was true in my case. I was a sucker for whoever did the food engineering behind Cheetos, for example. When the tartar sauce looked like a festive paint choice for a bathroom I pronounced it ready. Emma and I sat down and I plunked a crisp piece of perch on my daughter's plate. She took one look and and announced, "I forgot to tell you I'm on a diet where I don't eat fish."

I knew better than to take the bait. "You know the deal, Monkalula," I told her. "No dinner, no dessert."

"I don't care," she said. We said grace and she picked up a fork and began creating a line of peas in perfect parallel with her carrots, all the while ignoring her fish. I forked up a bite of fish and dredged it in the tartar sauce. It was sweet, crunchy, and amazingly tasty. I quickly ate every bit on my plate. "You sure you're not eating yours?" I asked. "Just try one. They're really good. Almost like Chicken McNuggets." She shook her head. I helped myself to hers, then got the remaining three fillets on the paper towel. By this time I was eating them with my hands. Ordinarily, I would have persisted in trying to get my child to eat. The fact that I'd never won that particular power struggle had never stopped me from engaging in it. But that night I didn't. For one thing, I remembered something from one of the many books about "oppositional" children I'd read, which was that if you already knew that the child wasn't going to do her homework or eat her vegetables regardless of what you did, you'd both be happier if you skipped the fight. I wish I could say that was what made the different. It wasn't. I just wanted all the fried perch I could get.

We skipped the fight. I ate the perch. Life was good.

The white perch run ended during the last week of April. The speed (overnight) and extent (total) of the exodus was stunning. That day with Dickie and Paula was not my only big one—on another outing I had boated forty-two keepers and released at least that many undersized perch from the hole known as the White Sign, named after an old and illegible placard on a tree by the water's edge. Three days after the big haul with Paula and Dickie, though, I went back to the scene of our triumph—same hole, same outgoing tide, fishing the same Dickie jigs—and got nothing. I pulled anchor and dropped downstream to the next hole, and the next. I might as well have been fishing my driveway.

Nobody knows how fish do this, how a multitude of creatures not known for their intellectual rigor, scattered over a wide, powerful river, coordinate their departure so precisely. It was as if all *Morone americana* in the Potomac had but a single mind among them, and that mind had decided to skedaddle. The desertion hurt my feelings more than I wanted to admit. I'd barely processed the revelation that these delicious fish were right under my nose and, if you put in the time, could be caught in large numbers. I'd been intent on laying in a supply that would last the summer. I'd had visions of holding a perch fry for one of the dinners that I and three other guys, friends for more than thirty years, held every month or so. I'd imagined how impressed they'd be upon learning I'd caught, cleaned, filleted, and fried the delicious fish they were enjoying. And now, nothing. "That's perch fishing," was all Gordon said. Easy enough for him, with sixty seasons under his belt.

I was reminded of something that happened the previous summer. Jane and I, wanting to model that divorcing parents could still be cordial toward each other, had taken Emma to the last day of the Arlington County Fair, one of Emma's rites of summer. Tickets in hand, Em was waiting in line to get on the rickety little roller coaster. For reasons she can't articulate, that ride has been a touchstone of Emma's childhood, the one ride she never misses. The small mob of waiting children was about to swarm the coaster's cars when a distant rumble sounded. Thunder. Within seconds, the fire marshal had closed the roller coaster and all other outdoor rides. Emma's face went red and hot tears raced down her cheeks. Jane and I tried to divert her with the Ping-Pong ball goldfish toss, the petting zoo, even funnel cake—something we'd agreed beforehand to veto. She remained inconsolable. Next we did something so dumb it bordered on child abuse: we tried to reason with her. Thunderstorms, we explained, are part of nature, and nature is beyond the control of any person—her parents, the man who ran the roller coaster, even the fire marshal who closed the rides down. "I don't care!" she wailed. "I hate nature!"

I hadn't really empathized at the time. If anything I'd been amused by her words, which seemed to imply that nature had feelings that could be hurt. Suddenly, I understood the depth of her sense of betrayal. The white perch had been my roller coaster, and when it suddenly shut down, I hated nature, too. Little did I know that another obsession, equally potent, was swimming my way.

FRIED PERCH

8 fillets from white or yellow perch*

(*This is the part where your typical recipe says "or similar, white-fleshed fish." That's bullshit. Nothing tastes like perch and if you're not making this recipe with it, you might as well give up and go with Mrs. Paul's Crunchy Fish Sticks. In that case, you'll be eating pollock, a few spices, and the requisite load of chemicals: Sodium Tripolyphosphate, Ferrous Sulfate, Thiamine Mononitrate, MSG, and something called "Tbhq," aka Tertiary Butylhydroquinone, a form of butane used as a preservative. I've never tried to light a frozen fish stick, but it might be worth a try the next time you're short of candles.)

2/3 cup unbleached flour
1/3 cup cornmeal
1 egg, beaten
1 tablespoon milk
Old Bay Seasoning *or* salt, pepper, garlic powder, and paprika (to taste)
Peanut oil (enough to fill your favorite skillet to depth of ½ inch)

Pour oil into skillet and heat over medium-high flame until a candy/ deep fry thermometer reads 370 degrees F. Getting the oil to this temperature is key.

While oil is heating, mix flour, cornmeal, and Old Bay, or seasonings of your choice in a ziplock bag. In a bowl, beat egg thoroughly with the milk.

Pat fish dry with paper towels. Dip each filet first into egg and let the excess "slide" off before placing in ziplock bag. Overly "wet" fish will not fry up crispy.

Place half the filets in the bag and double-check that the zipper is indeed closed (I speak from experience.) Shake and rotate the ziplock bag until filets are coated. Remove filets from bag, shake off excess and—carefully—place into the hot oil. (Tongs, gloves, and safety goggles are recommended for this.) Cook for a couple of minutes on each side or until desired color is obtained. Remove, drain on paper towels. Eat immediately with pre-made Bill's Beyond Tartar Sauce, an ever-changing ratio of mayonnaise, ketchup, and sweet pickle relish.

Chapter Two:
A "Savory Little Fellow" Rediscovered

"Odd" hardly begins to do justice to my relationship with Paula. We bonded over a shared love of deer, and that has been a constant. Paula knows more about deer than anybody I've ever met. She's also a "character" and has been fodder for any number of my *Field & Stream* columns. She's aware of all of this and feels free to ask for favors in return. She'll ask to be driven somewhere—Paula doesn't drive and for a long time didn't even have a photo I.D. Once, she called on a Saturday, told me to stop what I was doing, drive to Fletcher's, pick up a forty-pound box of frozen herring, and store it in my freezer for a few months. Which I did. This element of mutual exploitation is, paradoxically, what allowed us to become close. It afforded a safe boundary for the relationship. Our closeness is a prickly thing, studiously unacknowledged, not exactly intimacy and not exactly not. Call it a certain understanding. Whatever it is, we've been present in each other's lives for so long now that I'm no longer sure exactly when we met.

I do remember the dark days of 2005 when, after nine years of marriage and five years after Jane and I adopted Emma at birth, I left what had long been a contentious relationship. I left after realizing that I no longer believed that I could make the marriage work. I was miserable. We were always either recovering from a fight or sliding into the next one. We'd been to—by my count—seven relationship therapists. Each had a different approach or technique to help us communicate better and have greater mutual empathy. We never achieved this. Instead, we just learned new ways to play out the same struggle. I decided that I wasn't ultimately doing anyone—me, Jane, or Emma—any favors by staying in an unhappy marriage. As the one who initiated the break, I was the one to move out. I found a drafty rental house I could barely afford a couple of miles away. It was only at that remove that the full force of what I'd done hit me. The deeper canyons of the human mind have no particular use for reason and logic. As the one who had left, I should have felt some measure of relief. Instead, I was all but overcome with grief, despair, and depression.

One particularly overcast and colorless November day, weeks after moving out, I found myself sitting amid still-unpacked boxes, more alone than I'd ever been. I felt like a ghost, like I could walk down the muddy alley behind the house and leave no footprints. I'd stopped calling friends and they, understandably, had stopped calling me. Then after days of silence the phone rang. It was Paula, who, as usual, was already a good way into the conversation by the time I got the receiver to my ear. "They're moving," she was saying. November, the breeding season for deer, is like Christmas to deer hunters. The urge to mate causes wily older bucks that normally travel at night to lower their guard, sometimes searching for does in broad daylight. "The big guys aren't working yet," she continued, as if we'd last spoken moments ago instead of weeks. "They know the first does won't cycle in for a couple more days. But it's not gonna be long." I don't remember what else, if anything, she said. But she continued to call. During some of the darkest days of my life, it was Paula whom I spoke with more often than anyone else. Her calls during this time—short, always confined to what the deer were doing—were a lifeline, a reminder that I was not yet a ghost.

For a long time, the means by which Paula made enough money to live on were a mystery to me. Her seasonal gig working the dock at Fletcher's couldn't have covered much, even given her Spartan lifestyle. At some point I finally realized that her main source of income was selling bait, specifically herring. Herring run up the Potomac in large numbers each spring to spawn. And this oily fish is widely considered the ideal bait for striped bass and catfish. Fish of both species weighing up to fifty pounds were not uncommon in this stretch of river, and a good number of serious anglers came seeking them. For years, Paula's going rate was two herring for five dollars. Just last year she bumped that up to a flat three dollars per fish or—in a pricing strategy that only Paula could have thought up—seven fish for twenty dollars. She once confided that the only reason she kept working the dock was that it was the perfect cover for her business. Her customers, many of whom spoke little English, would wait off to one side of the dock, patient as smack addicts, knowing she would attend to them only after the boathouse's legitimate customers had been served. Like any drug dealer, Paula touched neither money nor product in the open. All transactions took place one step inside the dock's tiny wooden shack where the life jackets were stored. I never knew how Paula came by so many herring, and I knew better than to probe deeply. But she moved a lot of fish. Danny Ward, one of the guys who worked at the boathouse, once referred to her as "the Pablo Escobar of herring."

Paula's force of personality is such that the young men working the boathouse counter, for example, never complained when calls came in asking if Paula had bait, even though her private enterprise was illegal and had nothing to do with the boathouse. "The correct answer to the bait question is, 'I don't know,'" I once overheard her instructing a new kid. "Don't say 'yes' and don't say 'no.' Make 'em show up and find out for themselves. I might not have any when they call but could get in a new supply before they get here. Okay?" The kid nodded meekly.

I got to see her in action only once. I had come down to the dock to ask her what people were catching that day. As we stood talking on the dock, I noticed a Hispanic man standing in the shadow of the trees twenty yards away. He had several stout fishing rods and a bucket. Paula had seen him as well but didn't let on. Several times the man tried to catch her eye. Finally she turned toward him and barked, "*No más sardinas.* All gone for today."

The man nodded to signify that he had understood, then asked, "*Cuando?*"

"Maybe *mañana*," she said irritably, exhausting her Spanish. "Who the fuck knows? Whenever the hell I get 'em." She turned back to swabbing out boats.

My knowledge of Paula's story has accreted slowly over the years. She is not prone to trust or self-revelation. You wouldn't be either if you'd had her background. She grew up on the outskirts of Chicago, the oldest girl of four children, with an alcoholic father and a mother who was less than fully engaged with her family. Home being such an unpredictable place, she spent a lot of time in the woods. Her grandfather taught her much of what she knows. "He knew every plant, every bird by its call alone," she remembers. Her uncles took her fishing and hunting. But a lot of her woods sense came "just because I was there all the time. You learn to feel, you know, comfortable there after a while."

When Paula was thirteen, she once told me, she answered a knock on the front door to find a woman, the wife of her father's business partner, weeping hysterically. Paula's father had swindled the man out of every cent of his money. The man had committed suicide. Paula hadn't known about any of it. "She was screaming, 'Your father killed my husband,'" Paula said. She shrugged. I knew that shrug. It meant she had said all she had to say.

During her tenth-grade year at a Catholic girls' school she got expelled for organizing students against the war in Vietnam. She proceeded to do the logical thing, which was to enroll in public school. "Third day there, two cops showed up at my classroom and escorted me out. I got thrown outta public school for what I'd done at the private school! This was when Daley was mayor. Chicago was a different place back then. They could get away with shit like that." Apparently, Paula was not the only student in the Chicago school system to be treated this way. Years later, she said, there had been a class action suit by a number of students who had been unjustly expelled. They'd been given some kind of settlement money. Paula, never much of a joiner, didn't want any part of it.

It wasn't too long after this that Paula took a bus to New York. She'd meant to go for a short visit to a friend, but circumstances intervened. The bus somehow caught fire en route, destroying virtually everything in the luggage compartment. "They set up a table right by the side of the road and the bus company was handing out checks on the spot," she said, her tone suggesting she'd just hit the lottery. By the time she got to the head of the line, the amount and value of Paula's luggage had increased considerably. She walked away with enough to put down on a tiny apartment and decided to stay. She worked at all kinds of jobs, including exercising racehorses at one of the tracks. "It was either Aqueduct or Belmont, whichever one you could get to on the subway. I did that until I discovered it was a very good way to get hurt." Then she got a job with a printer, and worked in print shops over the years before starting one of her own. By this time she had also succumbed to the family curse, alcoholism. What did she drink? "Everything, honey. Anything I could get my hands on." Sometime in the 1990s, she ran afoul of the IRS. She's sketchy on the details, other than to say that she was paying the agency $7,000 a month by certified check and thought that they had an understanding. "Then they seized my assets, my accounts, everything I had. So I said, 'I don't need this shit, honey. Sayonara.'" And with that, Paula sort of rolled off the grid: no steady job, no house, no car, no driver's license or government-issued I.D. of any form. There are times, even today, when I wonder if "Smith" is her real last name.

One day, she simply stopped drinking. She'd lost one sibling to alcohol and another, her favorite brother, to AIDS and drugs. She knew she'd wind up crazy or dead if she kept on drinking, so one day she stopped. It wasn't too long after that, she says, that she turned up at Fletcher's. There she met Gordon, a retired federal fisheries biologist, who had grown up fishing at Fletcher's and was one of the regulars there. Gordon's father lived with him at the time. The man was dying and Gordon needed help tending him. In exchange for room and board, Paula helped take care of him. After Gordon's father died, she stayed on, and she has been helping Gordon fix up the house ever since. It's been nearly a decade now. On the surface they are an odd pair: Gordon is a gentleman of the old school, soft-spoken, upright, a courtly man who opens doors for women. Paula is pretty much the opposite in every way. But, as sometimes happens, their contrasting temperaments somehow make them compatible housemates. They both like to fish and to be out in the woods, and most days you can find one or both of them down at the boathouse.

Paula thinks of the area north and south of Fletcher's as "her" woods. She keeps track of the various people who frequent the area, like the striper addicts who sleep in their cars in the boathouse lot to save money. A man she referred to only as "Mudcat" was one such soul. "Guy was in the mason's union making thirty-seven bucks an hour," she told me. "But he'd rather chase rockfish. He used to borrow money from his own mother so he could stop working and just fish, and when he ran out of that he started sleeping in his car. He's like a rockfishaholic. He'll go hungry but buy fresh lobster tail for bait." Paula knows the homeless people. She knows the cops. And if she doesn't know the individuals who poach deer along the river, she knows their habits. She studies the kind of treestands they put up and the blinds they build of sticks and leaves. By the location and type of blind, she can tell whether they're using bow or gun and whether they prefer day or night. Sometimes she wrecks their blinds and steals their stands. Other times, she places a telltale vine or another piece of vegetation that they can't help disturbing, the better to ascertain when and how often they return. She buttonholes cops at the boathouse and keeps them up to date on the poaching tally.

Once, when we were out hunting shed antlers, she showed me some sticks amid the undergrowth and explained that it was a poacher's ground blind. I looked at it carefully. Having hunted for nearly twenty years, I have made and used ground blinds. I consider myself fairly woods savvy. For a ground blind, for example, you cut and place branches so they obscure your human shape and look like part of the landscape. You leave small openings, shooting lanes, where you think a deer or turkey will appear. I was pretty sure the fallen sticks Paula was looking at were not a blind and told her so. "Trust me, honey," she said. "The smart guys, they don't cut vegetation; they *arrange* it." She

39

walked in the direction the blind faced and kicked at something. Sure enough, fifteen yards away, right in the middle of a tiny opening, was a forty-pound mineral lick, the kind farmers put out for cattle. It was brown and hard to spot. Deer are just like cattle, constantly seeking out salt and minerals, which can be in especially short supply in the city. I looked around for Paula but couldn't find her until she called to me. She stood fifty yards farther on, hunched over the desiccated carcass of a deer, hide and all, probing it with a stick. It was months old, heavily scavenged, now little more than bones, hide, and small mounds of hair. From the pile, Paula lifted a crossbow bolt, which is like a normal arrow only shorter and heavier. The tip's three razor-sharp blades bore a light coat of rust. "Trophy guy," Paula muttered. "All he took were the antlers." She showed where whoever it was had sawed off the antlers and the front part of the skull. The cut started just behind the eyes, went two inches back and two inches up. It was eerily precise work, a shelf of bone surgically removed from the skull. You had to have done the procedure many times to be any good at it, and this guy had obviously put in the time. If I needed proof that Paula knew more about deer and the innominate poachers who hunt them right in downtown D.C. than the cops—or anyone else for that matter—this was it. I no longer question Paula when she tells me about deer and poachers.

Not long after the perch run ended I went fishing with Paula to help replenish her herring supply. We were armed with rods carrying a Sabiki rig, a diabolical little gizmo consisting of a length of fishing line with six dropper lines attached, each carrying a tiny gold hook dressed with a colored bead and an iridescent hackle. Just getting a Sabiki out of its plastic packaging and onto your line is a feat. The hooks seek each other out as if magnetized, and I've turned many a Sabiki into a useless bird's nest of tangles in a twinkling. Fortunately, Sabikis are cheap. And if you can get the thing into the water intact, a Sabiki rig is a baitfish-catching machine. You drop it right next to the boat, using just enough sinker to hold bottom in the current—usually an ounce or two. Once it reaches the bottom, you animate the tiny dressed hooks by popping the rig up with your rod tip and allowing it to fall. Strikes usually come on the fall, when the lures seem most vulnerable. Herring feed on zooplankton, so nobody knows why they hit Sabiki rigs. Maybe it's a chance to try something new, maybe there's something about the gold flash of the hooks that aggravates them. Whatever the reason, when the fish are running thick it's not uncommon to have two or three on the line at once.

During a lull in the action, I idly asked whether herring were any good to eat. "Oh, yeah," Paula said. "Kinda bony, but I like 'em. You can't fillet the bones out but they soften up when you cook them." Why, then, didn't she eat them? "You kidding? I get three bucks apiece for a fish that has maybe two bites of meat on it. They're worth a hell of a lot more to me as bait than food, honey." She said she liked herring roe better than the more popular shad roe. And while nobody today fishes for herring except for bait, a hundred years ago people came from all over for the Potomac's herring run. "Gordon and his family used to catch them like crazy when he was a kid."

This was a minor thunderbolt. Here I was helping Paula load up on fish she would sell for bait—bait I could be *eating*. How had a local, readily available protein source escaped my notice? I regularly hunted deer, but that involved driving an hour or more each way. Herring were almost in my backyard, a fifteen-minute drive. I remembered eating creamed herring as a child and fancying myself something of a connoisseur because I liked it. But I was like most Americans. Herring had simply fallen off my radar.

Gordon confirmed that his family used to fish herring for food. "Oh, it was a big deal," he said. "There were tackle shops on either end of Chain Bridge where you'd rent snagging poles. Fourteen- or sixteen-foot pieces of bamboo with a length of heavy carpenter's plumb line and a weighted treble hook on the end. You'd stand out on a rock and rip that thing through the water, snag the fish, and throw them into a basket. I always thought a dip net was more effective. Stick it in, scoop 'em up. As boys we'd catch until our arms wore out." Buyers paid boys a penny apiece for the fish. When the first herring showed up in late March, Gordon's mother would always fry some with eggs for breakfast. The season lasted two and a half months, mid-March to the first of June. When the family had finally had their fill of fresh herring, Mrs. Leisch preserved them in ceramic crocks for use during the year. "She'd put down a layer of salt, a layer of fish until she filled it up, then start on another." When she wanted to cook the fish, she placed that quantity in fresh water overnight to draw the salt out.

The more I found out about herring, the more they seemed a locavore's dream: an abundant, potentially sustainable, extremely local fish. Human consumption of herring dates back at least 5,000 years, and they were a staple in Europe from the Middle Ages on. Even today, in some cultures herring is known as "two-eyed steak." The Swedish, Dutch, Danes, and Norwegians consume vast amounts, eaten raw, pickled, smoked, and—for those exceptional individuals straddling the thin line between true connoisseur and certifiable whack job—buried underground until the fish have fermented.

For most of American history, the fish were hugely important, an abundant and inexpensive source of protein. Among the rivers most famed for their herring runs was the Potomac. George Washington, never one to pass up a quick buck, was an early participant in the commercial fishery. A May 1772 entry in his ledger records the sale of 11,000 herring. In 1895, the *New York Times* wrote, "In the Maryland and Virginia regions adjacent to the Potomac, salted herring holds about same place in the domestic commissariat that salt pork does in New England." The article ends with the observation, "No well-regulated household in this region finds it convenient to do without herring at this season, and there is always regret when the savory little fellow returns to the sea." In 1891 the herring take from the Potomac alone surpassed 7 million pounds. The world's largest haul seine was in use on the Potomac at Stony Point on the Virginia shore at that time. It was two miles long and took a team of horses to haul it in.

The day after learning of herring's edibility I was back out in the river, busily embedding Sabiki hooks in my hands, neck, pants, hat, oars, and anchor line (the hardest to get out) and—eventually—in the mouths of a few herring. I eventually figured out that keeping the line under tension at all times, even when letting the raised rig fall to the bottom, reduced tangling. I was soon sliding herring into the basket at a steady rate. Almost upon dropping the rig, I would feel the electric wiggle of a herring. The fish average a quarter to half a pound and are on the menu of virtually any swimming thing that exceeds them in size. Herring seem strangely resigned to their fate as baitfish. Each one not slipped directly into the basket fell to the deck of the boat and then flapped from bow to stern and back again, one hand clapping madly in a bid to return to water. The display lasted less than a minute, however, and then the fish lay down and died as if practiced in it. In death, a herring lacks the stunned and vaguely accusatory look of a perch. It looks pretty much the way it did alive. In short, a great starter fish for the squeamish locavore. It's all but impossible to feel more than a passing twinge of guilt at the death of a herring. Something was bound to get it sooner or later.

On my second or third outing, I was boating fish at a nice clip when abundance mania kicked in. "Abundance mania"—a phrase so apt I'm surprised no one thought of it before me—describes the cocktail of neurotransmitters that unleashes the irresistible compulsion to collect more and more of something having three characteristics:

- It has just come into season.
- It's suddenly everywhere.
- It won't be for long.

I had already felt abundance mania when catching perch. Though I didn't know this at the time, I would experience it in numerous picking-and-gathering situations to come. At the moment, the object was herring. I once saw an interview with Richard Pryor in which he was asked "how cocaine makes you feel." He replied, "It makes you feel like doing more cocaine." Abundance mania does the same thing. Catching a bunch of herring made me want to catch a bunch more herring. My state of mind combined intense focus and an insatiable appetite to collect the thing in question, with an overlay of euphoria. When you're in this state, when you've got a fish on almost before your rig hits bottom, the only thing you can think about is the next fish. And the next. And the next. The idea of saying "enough" never crosses your mind. You know that you've become a lab rat pushing the lever that squirts an addicting chemical into its bloodstream, but it doesn't slow you down. What finally interrupted my mania was a brief moment of clarity during which I realized that every fish I caught was a fish I would also have to clean. I stopped immediately. Hoisting the basket back into the boat required both hands. Then, because I hadn't reeled in a fish in sixty seconds, I had to drop the rig down and catch a few more. Days later, relating the story to Gordon, I learned that any rig employing more than three hooks was a violation of local fishing regulations. (Incidentally, it was no great surprise that I learned this fact from Gordon, not Paula.) I have since modified my Sabikis to conform. It's a trade-off. I catch fewer fish but also sustain fewer injuries.

Onshore, I found that the fish filled my cooler to the point where there was almost no room for ice. I sped home, stopping for more ice at a 7-Eleven, and divided fish and ice between two coolers. I undressed by the washing machine in the basement. I knew I reeked—several people had motioned me ahead of them in line at the 7-Eleven. But I'd been exposed to the fish so long that the odor no longer registered. Herring scales winked up at me from my discarded shirt and pants. Scales lodged in the hair on my arms and chest. I felt happy as I loaded the machine. I walked upstairs and into a hot shower, where more scales rode the water down the drain. I was tired and hungry, but the last thing I wanted for dinner was herring. I grabbed a package of venison from the freezer, stew meat from the leg of a doe I'd killed six months earlier. I did a speed-defrost, dunking the meat in a large bowl of warm water. I fried some up and made a venison sandwich with pickles, mustard, and mayonnaise. I washed dinner down with one of the beers I'd home-brewed from a kit two months earlier. I fell into bed and slept the sleep of the fulfilled fisherman, which is similar to the state of a loose herring flapping around the boat when it finally gives up.

The next day, I was eager to try both cooked fish and roe. Most of all I wanted to inaugurate my new smoker, an electric Brinkmann Gourmet that I'd bought at Home Depot for sixty bucks. I'd bought it after happening upon a foodie radio program on NPR, during which the guy—who sounded as if he'd be happier mixing cement than a béchamel—had said that oily fish were the best candidates for smoking. One of the more encouraging things I'd learned about herring from Gordon was that there was no need to gut and clean them. They could simply be filleted. He also said to leave the skin on and his say-so was reason enough, although I was curious about the rationale. As I worked, this became self-evident: herring skin was so thin that it would be next to impossible to remove. I cleaned fish for nearly an hour, and by the time I finished I had about ninety fillets.

The first order of business was to try some fresh herring. I slid four fillets into a pan with some oil, sautéed them over medium-high heat until they had browned, and arranged them on a plate with toasted sourdough bread, butter, and a bit of mustard. It tasted . . . okay. To be honest, I was disappointed. I'd hoped to find it wonderful, but it was neither objectionable nor particularly appetizing, the taste at once fairly mild and fairly fishy. This, I decided, was the invariable characteristic of an oily fish. And perhaps why few people of my acquaintance ate herring. It didn't taste that different from sardines, and I later discovered that in fact small herring are sometimes sold as sardines.

I approached the two sacs of roe I'd saved with trepidation. They were kidney-shaped and sheer, with tiny red veins running through them. The eggs inside were pale yellow and appeared to have the texture of grits. I wished I'd known what the standard procedure was, because I knew neither how long to cook them nor whether the sacs should be kept intact or mashed in an attempt to cook the eggs evenly. I have always preferred ice cream mashed and softened, which may be why I did the same thing to the herring roe with a spatula, removing the pan from the heat when the roe started to turn gray.

For a guy who has eaten chicken eggs his whole life without giving them a second thought, I was surprisingly creeped out by herring roe. Maybe it was a numbers thing. One chicken egg meant one unborn chicken. But the roe from a single herring represented thousands of potentially meaningful herring lives cut tragically short. I found myself coining an advertising slogan for herring roe—"A school-full in every spoonful!"—and took a bite. For a food with no particularly strong flavor—it tasted of the fish itself, only more so—I found it surprisingly . . . repellent. But then again, I once had real Iranian caviar and didn't like that either. I'm convinced that scarcity alone is what makes some foods beloved of gastronomes. If peanuts were as rare as caviar, the height of debauchery might involve wealthy degenerates scarfing down mounds of Jif from porcelain plates. In any case, herring roe and I had parted company.

Undeterred, I moved on to smoking. First I rinsed and dried the fillets, then arranged them on the smoker's two circular racks until there wasn't an uncovered square centimeter. At the last minute I salted the fillets liberally, reasoning that it couldn't hurt. I plugged the smoker in and soon felt the warmth coming off the lava rocks sitting atop the electric heating element. I covered those with a half pound of hickory chips that had been soaking in water and put the top on. My new smoker looked like a big red suppository leaking clouds of smoke. I went inside and started working on a column about traveling to rural west Texas for a quail hunt with two other hunters and four highly trained dogs. In two days, we had failed to kill a single bird, which surprised the hell out of my companions but was in fact how most of my quail hunts have gone.

Three hours passed before I remembered the smoker. I tore outside. Lifting the top, I released a ball of smoke. When it cleared, I saw that my beloved fillets had shrunk to one-third their original size, were nearly black, and were curling up at both ends. Moaning at my carelessness, I removed the racks to cool. I told myself exactly what I thought of myself, then opened an early beer to ease the sting of self-censure and bitter disappointment at the lost fish. Half an hour and two beers later, figuring that I had a responsibility at least to taste my work, I bit into a charred smoked herring. It was overdone, of course, somewhat crunchy and dry. And yet beneath the surface the meat still had an appealingly oily, smoky richness. What's more, it had lost its fishy taste. I'd never had fish jerky and still haven't, but I imagined this was roughly what it would feel and taste like. It was, I decided, against all odds, delicious. I would have liked it to be a bit less done, of course, but it possessed a pleasing combination of salt and fat, two essential traits of any commercially successful snack food product. And it was further seasoned by the knowledge that I had caught it, chilled it, scaled it, filleted it, washed and dried it, seasoned it, and smoked it myself. I felt slightly godlike, a state I can't recommend highly enough.

Stoked to smoke more herring, I redoubled my efforts at catching the little fish. The bad news was that, as with everything else in the Potomac, the runs of herring today are but an echo of those as recent as thirty or forty years ago. The good news was that when they are around, you can catch a lot in short order. I decided to bone up on smoking, too. I found a website, 3men.com, that was a trove of information about smoking everything, including fish. I began placing the fillets in an all-purpose brine the site recommended: two cups salt, one cup brown sugar, and a dash each of lemon juice and garlic to a gallon of water. It was recommended that after brining for half an hour or so, you allow the fish to dry in a "cool breezy place protected from flying insects" until a thin glaze known as a pellicle formed. The pellicle was said to promote the retention of moisture and texture during smoking. The closest thing I had to a breezy place was the backyard, but it was anything but protected from flying insects. As soon as I set the racks down, flies appeared as if I'd just received a truckload of fresh horse manure and was throwing a block party. My God but those flies loved herring. I rushed the racks back inside and pondered. It wasn't possible to screen the racks. The best I could do was create hazards to aviation in the flies' vicinity. I hauled out an old attic exhaust fan that took twenty seconds to reach full throttle, at which point it roared like a vintage fighter plane. It damn near blew the fillets right off the racks. I moved it around, experimenting until I found the right distance. At five feet, the fillets stayed put while the flies repeatedly tried to land on the meat, only to be beaten backward. I was delighted at having created a localized tornado and the fish developed a nice pellicle in about ten minutes.

I began producing batches of gorgeous, mahogany-colored smoked herring. Two to two and a half hours seemed to be the ideal smoking time. I thought the quality was, in a word, astounding. I started eating smoked herring sandwiches for lunch and found myself opening the fridge at all hours of the day for just one more. Eating smoked herring was surprisingly similar to fishing for herring. You always wanted just one more. They were dense little things. I could put a whole one in my mouth—and routinely did when headed out of the house with both hands full of fishing tackle, to be savored at leisure while I was driving. But there came a point when I began to doubt my own assessment of my work, questioning whether pride of authorship had clouded my objectivity. I decided to take some to Gordon and Paula. I was a little nervous, not least because Paula was incapable of diplomacy. If she thought my herring sucked, she'd tell me straight out. They both pronounced it "excellent." Paula, who has surprisingly high standards of food preparation for someone who eats roadkill, found fault only with the fact that I hadn't removed every last scale. I could live with that. A single scale was exactly one more than Paula could tolerate. I cranked out about six batches of smoked herring before the fish left the river in late May. Paula called at one point to compliment me on my latest batch. I wasn't home and was surprised to hear her on my voice mail. Paula almost never left messages. "I don't know, there's just something about talking to a machine that gives me the creeps," she once told me. But she raved about the herring. "You know, really, this is the best thing you do," she said, in a voice that sounded pleased that at last I'd found something I was halfway good at. Like nearly all of Paula's compliments, it was barbed. With the praise for my smoked herring came the clear implication that everything else I did was okay at best. For once, I chose to focus on the unbarbed part of her approval. With Paula you learn to take what you can get.

SMOKED HERRING
(adapted from 3men.com)

1 gallon of water at room temperature
2 cups salt
1 cup brown sugar
1/3 cup lemon juice
1 tablespoon garlic juice (or 1 tablespoon garlic powder)
1 tablespoon onion powder
1 tablespoon allspice (it is best to sift this into the water to avoid clumping)
2 teaspoons white pepper

Herring filets, the more the better

In a glass, plastic, or ceramic container (basically anything but wood or metal), mix everything but the herring thoroughly until dissolved. Place the herring in the brine solutuion, ensuring that all pieces are completely submerged. Use bricks, plates, or other weights on top of the fish to maintain complete submersion. Put container in refrigerator or place ziplock bags of ice in brine solution to keep it chilled. Let fish rest in brine 6 hours. Or, if you're bored, two hours.

Remove fish from brine, gently pat dry with paper towels, and lay pieces on the smoker racks. Elevate racks—beer cans work nicely for this—to allow for air circulation. A fan speeds drying. After one hour—15 minutes with a fan—you will notice the fish has developed a glazed "skin." This is called the pellicle, and you want it to seal in moisture and flavor. When the fish is sticky to the touch it means two things: that the fish is ready for the smoker and that you should wash your hands before sorting laundry while the fish smokes.

Smoke fish for about 2 hours at 200 degrees F.

Use your favorite wood chips when smoking; hickory, alder, apple, and cherry—or combinations of these—work well. (Never use soft woods, such as pine or poplar. Ditto for engineered wood siding products such as SmartSide and Hardi Plank.) Soak wood chips in water for 10 minutes before putting in smoker or grill. Add more wood chips about every 30 minutes, depending on what's on TV.

Oily fish like herring are pretty forgiving. They're best at around 1½ to 2 hours. But I've fallen asleep, let them go four hours, and still found them tasty. They will also be smaller and drier. This is a good option if you're packing to run away from home.

Chapter Three:
The Homicidal Gardener

"How fair is a garden amid the trials and passions of existence."
—Benjamin Disraeli

With the spring run over and a store of frozen perch and smoked herring put by, it was time to figure out other edibles I could hunt, gather, or otherwise procure. Planting a garden seemed to be a sensible first step, even if I wasn't enthralled by the notion. Agriculture, after all, is what replaced hunting and gathering, giving rise to civilization, indoor plumbing, and ranch dressing. Man cannot live by meat alone, although I would have been willing to give it a try, especially now that I'd mastered smoked herring. I had half-custody of Emma, however, and at this point in my life I still labored under the delusion that children need to consume the occasional green vegetable. By force, if necessary.

While I knew zilch about gardening, I also harbored the notion that I might have a knack for it. This belief was grounded in having grown four killer marijuana plants in the backyard of the house I'd shared with Jane before we got married. I'd started about a dozen in peat pots and when, to my surprise, they'd thrived, I transplanted them to manure-filled holes on the south-facing slope of the backyard, hiding them among some kind of low landscaper's shrubbery that grew there. Someone had told me you needed to kill off the males before they flowered, which made the females work that much harder, producing superior bud. I actually learned how to tell the sexes apart, thanks to the billions of Internet pages devoted to marijuana cultivation. Anyway,

I fed the surviving females Miracle-Gro daily and hoped that the guy mowing his lawn ten feet away on the other side of the fence wouldn't notice the pungent odor of ripening cannabis. When a friend tried the finished product he said, "Dude, you could get four hundred an ounce for this shit." I felt as though I'd just won a 4-H Club blue ribbon. The same guy pointed out that in the state of Virginia, the police could basically take away your house if you were found to be growing pot. That marked the end of my marijuana cultivation career.

One of the good points of the otherwise unremarkable house I eventually purchased after my marriage ended was its backyard. It was a full forty yards deep, a big chunk of real estate in Arlington, Virginia, and a large swath of it received full, or nearly full, sun. It seemed like a good spot for a garden. I happened to mention this to my fishing buddy, Greg, who had experience as a gardener. He confirmed what I'd suspected, which was that the first thing I needed to do was plow up the lawn with a rototiller. "You want to rent a rear-tine model," he said. "The others won't be powerful enough." I had no idea how a rear-tine rototiller differed from others, but I felt knowledgeable specifying one when I called a rental shop.

"I assume you know you'll need a truck to move this thing," the man said. I didn't know this. Nor did I have a truck—I had a 2003 Subaru Forester. But I did have a friend around the corner who would lend me his pickup. Bright and early the next day, I set out. Few things in a man's life so lift his spirit as as heading down the road on a spring morning to rent a large, powerful machine with which he will destroy something. The rental contract resembled a bail bond application. I acknowledged that I could be maimed or killed by the machine and that they could seize my possessions and hunt me down like a dog if I tried to steal it. Then I was given a thirty-second lesson in its operation, which was inaudible over the hearty roar of the 6.5-horsepower Troy-Bilt pony engine. It seemed like the Abrams tank of rototillers. It sported lethally crooked twelve-inch tines, thirteen-inch pneumatic tires, and a cast-iron tine shield designed to prevent your legs from being turned into mashed potatoes. To have this much power at my command was intoxicating. I had marked off three beds in the back-yard, each five feet wide and twenty-five feet long, using jade green Krylon Indoor/Outdoor spray paint, a much more vibrant color than the lawn itself. To move the rototiller, the engine had to be on and the tiller disengaged. I backed the truck right up to the slope of my front yard, dropped the tailgate, and drove the thing onto my property. For an instant, I was tempted to try rototilling the sidewalk, just to see what it would look like. I was certain the machine was capable of this but managed to rein in the impulse. I was less successful controlling myself when it came to the lawn. Having thoroughly plowed the three beds I'd designated with the spray paint, I went on to do two more of equal size. These last two were mostly in the shade, but what the hell. I figured there must be something edible that liked shade. By the time I was done, I had rototilled nearly 500 square feet of garden and felt like a god. (Just so you know, the shaded beds never grew anything. Not even grass, once I conceded failure and tried to reintegrate them into the lawn. It didn't work. To this day there are two corrugated patches of dirt in my backyard, forsaken even by most weeds.)

As it turned out, this was but the first of three times I would rent the rototiller. A week later, I got back the soil analysis that I'd sent weeks earlier to the county extension service and promptly forgotten. The report said that my soil was highly acidic and recommended that five pounds of lime be thoroughly mixed into each hundred square feet of soil. By this time, I had become a man to whom the phrase "thoroughly mix in" meant only one thing: another shot of rear-tine rototiller. A week after that, while talking to a neighborhood gardener about my new garden, the woman interrupted me in mid-sentence. "Wait, are you telling me you you didn't use any soil amendments?" she asked. Her tone suggested I might as well have poisoned Emma's Cheerios. The local soil, she explained, was essentially clay. It was, she said, like asking your plants to send down roots through concrete. Never having heard of "soil amendments" but fearful of being labeled a sadistic gardener, I went to a nursery, where I found the prices for soil amendments appalling. After talking to one of the salesmen, I bought two cubic yards of Ortho-Mix, a "reclaimed" product that, while half the price of the "organic" stuff was, he said, just as good. I drove the stuff home—I was borrowing my friend's truck a lot—and rototilled it into to the beds. It would be weeks before I discovered that Ortho-Mix was nothing more than sewage sludge that had been "processed," a procedure that no one has ever explained to me. Not that I want them to. I tried to give Ortho-Mix the benefit of the doubt, much as one might hire a young criminal after he had completed six weeks of vocational education. The fact that I was growing vegetables in a medium largely composed of material that had passed through somebody else's digestive tract was something best not thought on too deeply.

The euphoria of rototilling—as with most opiates, the rush diminished with each successive rental but never completely went away—would turn out to be my favorite part of gardening. Fortunately, I was unaware of this at the time. I started planting. Like many novice gardeners, I found myself buying more seed than I could possibly use. I just couldn't resist another little envelope of pumpkin or watermelon or collards. The packets' pictures of the beautiful vegetables inside, just waiting to be unleashed, got me every time. I bought seeds for vegetables I wouldn't eat on a bet. Beets, for example.

Seeds were a hell of a lot more fun to buy than to plant. Especially carrots. Planting carrot seeds is no more difficult than etching a copy of Leonardo's *The Last Supper* on a watch battery. They may be sown for example, at any depth you like between one-quarter inch and one-half inch. The seeds themselves, nearly invisible, are to be sown three per inch, in rows fifteen inches apart. Naturally, you will want to check the seedbeds daily and moisten the surface if it seems the slightest bit dry using a "rose-type" nozzle so that you don't blast the tender seedlings. (I Googled "rose-type nozzle" for twenty minutes before I found, courtesy of the Columbus Bonsai Society, that it's an attachment that spreads the water out evenly, even at low pressure, which is where your run-of-the-mill nozzle shows its flaws. It has something to do with the "cohesive" nature of water and, I suspect, the origins of matter itself. Anyway, the folks in Ohio gave a glowing review of the Masakuni Watering Wand, which is a mere thirty dollars and "available from most online bonsai distributors.") Assuming you haven't blasted your carrot seedlings to kingdom come with a fire hose, you thin them to one plant per square inch once they attain a height of two inches. And one learns—although in my case, not until well after planting—that the soil must first be thoroughly loosened to the depth of the mature carrot, because carrots are a cheating, lying vegetable. A mature one looks sturdy and robust, fully capable of driving its way into the earth like a nail. But that's not how carrots grow. What they do instead is send down a delicate, threadlike, easily discouraged root. And it's only when this thing reaches its maximum depth that the carrot begins to thicken. If, like me, you've been fool enough to buy Long Imperator carrots, for example, that means loosening the soil to a depth of at least ten inches. Jesus! Growing carrots was like dating Winona Ryder, attractive at first but so high-maintenance that you began to wonder what you saw in her in the first place. My *Rodale's Vegetable Garden Problem Solver* advised weekly inspection with a magnifying glass to check the feathery leaves. "Small dark brown, black, gray, or tan spots" indicate leaf blight. Yellowing leaves, a lack of nutrients (kelp or a water-soluble organic fertilizer may help). But they could also be a sign of "aster yellows" or the dreaded "root-knot nematodes." All of this was terribly interesting, but I'd be damned if I was going to do it.

Knowledge of what a pain in the ass growing carrots was gave me a new appreciation for the ones in the supermarket. I was also glad that my survival did not depend on plants so fragile. As I looked with new eyes at supermarket carrots, however, I found myself wondering about something else I'd never considered. Namely, why do we, the food-buying public, allow vegetable growers to package fruits and vegetables in plastic bags that, although they appear transparent at first glance, are actually lined with colored pinstripes—orange, yellow, green, and brown—to make the vegetables look fresher and more colorful than they are?

Wondering about this, I spent way too much time researching variations on "carrot packaging orange stripes enhanced," expecting to find outraged consumer groups who objected to the practice. Near as I can tell, I'm the only one who is at all worked up about this. We don't rein in or punish the companies that deceive us like this. We give them government subsidies.

I did, however, come across a 2003 MSNBC news story about the carrot industry's turnaround moment. I refer, of course, to the creation of fake baby carrots. On the off chance that you don't follow the industry closely, here's the deal. In the late 1980s carrot consumption flatlined. We were eating carrots but not a whole bunch of them. Mike Yurosek & Son, one of California's largest growers, was looking for a way to juice sales. The company found it in the "baby carrot," which quickly increased carrot sales by a whopping 50 percent. It was the most dynamic carrot development in decades. And not only did consumption of carrots increase dramatically, but it was found that baby carrots could be sold for twice as much per pound as regular carrots and sometimes even more. The real genius of the invention of baby carrots is that "baby carrots" aren't baby carrots at all. (True baby carrots exist but are a small speciality market.) Read the fine print and you'll see that what that bag says is "baby-cut" carrots. A baby-cut carrot is nothing more than a two-inch piece of a bigger carrot that has been cut and peeled—"abraded" is the term of art—by a machine that essentially grates off the outer layer and rounds the ends so it looks like a baby carrot. And the beauty part is that you can get three or four "baby-cut" carrots out of a regular carrot.

I felt a fatherly duty to expose Emma to the idea of gardening. If she hated it, that was her right. At least I'd have done my part. She had been mildly curious about my rototilling sprees and I hoped that this might lead to actual gardening. In our particular historical moment, anything that gets a child playing in the dirt should be encouraged. You want to subsidize something? Subsidize that. Thus it was the one afternoon I called her over as I worked in the yard. "Monkalula," I announced solemnly, "it is time to plant the carrots." I decided against burdening her with the joy-trampling exactitude of planting as instructed by the seed packets and gardening books. We were just going to get the damn things into the ground and hope for the best. We each found a stick with which to scratch five rows each across one of the raised beds. Next, taking seeds between thumb and forefinger, we sprinkled them into the scratched furrows. At least we may have been doing this. The seeds were so tiny that you wondered whether they were subject to gravity at all, so tiny it was hard to see them in your own hand. Once released, they disappeared against the backdrop of the earth. We sprinkled until we emptied two packets, then knelt and teased soil over the furrows with our fingers. The next step was to water, something Emma was eager to do. I handed her the running hose and was about to tell her to water gently, as our Masakuni Water Wand had not yet arrived. But she had already buried her thumb in the nozzle and was blasting the seeds with such violence that it was like a mini diorama of the Birmingham riots. She was undoubtedly launching some of them ten feet out of the garden. One of my worst faults as a parent is my tendency to overinstruct. But the unreasonably detailed and horatory nature of the carrot-planting instructions I'd read had freed me for once from the compulsion to dictate. "Good job," I said approvingly. "They're nice and wet now." The great thing, I decided, was that my daughter and I had just planted something together. Anything that actually survived was gravy.

Late that evening, after Emma had gone to sleep, I strolled out back and surveyed my five beds, all more or less seeded, now quiet in the still of the suburban night. I tried to imagine tiny vegetable shoots already bursting out of the seeds and pushing toward the surface. I felt as if I were in the opening scene of the movie *Patton,* where George C. Scott, facing an unseen assembly of untested recruits, tells them, "All real Americans love the sting of battle." Like him, I knew what these young shoots did not, that they would shortly enter the crucible of competition, fighting to get as much light, water, and nutrients as they could if they hoped to survive. Trying to channel my own inner Patton, I growled, "Get motivated, motherfuckers" to the newly planted seeds in my beds. "In the weeks and months ahead, we will separate . . ." Here my speech stalled. I was not quite sure what we'd be separating. There had to be some vegetative equivalent of the men from the boys, but it was beyond my current level of knowledge. It was about this time that I noticed the glowing orange dot of a cigarette from the patio of my closest neighbor, barely forty feet away, sneaking a last smoke before bed. She had undoubtedly heard every word I'd said. I turned and slowly retreated inside, thinking, Great. You are now officially the crazy single dad who waits until his child is asleep to sneak outside and issue profane pep talks to non-existant plants.

The damnedest thing happened to not a few of my carrots: They sprouted. Not, I hasten to point out, the ones in the fifteen-foot carrot "strip" I bought and secretly put down to replace the carrots that Emma had hosed into eternity. I had bought this high-tech, foolproof carrot contraption so that my daughter's first gardening experience would be a success. The packaging promised that each of the 570 tiny seeds had been placed the optimal distance from its fellows. It was sheathed in some environmentally friendly fabric packed with all the nutrients carrots require. Those carrots never even woke up. Instead, it was the ones that we planted together that had somehow sent up their lacy green tops. I noticed them on a June afternoon while mowing the lawn and was so taken that I let the mower stall and dropped to my stomach to marvel at them "Em!" I hollered. "C'm 'ere!" My daughter was in her favorite spot in the yard, the crotch of the slowly dying dogwood tree in the front yard.

"What?" she called back, in what I realized was becoming her default tone—a combination of irritation at her play being interrupted and suspicion that whatever I had to say would not be something she wanted to hear. She had adopted it for a perfectly good reason, which was that more often than not when I summoned her, it wasn't to praise her, give her a treat, or invite her to do something she'd enjoy. It was far more likely to be on the order of telling her to start her homework, clean up her room, or get into the shower. It was humbling—shameful, really—to realize that I was the author of how my daughter perceived me. I vowed to spend more time enjoying this curious, bighearted, spirited child, and less trying to bend her to my will. "You're not in trouble," I called back. "C'm 'ere! Your carrots came up!" My excitement somehow conveyed, for she came running.

"Look," I said, pointing. She flopped down beside me for a closer look. The foliage was all of an inch long, but unmistakable. When I heard my daughter's sharp intake of breath, my heart leaped. All was not lost. There was yet time for me to change course, be a better father, be something more than just the hairy thunderer who pointed out her failures. We were in business.

"Let's water the sunflowers!" she said.

I had forgotten all about planting sunflowers. I had dropped a few seeds in the hard clay by the air conditioner condenser or whatever that thing is that blows hot air all summer. Its only advantage was that the spot that got maximum sun. The sunflowers hadn't sprouted, but I liked the way she referred to them as if they were already facts. I turned on the hose and she applied her thumb as before. She aimed it at the sunflowers, the air-conditioning unit, the cement walkway, and most of the bricks in the back wall of the house. For once, I let her waste water. I simply stood and enjoyed the delight with which she watered bricks.

I was astonished at how swiftly and directly the gentle act of vegetable gardening led to murder, but lead there it did.

By high summer, from my office on the converted porch, I had but to turn my head to see a bounty of squash, tomatoes, eggplant, beans, kale, peas, peppers, watermelons, and carrots. Even some of the damned beets had come up. My greatest love, like that of many gardeners, was reserved for my tomatoes. Until this point I had thought that a tomato was ripe when it achieved the proper color. Now, however, having learned what a truly ripe tomato tasted like, I revised my criteria. A tomato at its absolute peak of ripeness, I'd discovered, was not only something I'd never had before. It was almost a different species.

The fruit, having little fragrance until a certain moment, gave, at the moment of peak ripeness, an earthy, vegetal, almost sexual odor, and the flesh had a particular voluptuous firmness. Such tomatoes are not sold in the supermarket. They couldn't withstand the handling. And the ripeness was so short-lived, no more than a day or two. But, my God, they were good. I couldn't get enough of them.

The problem was that there were five or six squirrels living in the big red oak at the very rear of my property. And the squirrels liked tomatoes, too. What they liked above all things was to wait until a tomato gave off that odor of perfect ripeness and then take a few deep, chisel-shaped bites out of it. Which they then spat out. They did this so consistently that I began to wonder: Was ruining tomatoes simply one of the great pleasures and privileges of being a squirrel or was it, rather, a duty? Were young squirrels taught by their mothers that ruining the tomatoes tended by a species that sometimes hunted and ate them was a revenge they owed their ancestors? Maybe it was a nutritional thing. Maybe their mothers said, "You should always take a bite of ripe tomato, dear, for the phytochemicals. You don't have to eat it, just swish it around your cheeks. And if it pisses off a human, well, so much the better."

One afternoon on the porch, I happened to look out and see three squirrels frolicking in my garden. One was new to me. It had a different hop—bouncier, more vertical—from the squirrels I knew. I trained the Nikon 8×42 binoculars I keep at the desk (handy for bird-watching and spying on your neighbors) on the squirrel. It had disappeared into the kale. I could track its progress, however, by the waving stems and leaves. Magnified eightfold, it reminded me of Kong among the palms. It reversed course, returning as it had come, through the tomatoes. Then it stopped, standing nonchalantly with one elbow (I'd never thought of squirrels as having elbows) resting on the lowest wire of a tomato cage, one paw resting on its hip. It looked strangely relaxed and jaunty like a guy hustling fake Rolexes who wasn't worried about the cops. Except for its jaws, which were working rhythmically and at superhuman speed, doing the squirrel bite-and-spit on one of my tomatoes.

The planting of crops on any scale makes of one a farmer, and it is a fact that farmers live in a state of continual enmity with the animals that prey upon their crops. Squirrels weren't my only foe. Mice and voles gnawed on things—I could see the evidence on my pumpkins and watermelons. And it was birds, I was sure, that pecked to death a good many of the uppermost tomatoes. But squirrels seemed both to do the most damage and with the greatest insolence. They alone destroyed tomatoes for the sheer joy of it. The rodents had already killed half of the green tomatoes I had carefully caged. In most cases, the cause of death was a single chiseled bite near the crown of the tomato. Every time I threw another ruined tomato onto the compost heap, I thought of my labor: the getting and planting of seed, the watering and the worry, the Miracle-Gro and the tying with twine of frail tomato plant limbs to cages. The rototilling and rerototilling and re-rerototilling, I thought of the growing weight of my magnificent Early Girls and Beefsteaks and Better Boys—all the young tomato lives cut short by these bastards.

That day, as I watched this squirrel take its time selecting which tomatoes to ruin, something finally snapped in me. The bow I hunted deer with hangs from a hook in my office. Archery skill has a short shelf life and requires constant practice. Shooting a bow is also fun. With the opening of deer season just three months away, I was shooting daily. Before I knew it, I had quietly opened the window and was reaching for the bow. I removed an arrow from the bow's detachable quiver, unscrewed the field point (a conical 100-grain tip, designed to be shot into a foam target) and replaced it with a judo tip, designed to be shot at small game. A judo tip has four tiny spring-loaded wire arms emanating from the center like a lethal flower.

Thanks to my Bushnell rangefinder I knew that the squirrel presently sampling, systematically but leisurely, each and every one of my remaining tomatoes, was exactly eighteen yards away. (Lest my owning a range finder strike you as bizarre, you should know that virtually all bowhunters own and depend on these devices. An arrow drops, for example, six inches between twenty yards and thirty yards, the

61

difference between a hit and a miss.) I watched as the squirrel hopped its strangely vertical hop to the next plant and began sniffing its fruit.

I returned to my desk chair, turning sideways, squaring my body for the shot. The compound bow that many modern hunters use incorporates the first significant design change in this prehistoric weapon in thousands of years—a levering system of cam-shaped wheels and pulleys to bend the limbs, creating significantly more power and arrow speed than a traditional longbow. With longbows, the farther the string is pulled back the greater the force required (the draw weight). Because it's difficult to hold a bow at its full draw weight, most longbow archers are taught to shoot the instant the string touches their nose. A compound, by dint of its design, can be held at full draw reasonably comfortably for half a minute or so if need be.

I drew and did precisely this, waiting until the squirrel was standing upright and facing me as it chewed. I aimed for the middle of its tiny chest. And then I released my arrow. Eighteen yards away, there was a momentary bicycling of squirrel legs followed by absolute stillness. My heart raced and a rush of conflicting emotions flooded my system: exhilaration and shame, wonder and horror, pride and disgrace. I was astounded at the depth of my reaction. I have killed any number of whitetail deer with less emotional upheaval. I put the bow away, paused long enough at the porch door to make sure no one was around— unlikely at 12:30 on a weekday—and went out to verify my kill.

But there was no squirrel lying where I had shot. Looking around, I saw the shaft waggling to and fro from inside one of the tomato cages. It had evidently struck low, hitting the squirrel in the thigh. Wounded but very much alive, it had moved to the relative safety of the cage. I moved to grab the arrow shaft, at which point the squirrel unleashed a series of unearthly screams and began thrashing, the arrow's neon-lime-colored vanes waving like a distress flag. This was shocking. The squirrel sounded something like a bawling house cat—equal parts agony and fury—and was most startlingly alive. I staggered backward, shocked. Jesus! I'd never have believed a squirrel capable of this much emotional range, not to mention volume. I had to kill this thing quick, before it roused a neighbor. It wouldn't be the easiest thing to explain, especially after my profane pep talk to the carrot seeds. I ran to the shed and grabbed the likeliest garden implement for the job, a hoe. I returned intent on lifting the cage with my left hand while bringing the hoe blade down on the squirrel with my right. But at my first touch of the cage, the squirrel made a break for it. The animal had lost the use of the impaled leg, but was still moving with impressive speed for a rodent with a thirty-inch arrow in it. I was sure it couldn't get through the chain-link fence with the arrow and ran to intercept it there, planning to hoe it to death. By sheer luck or some miracle of squirrel reasoning, once the rodent passed through the fence, it twisted its leg in such a way that the arrow also passed through without hindrance. It couldn't have done this any better than if it had spent its life practicing the move. My appreciation for the squirrel's gymnastic abilities was, however, tempered by a horrifying realization, *The goddamned squirrel is now in my neighbor's yard!* Once through the fence, it headed straight to a thick bed of English ivy. Had the arrow dislodged, I could have called it quits, trusting a hawk or one of the neighborhood foxes to finish off the squirrel. As it was, the lime-green flag was still waving, semaphoring my demented cruelty. There was only one thing to do. Hoe in hand, I vaulted the fence, fully adrenalized and determined to do the damn thing in at last. I slashed at where I thought the squirrel was but somehow missed it amid the exceptionally dense ivy. In response it unleashed another torrent of squirrel profanities, stunning in variety and operatic in scope. It was all there—fear, suffering and, most of all, an unmistakable threat to exact revenge. Impressed as I was at discovering the squirrel's emotional range, I was still bent on killing it. I brought the hoe down again and again, but either each stroke missed or the ivy was so thick it dissipated the force of the blow. This was hand-to-hand combat. And the squirrel did not seem to care in the least that I was 170 times its size.

I slashed again, this time breaking the carbon-fiber arrow, but not completely. The two parts were still connected by a few strands of the material. It was at this moment that the list of laws I was breaking ran through my head: discharging a firearm inside a township (a bow is considered a firearm in most locales), hunting in a nonhunting area, hunting out of season, and God only knows what else. Criminal trespass was a possibility, given laws I'd heard of that granted certain rights to animals. Animal cruelty was probably in there somewhere. There was no way any authority would view me as a farmer protecting his crop. My vegetables—the tomatoes, corn, basil, carrots, and others I'd planted—had become dear to me over the time I'd nurtured (and, yes, on occasion threatened) them. But in the eyes of the law, I was a criminal. And as long as that squirrel had my arrow lodged in its leg, the little fucker might just as well have been wearing a wire. I was starting to panic. The neighbors in whose backyard all this was taking place were an older couple who rarely came out. But eventually even they would have to hear the squirrel shrieking—it was unbelievably loud—and emerge to investigate. There was a moment when the enraged squirrel's invective became so forceful that I was actually afraid that the tables had turned and it was coming after me. I raised the hoe high over my head now and brought it down as hard as I could, over and over, desperation fueling each swing.

Suddenly, the squirrel—arrow still attached—scampered out of the ivy bed and into the azaleas growing right next to my neighbors' house. I was trying to invent a plausible reason as to why I was hacking their azaleas to bits when I heard a car door slam. It was Jane's car. Jane was out front. I'd forgotten that it was Wednesday, early-release day at Emma's school, and my turn to have her for the afternoon. I jumped the fence back into my yard, threw the hoe in the general direction of the garden, and made for the front yard to head them off before they came upon the scene. I must have still been in fight-or-flight mode because Emma—after happily shouting "Daddy!"—took a look at my face and said, "Is everything okay?"

Of course it is, I told her. Everything's fine! Fortunately, Jane was late for something and was waving good-bye as she pulled away. Emma busied herself climbing to her accustomed perch in the diseased dogwood tree. I sat on the steps and tried to calm down and take stock of the situation. The only thing I knew for sure is that nobody hearing or seeing what had just taken place would entrust me with the welfare of a child. I found myself praying that the squirrel would die quickly and in a place where I could find him before anyone else did.

This, of course, was not to be. Later in the afternoon, while Emma was watching *Spirit: Stallion of the Cimarron* for the eight-thousandth time, I hopped the fence again, hoping to find the dead squirrel and my broken arrow. Nothing. Now I began to pray that the wretched thing would die where nobody would find it.

Two days later, Dave, my across-the-street neighbor, came over. "You lose an arrow?" he asked. As a matter of fact, I said, I had. "The reason I ask is I found a squirrel dead in my chain-link fence along the alley." He told me he had found it yesterday morning. "It had part of some kind of arrow in it, kinda creepy, you know?" I nodded in the most noncommittal way possible and waited. "So I called the cops. I thought maybe some whack job had a crossbow or something and was going around killing squirrels." I nodded again, as if I understood perfectly and was not, in fact, wondering what sort of defense I might attempt at my trial. I ask what happened. "Well, they didn't send out a cop, just an Animal Control officer." He sounded disappointed, as if he'd been hoping for an Arlington CSI team. This person, Dave said, had examined the arrow fragment (the arrow had apparently finally broken completely, thank God, which made identifying the kind of bow it had come from more difficult) and the squirrel, which had died while stuck in the chain-link fence. I asked what the Animal Control officer had deduced from his examination. "Well, he said it had obviously been shot at point-blank range with a crossbow and died immediately." Dave said that they were going to do an investigation. My face must have betrayed me. A look of comprehension suddenly creased Dave's brow. "Hey, I didn't know it was you!" he protested. I nodded as if this were understandable. I was done talking to Dave.

It was at this moment that I decided to abandon any further attempts at squirrel control. If the squirrels wanted my tomatoes, they could have them. I turned and walked up my front steps. "I really didn't know it was you," Dave called after me. "You never know what kind of whacko could be running around!"

RAW RIPE CHEROKEE PURPLE TOMATO

Plant some Cherokee purple tomato seeds, now available from Burpees. This is an extremely ugly tomato that is thought to have been given to settlers by the Cherokee people in Tennessee. It has a deep purplish red color, with green or greenish black shoulders. But the meat inside is dense, sweet, and smoky-tasting. Eighty to eighty-five days later, go out into your garden and sniff the tomatoes. When you find a tomato that gives off a vegetal funk unlike anything you have ever smelled in a grocery store, that's the tomato you want. Pick it, rubbing it gently against your pants leg to get the dust off. Eat it as you would an apple, slurping up the juice before it leaves your hand. This is as close to heaven as many people will ever get, in this life or the next.

Chapter Four:
Of Cattail Disasters and
the Blue Goose Incident

After Paula had shown me the watercress patch that day, something in me had shifted. I'd begun paying more attention to plants on our outings. And now that I had embarked on gardening and recreational squirrel homicide, the idea of learning more about foraging seemed especially attractive—if only because the penalties for killing plants were comparatively lenient. As with so many of the new skills I took up, I completely misjudged the level of knowledge needed. I knew that certain plants were edible, even tasty, and that others could lay you out like one of the perch I had recently killed. How much more could there be to know? A lot, as it turned out. Reams. Most of which was insanely confusing.

I had known Paula for several years before I realized how much of their own food she and Gordon got themselves. "You should see our grocery bill sometime, honey," Paula once bragged. "Sugar, coffee, cooking oil, bread, milk, that's about it."

Gordon had grown up here, and told tales about how, as a boy, he had carried a disassembled shotgun aboard the local bus in a paper bag to hunt squirrels and rabbits inside the Beltway. "Hell, there were places you could sight in a deer rifle inside the Beltway then," he once told me. If you tried that today, you'd have a Homeland Security SWAT team jumping out of a helicopter before you got your third round off.

Paula had her own tales of adventure regarding hunting and D.C. public transit. When parts of "her" territory were overrun with Canada geese a few years ago, she would occasionally grab one, wring its neck, stuff it into her backpack, and take it home on the bus. "You gotta be fast and know what you're doing with Canadas, though," she said. "They can hurt you." One day, she said, she had taken a big, fat goose on the Mall, wrung its neck, and was headed home on the bus. "But about the time we got to Georgetown, I hear this sound coming from my pack. The goose ain't dead. It's coming back to life. It's going *aw-uk, aw-uk*. And people are trying to figure out what this sound is and where it's coming from."

"Are you serious? What'd you do?"

"I didn't know what the hell *to* do. And people are starting to look at me, 'cause they're starting to realize where the sound's coming from. So I did my crazy-lady act just to buy some time."

"Your crazy-lady act?"

"Yeah, you know." She demonstrated. Her eyes suddenly got wide and moony. Her neck went limp. She swung her head to and fro, moaning a sort of unhinged stream-of-consciousness about buses and birds and someone called the Gravy Man chasing her. It was so good it freaked me out, despite having known her for more than a decade.

"Well, it only works for a little while. I got off the bus, but I was right in the busiest part of Georgetown. So I walked around a little, found an alley, waited till no one could see me, and finished choking that goose. Then I got on the next bus and came home. Me and Gordon ate that bird for a week."

In addition to wild game, however it was gotten, I knew that Paula also harvested mushrooms and wild greens when she happened across them. These were generally eaten fresh. When fruits and nuts came in season she put in a lot of time gathering them in quantity and pre-serving them for use throughout the year. Paula had an inventory of trees and bushes she had discovered during years of tramping all over the metropolitan area. Some were in parks and in other public places but many were on private property. If people were either unaware of the peach or apple tree in their own yard or too lazy to make use of it, Paula considered it fair game. I knew this from having trespassed extensively with her. We once drove to a house and used a ladder to hit the pear tree in the front yard. On a busy street. In broad daylight. Amazingly, no one said a word to us. Brazenness often carries the day.

In addition to apples, peaches, and pears, Paula had places where she got sweet and sour cherries, figs, and persimmons. She picked serviceberries (a native, something like a blueberry, that grows on small shrublike trees from Canada to Alabama); blackberries; and wineberries, introduced raspberries that often grow more profusely than native ones along highways and waterways. She gathered large quantities of black walnuts. The trees are common, but the quality of the nuts varies widely, even on adjacent trees of similar size. Paula is picky about her walnut trees.

Walnuts were a lot of work just to hull and dry, a messy job in itself. You waited until the outer hull had gone from hard and green to soft and brown. Then you put on boots or heavy shoes and rolled the hulls under your feet on the street, at which point you had the wet nut itself. If you handled the hulls or nuts at this stage, you acquired a brown stain on your hands that lasted for weeks. Then you had to dry the nuts, putting them in a box or basket and rolling them around every few days to make sure they dried evenly. It could take weeks to dry a big batch to the point where they were ready to crack. Cracking and picking were the real work. Walnuts are amazingly hard and are cracked by being struck with a hammer. I learned the hard way to wear safety glasses to protect my eyes from walnut shrapnel. Most time-consuming of all was picking out the meat, as the nuts have many interior chambers. Armed with a pick the size of a dental tool, I coaxed forth tiny bits of meat, along with tooth-cracking bits of shell that invariably adhered to them. (I made my own pick by hammering a four-inch nail lengthwise through a two-inch section of broom handle and then using a grinding wheel to form the tip into a spatulate shape. This was another of the few times I've managed to impress Paula. She said nothing but awarded the tool a raised forehead and an appreciative grunt.) It could take me fifteen minutes to get a tablespoon of walnut meat, which was a little crazy when you could buy shelled black walnuts at Costco for ten bucks a pound. Paula insisted that wild black walnuts tasted better, mostly, I thought, to justify the time she spent on them. She would even process hickory nuts, which yield so little meat for the effort that they make cracking and picking black walnuts look like a good use of your time. I know of no other human being who shells hickory nuts, although somebody must, since you can buy shelled commercially grown hickory nuts online for twenty-four dollars a pound, plus shipping.

Paula's knowledge of wild edible plants was wide but, like the woman herself, anything but systematic. She had learned on the fly, and she limited her foraging to the specific things that interested her. For me, foraging had quickly become the most daunting aspect of getting my own food. The body of knowledge about wild plants was endless. Worse, more so than in any other of my attempts at food-gathering, it required quite a bit of education before you could safely eat anything. A child could catch and eat a fish the very first time he put a worm on a hook. That same child could shoot and eat a rabbit, a squirrel, or even a deer the first day he went hunting. A child could also pick and eat a wild plant the same day he or she opened a copy of Peterson's *Field Guide to Edible Wild Plants*—but that child might not survive the night. Most books advised the novice to forgo eating any wild edibles for the first year unless an experienced forager had confirmed the plant in question. My problem was that the only experienced forager of my acquaintance, when asked to confirm a new plant, often responded with an irritated, "How the fuck should I know?" So I kept reading, trying to identify any single plant in multiple field guides before ingesting any of it.

The Peterson guide tried mightily to strike an encouraging tone for the novice forager ("Do not let the fear of being poisoned deter you from experimenting with wild edible plants"). The trouble was that for every reassuring sentiment there were half a dozen warnings about side effects of misidentified plants, which ranged from upset stomach to sudden death. The book's first section, for example, was "Poison Plants," which, like an Old West gunfighter notching each kill on his gunstock, awarded an asterisk to each plant with a documented death to its credit. Of the ninety plants listed, twenty-four had asterisks.

Other wrinkles in the vegetable kingdom arose with each new page. "Edible," for example, did not necessarily mean "tasty." It could also mean "suffered through for nutrition's sake during emergencies." I really hadn't been thinking about emergencies. I'd been thinking about some tasty tuber that I might fry up like a potato chip to accompany the home brew I was planning on fermenting. As I studied the drawings and photos of the oft-confused cow parsnip (a prime edible) and water hemlock ("Our deadliest species. A single mouthful can kill."), I tried to memorize the section under "treatment," which, if nothing else, thoroughly covered possible contingencies. If you thought someone had eaten a poisonous plant, you were to call your doctor immediately with the name of the plant or a good description. You should also be able to specify how much and which parts of the plant were eaten, and how long ago. Should no doctor be available, your best bet was to induce vomiting at once. You stuck our finger down the victim's throat and gave syrup of ipecac, "mustard water," soapy water, or diluted coffee grounds. Once you had successfully induced barfing, it was off to the hospital rapidly, hydrating en route. Should it not be possible to transport the victim to a hospital, you were to "repeat the vomiting process described above several times until his stomach is thoroughly cleaned out and his vomit is clear." Should the victim fall unconscious after this, you were to cease efforts at inducing vomiting, tilt the head back and to the side so that the victim could not swallow his or her tongue, and get ready to give mouth-to-mouth resuscitation.

By this point, I wanted to close the book, quietly place it deep in the trash, and substitute just about anything—Dumpster diving; shoplifting; growing and eating the sprouts from my own Chia pets—for the dangerous and arduous task of learning edible plants.

The issue of identification alone was overwhelming, calling to mind a sick person rummaging through a medicine cabinet full of unlabeled prescription drugs. In boldface type the reader was warned: **Do not attempt to use any plant that you cannot positively identify.** Look-alike poisonous plants, it turned out, were just the tip of the iceberg. The vegetable kingdom was a far more dynamic place than I'd ever imagined, full of hardy survivor species with no desire to be eaten whatsoever. Those most likely to be on the menu of animals or people at certain stages in their development, for example, adapted to this threat by making themselves harder to identify at precisely these most-edible stages. It was typically the young shoots in spring or the developed roots in fall that offered the best food value, which was to say before the plant's characteristic shapes or distinctive flowers appeared, or after the flowers were long gone and the plants had begun to die back. The symmetry of confusion was almost perfect, because at those times when a plant was most easily identified, it was usually at its least edible, hard at work manufacturing bitter chemicals, poisons, or thorns to discourage would-be foragers, whether animal or human. It was a wonder that early man had stayed around long enough to become middle man, let alone late man.

Paula had taught me the most readily available nuts and berries, along with some other plants, but the more I learned on my own the more I felt the need for a counterweight to her idiosyncratic approach. Someone with a more scientific and systematic understanding of the greater range of what was out there. A *Field & Stream* assignment that sent me to a wilderness awareness course led me to the "primitive skills community." The unfamiliar phrase conjured people dressed in skins who lived in huts made of sticks and leaves and used smoke signals to invite each other to social engagements. This was inaccurate, of course. Most primitive skills enthusiasts turned out to be well-paid middle-class professionals in various technical jobs, from scientific research to software development, who were drawn to learning how people got along before technology took over: how to knap arrowheads, tan hides, build traps, and forage. Michael Pollan calls this "playing at self-reliance" but correctly notes that "something in us apparently seeks confirmation that we still have the skills needed to provide for ourselves."

Anyway, through a chain of people I'd met in that community, I heard about Rick Hueston. He lived in Baltimore but worked at the Pentagon, just three miles from my house. "He's into all the skills, was a Special Forces type who taught survival in the military and now has some high-clearance job with Army Intel. But what he's really into is plants," one acquaintance told me when he gave me Hueston's number. I called and got a soft-spoken man who said everybody called him Hue and listened as I described my desire to get more of my food myself. Then, immediately and casually, he agreed to to teach me what he knew about edible plants. He made no mention of compensation. In fact, he offered to stop by my house after work two days later. If you know anything about the work culture of the D.C. area, generously extending yourself to a stranger like this has a well-known and highly specific meaning. It means you're about to be played like a kazoo. Nobody in this town fears the guy who would happily throw his mother under a bus for a promotion or a corner office. That's normal here. This is a place where politicians proudly cite Ayn Rand as a favorite author and spout aphorisms like this one: "If any civilization is to survive, it is the morality of altruism that men have to reject." In other words, "me first."

If you really want people here to lie awake at night in a state of fear and paranoia, do something nice for them and ask nothing in return. By this point, however, I was desperate for instruction. So I thanked Hue for his kind offer, accepted, and prepared for the worst.

As the appointed afternoon approached, I stocked a fanny pack with what I usually took along on forays with Paula: my Peterson's, a notepad, a water bottle, and a digging stick I'd fashioned from a deer antler. Despite the warm weather I put on heavy boots and pants, my protection against poison ivy and briars. (I'm deathly allergic to poison ivy, a condition that seems to be worsening as I age. The last time I was exposed it went systemic, erupting in places like behind my ears and in the folds of my eyelids. I'd had to get shots of cortisone and Benadryl in the butt followed by ten days of steroid pills.) When Hue pulled up, I walked out to greet a lean guy a few years my junior in business casual slacks and dress shirt who started pointing out edible plants almost before we'd finished shaking hands. "You got wood sorrel growing there in the cracks of the sidewalk," he said, picking a four-inch stem with clover-like leaves and tiny yellow flowers. "Good trail nibble, nice sour taste. You can add them to other greens for a salad or make a kind of lemonade by steeping the leaves for ten minutes. Peterson's says to use hot water. Thayer"—the author of another guide to wild edible plants—"says cold." I accepted the sprig, took a little bite, and found it agreeably acerbic.

Before we were halfway up the steps from the street to my front yard he identified star chickweed, seaside plantain, and gill-over-the-ground, a particularly prolific uninvited guest in my lawn. I asked what this last one was good for. "Mostly crowding out other plants," he said. "It's not native but it thrives here. In the same family as catnip. You can make a nice tea out of the dried leaves."

For a guy with such an unassuming air Hue was certainly destructive, popping my foraging fantasies left and right. Foraging, I was almost certain, required that you travel great distances until you stumbled on some secret glen—perhaps like the one where I'd discovered watercress, only minus the old appliances and droppings of deer and homeless people—where choice, ripe edibles grew. Hue, essentially, was telling me to forget that. Foraging was actually more about the stubborn little weeds that grew through your own sidewalk. In fact, so far the trait common to all the plants Hue had named was commonness itself, an almost wilful pedestrianism on their part. To a plant, they were small, low, and—this may be unfair, but it needs to be said—homely. They were, in fact, plants I'd been seeing and dismissing as unworthy all my life. Damn. You could forage while taking out the garbage. We hadn't even made it to my front door. Had Euell Gibbons started this way?

By the time we'd gained the porch steps, Hue had ticked off three more edible species: wild lettuce, Pennsylvania bittercress, and deadnettle. "See the square stem on deadnettle?" he asked, plucking one and handing it to me. The stem was indeed almost perfectly square. How odd. "Everything in the mint family has a square stem. Deadnettle's not in your Peterson's but it's a pretty good potherb, full of vitamins, iron, fiber. Other than that, I'm not a big fan of it." He picked a piece, bruised it between his fingers, and held it up for me to sniff. It smelled of mildew, with overtones of wet laundry and basement mold. Something about that smell suggested that my romance period with wild plants was already over.

By this point I just wanted to get inside and leave my front yard behind. Hue, however, was intrigued by the neglected flower bed along the front wall of the house, which had a few straggly azaleas and some other sort of flowers that had been there before I took possession of the house and instituted a comprehensive program of neglect. In the meantime, it had been colonized by assorted weeds, some of which were now three feet tall. Dominant among them was a thick-stalked, leggy plant with a multitude of brown, circular, thistle-like "stickers" that adhered to anything they touched. I knew this weed by sight if not by name because it grows everywhere, and I'd carried home countless hundreds of those round stickers Velcroed to my clothes. Now Hue named it. "Common burdock," he said. "Another introduced plant with several edible parts." (Who, I wondered, was introducing all these plants? And where, specifically, was the individual who had introduced this particular pain in the ass?) The pattern emerging, while unpleasant, was clear. Based on what I'd learned so far, the uglier and less inviting a plant looked, the more likely it was to be edible, though it seemed highly unlikely that it would actually be fun to eat.

Hue asked if I could name any of the plants in my yard. He did this not in a challenging way but simply to gauge the extent of my knowledge. I happily marched over to the dark green stalks of wild onion, vivid against the moribund yellow of my zoysia grass, and plucked a few. "Onion grass," I said. Hue nodded, bruised the stalks, and held them up to my nose.

"Smell," he said. I registered an agreeably stinky odor. He gave me an is-that-your-final-answer look. I shrugged. It sure smelled like onion grass to me.

"That's wild garlic, not onion," Hue said. Not unkindly, by the way.

We still hadn't made it into the house. I had one hand on the door-knob and wanted nothing so much as to go inside and shut out the world of ugly-ass edible plants. But Hue had just discovered pokeweed growing along the chain-link fence I share with a neighbor and more wild lettuce growing directly beneath my kitchen window. He picked a leaf of the lettuce, tore it in half, and held it up as a milky white substance bled along the torn edge. "Latex," he said in response to my questioning look. "All the lettuces have it." So rubber came from lettuce? That was a handy conversation-stopper to have at one's disposal. He then said, "I'm glad you're not using any herbicides in your fertilizer, if you do fertilize." I was curious how he knew this from looking at my lawn. He explained that most lawn "fertilizers" also incorporate various toxins to kill dandelions and other "weeds." The thriving dandelion population in my yard indicated the absence of such poisons.

At long last we went into the house and had a cup of tea. To fore-stall the complete de-romanticizing of foraging, I asked Hue about his background. As he talked he revealed a number of traits I liked immediately. He seemed without guile, something I find attractive in competent men, and equally unassuming. He had a military back-ground and had been in on the invasion of Grenada in 1983 and Des-ert Storm in 1991, where he won a Bronze Star. "They were handing those out like coupons," he said dismissively when I asked about it. "I didn't do anything special. Grenada was actually scarier. They were shooting RPGs instead of bullets. A rocket-propelled grenade is like a beer can coming at you." I have been around enough men who've survived combat to know that it imbues some with a kind of aura you can recognize if you're attuned to it. It's as if, having been tested and acquitted themselves honorably in the most dangerous circumstances a man can face, they no longer have any need for external validation. They don't take up as much space in the room as other men, aren't as concerned with the pecking order, are less easily hooked by the petty irritations of everyday life. These traits, however, don't make a man more accessible. I would come to feel that I knew Hue intimately but not well, if that's possible. I suspect that no one knows him well. He strikes me as one of those men who never set out to be a loner but ended up there anyway.

It was troubling, as I researched foraging, to discover how many of the best-known foragers traced their interest to a traumatic childhood of one sort or another. Euell Gibbons—known as the father of modern foraging for his 1962 book *Stalking the Wild Asparagus*—spent part of his youth in dire poverty in central New Mexico during the Dust Bowl era. He started foraging to help feed his mother and siblings while his father was off trying to find work. Sam Thayer, whose two diligently researched field guides, *The Forager's Harvest* and *Nature's Garden,* have become the go-to reference for modern foragers, grew up in a household where the only foods his parents could be relied on to provide were cereal and milk. Paula's father was an alcoholic. I'm as damaged as the next person, but I wasn't sure I had the makings of a good forager in me.

I hadn't known Hue very long when it emerged that his interest in foraging also stemmed from a childhood wound, though less outwardly dramatic than most. He grew up in Buffalo, New York, and his parents divorced when he was seven. The couple didn't handle the split well themselves, nor did they give much thought to how it might affect their children. That they handled it by not handling it wasn't unusual, but neither did it lessen the trauma to a child. "They didn't even announce it," Hue remembers. "My dad just stopped showing up. I guess he was more interested in being a good doctor than a good father." Hue had two younger sisters and, as the eldest, may have felt especially responsible—as do all children, to some extent—for the breakup. He just wanted out, so he ran away from home. "But I forgot to bring anything to eat," he said, "and when I got hungry there was no place to go but home." It doesn't take any great stretch of the imagination to see how such a child might vow to become as self-sufficient as possible.

The boy immediately began to apply himself to the study of edible plants, natural history, and outdoor skills. If he wasn't in the woods, he was in the library. In college, he went into the woods of New Hampshire with nothing but a wool blanket and the clothes on his back. He made a rough shelter in the crotch of a tree with sticks and leaves and went hungry for the first week. By the twentieth day, he was making bread from acorn flour, making tea from dried herbs, and not only feeding himself but storing food. It was, he said, paradise.

In the army, he attended a number of survival schools, even though by this time he knew more about wild edibles than his instructors. During one that involved spending a night alone in the Arizona desert, Hue decided to perform a vision quest of the kind he had read about in the books of Tom Brown, a well-known figure in the primitive skills movement. He fasted, prayed, and meditated for twenty-four hours, seeking a deeper understanding of the world and himself. Hue ended his quest thinking he had failed. There had been no vision, no epiphany. The only thought that occurred was that maybe he needed some help. A teacher.

The next evening, having completed the course and eaten dinner at his favorite diner in Bisbee, Hue was walking down an alley when he encountered a Native American man coming the other way. The man was middle-aged and had hair almost to his waist. Hue stood to one side to let the stranger pass. The man mirrored his movement. Hue stood to the other side. The man did the same. Tired of the Laurel-and-Hardy routine, Hue asked the guy if he intended to pass or not. The man regarded him for a moment and said, "I hear you're looking for a teacher."

The Indian's name was Sunday and he became both friend and teacher to Hue until his death seven years later. Under his tutelage, Hue learned about medicine wheel philosophy. He learned about the distinction between a man's "dream"—his own idea of happiness for himself—and his "vision," the fate that the cosmos nudged him toward. Hue once told me that he'd wanted nothing more than to be a father. He has been married three times and had children with the first two women. But he was often deployed while his children were growing up and the first two marriages failed. "I've loved every woman I've ever been with," he said. "But it never worked out. They were too . . . independent or something. After a while, you realize that it's not just a coincidence." Hue came to believe the universe was telling him his dream of fatherhood was not to be and that he should instead fulfill his vision of passing on the knowledge and skills he had learned so that they wouldn't disappear. This, I finally realized, explained his willingness to help me.

One of the plants Hue talked a lot about was cattail, a species even non-foragers often know. Most wild edibles go from "almost ripe" to "you just missed it" in the time it takes to hit a fast-food drive through window, but the cattail is edible in one form or another—shoots, stalks, flower spikes, pollen, and roots—almost year-round. Experienced foragers almost seem to compete over who loves the plant the most.

It was Euell Gibbons himself who threw down the cattail gauntlet in 1962, when he called it "the supermarket of the swamps." Peterson's deems it "one of the best and certainly the most versatile of our native edible plants." On the website of the not-to-be-outdone *Backwoods Home Magazine*, it's called "the Super-Walmart of the Swamp." Sam Thayer offers a more balanced perspective, calling Gibbons's assessment a "slight exaggeration" even as he notes the plant's remarkable versatility. The plant yields four vegetables over the course of a year: the immature flower spikes, the buds, the leaf "hearts," and the shoots of the rhizomes. The rhizome itself is starch-laden and can be turned into a good flour, and the golden pollen, which is high in protein, can be eaten raw or dried and used as a flour as well. ("Rhizome," by the way, is a word much in use by foragers. I finally figured out that it's basically a way of saying "sideways-growing root," although technically it's a "horizontal stem, often growing underground.")

Archaeological evidence in Europe of ground cattail material dates back 30,000 years. Cattail rhizomes contain ten times the starch of an equal weight of potatoes. The seed heads, the brown "tail" of the cattail, are full of a downy material. Birds line their nests with this down. Aboriginal people lined their moccasins and beds with it and also used it as a combination diaper/baby wipe. As recently as World

War I, the U.S. Navy filled life vests with cattail down. The sticky stuff at the base of the green leaves is reportedly useful as an antiseptic and coagulant. The dry stalks, being uniformly straight, are good for arrow shafts and fire-starting friction drills. I'm sure a cattail-powered car is under development at this very moment.

With Hue's help, I discovered firsthand that it's more fun to rhapsodize about cattails than actually eat them. We agreed to meet one Saturday so he could teach me how to make cattail flour. To shorten the time he'd spend driving, I suggested we meet at my mother's house, in Bethesda. Hue showed up with a trash bag full of cattail rhizomes. We proceeded to wash them and strip off the outer layers. This left the inner cores, white and pencil-thick. They were full of both starch and tough fiber. We sat together on milk crates over a bucket of water on the back porch, holding the cores under water and "worrying" them between our fingers to extract the starch. The cattail slime rose to the surface. The starch sank. When you felt you'd done justice to a given piece, you tossed the fibrous remains aside and moved on to the next. We did this for about a week. Actually, it was probably more like ninety minutes. All I know is that by the time we were through my hands looked like prunes and my back was so stiff I doubted my ability to ever stand fully upright again. We poured off the water and beheld the fruits of our labor, a putty-colored orb of cattail sludge about the size of a golf ball. My heart did not leap at the sight.

At this point, if we'd really been after cattail flour, we would have dried the sludge until it turned to powder. Being of middle age, I wasn't sure I had that kind of time. Hue's solution was to combine the cattail sludge ball with an equal amount of regular flour. This didn't dry it, of course—the sludgeball merely doubled in size. Next he told me to fold in an egg, a little sugar, and some salt. I did. Then, under his eye, I poured this mixture out into three "pancakes" in an oiled skillet over medium-high heat. The batter seemed completely unaffected by heat, suggesting an untapped source of flame-retardant textile. The stuff had a gummy viscosity that it retained in the pan even as I came very close to burning the pancakes. I flipped them. When the still-mucilaginous little pancakes smelled as if they were about to burn again, Hue declared them done.

We plated and served the pancakes. Hue took a bite of his and said, "Hmm," in a fairly contented tone. Bear in mind, however, that this was a man who maintains that all rodents, generally speaking, are pretty good eating in a survival situation. I took a small bite. It tasted like a cross between a regular pancake and an unknown vegetable. My sister, Olivia, who knows a great deal about cooking, tried a tiny bite of mine. She cocked her head and assumed an expression of diligent interest. "I'm tasting some corn and"—she paused, rolling it around in her mouth—"a bit of cucumber." As there were three of us and three pancakes, I told her she was welcome to one. "No thanks," she said brightly, and marched off to the den to make herself a Manhattan.

In the days that followed, I decided to try making cattail flour on my own. Don't get the wrong idea. It wasn't that I liked the stuff. But I did have a desire to show my teacher that I was, despite appearances, serious about this foraging stuff. Jogging one afternoon along the bike path about a mile from home I spotted a stand of healthy-looking cattails. I resolved to return and harvest some rhizomes. (I had taken to working the term into everyday conversations as often as possible to display my deep connection to the natural world.)

My chance came during Emma's dance class at a nearby Unitarian church. It was a midweek afternoon class. I was the sole dad in attendance and, as a single dad of but one year's standing, keenly felt my outcast status among the moms. I had shown up in running clothes with a fanny pack in which I had my digging antler and some plastic bags. I figured the hour-long class would give me plenty of time to jog the mile or so up to the cattails, harvest some, and return in time to pick up Emma.

It was a warm March day. I took off on my jog and, not wanting to be seen pulling up plants by passersby on the bike path, I moved to the back side of the pond and knelt at the water's edge. The place was absolutely choked with cattails. I began to dig and was immediately struck by how deeply attached the cattails were to their environment. I could barely budge anything with my antler, which is a surprisingly strong material. The leverage I exerted on it would have bent a metal trowel in no time. My antler had a smooth, pointed tip, but the handle was rough with the coarse "pearling" that occurs at the bases of deer antlers. Following a root down into the mud as deep as possible, I applied full pressure. No movement. I pulled the stick up and found that I'd cut my hand on the little bumps in the antler.

When your foraging teacher has been awarded the Bronze Star, you don't let a scratch stop you. Besides, Hue had said that cattail slime had antiseptic properties. Between running and digging, I had begun perspiring heavily. Actually, I was soaking wet with sweat, which was dripping off me like a one-man spring rain. My eyes stung from the perspiration finding its way there. I reflexively rubbed the back of my muddy hand across my brow, realizing only afterward what I'd done. Great, I thought, that should endear you to the moms. Having knelt the whole time at the water's edge, I was also covered in mud up to my knees. I kept digging.

These cattail rhizomes were different from the ones Hue had given me—darker in color and harder to break. But I was damned well going to come away with something to show for having muddied and bloodied myself. With a final shove and twist of the antler I succeeded in breaking off a few roots. This effort cut my hand a second time, and deeper. Shoving the roots into a bag, and the bag into my fanny pack, I suddenly realized I'd lost track of the time. I needed to boogie if I was going to get back before the end of dance class. Like many men my age, I take a baby aspirin daily as a blood thinner. It seemed to be effective, because the minor cuts on my hands were now bleeding steadily. I splashed warm pond water over myself in what I knew was a futile attempt to clean up and then took off up the path at a brisk jog.

A few paces along I realized things must be even worse than I'd thought. A mother and toddler coming the other way on the bike path spied me and, even at a distance of fifty yards, the woman's eyes widened with fear. She moved the child behind her to shield it and gave me a glare of maternal challenge as I ran past, giving them as wide a berth as was possible on the narrow trail. I really needed to speak to my doctor about the baby aspirin, because now the blood was running down the inside of my forearm. The bike path passed under a road and I noted moss growing on the damp concrete of the underpass. I'd read somewhere of aboriginals using certain mosses as styptic agents, so I grabbed a handful on the off chance that this was such a plant. It wasn't.

Ten minutes later, I jogged into the parking lot of the church. From the relaxed way the mothers and girls in their leotards were scattered about, I knew instantly that the class had been over for some time. I spotted Emma, anxious and alone at the far end of the group. "Em!" I called, waving at her with what I realized a second too late was a hand full of blood-soaked moss. "Here I am!" I jogged over, avoiding eye contact with the moms. If I looked at them, I knew, I'd try to explain the perfectly good reasons I had for being covered in mud and blood. I also knew, from years of experience, that explaining my actions nearly always made them sound creepier and less defensible than if I'd kept my damn mouth shut. The relief that had initially lit up Emma's face was quickly replaced by alarm. "Daddy, what happened?" she said, sounding more like my parent than my child. "Where were you? Are you okay?" It turned out that the class ran forty-five minutes long, not an hour, which meant that Emma had been sitting there by herself for fifteen minutes, an eternity to a child.

I panicked. I'd had sufficient time on the run back to accept that there was nothing I could do about my appearance. But I'd been sure the class was an hour long. Next thing I knew, I was rapidly doing exactly what I'd vowed not to do. I was explaining. I spoke as if to Emma alone, knowing that every woman there was listening. I recounted digging for cattails, how my antler digging stick had cut my hand, how I'd bled because of the baby aspirin Daddy took for his heart. I told of my muddy hands and the stinging sweat in my eyes, which I'd wiped without thinking that . . .

I had the strange experience of hearing my own voice as I spoke, as if I were wearing headphones. I knew I was gushing a torrent of language that was making what had happened sound increasingly implausible, but I couldn't stop. I did have the sense to quit squeezing the moss, from which blood droplets were dripping onto the gravel of the Unitarian church parking lot. By this time, a mom with whom I had a nodding acquaintance had come over and wordlessly extended a wad of tissue. I thanked her, wiped my brow (careful not to look and see exactly how much blood and mud had been on display) and then wrapped it around my injured hand. I knew I needed to go before I explained how certain Australian aboriginals used moss—not all mosses of course, but certain kinds, of which I'd hoped that this was one but alas it was not—as a styptic agent. "Daddy?" Emma interrupted in a whisper. "Can we just please go?"

Yes, I said, brightly. Yes, of course we can go. We got into the car and we went. In the car, Emma again asked if I was okay. Yes, I told her.

"Are you okay, Monk?" I asked tenderly.

"Yeah," she sighed. "I guess. But I think you scared some of those people."

A few days later I showed the rhizomes, unexamined since being shoved into the refrigerator, to Hue. "These aren't cattail," he said. What? Of course they were cattail. They were growing in water. They looked like cattails. They had cattail-like rhizomes. What the hell else could they possibly be? "I can't tell you what they are," Hue replied calmly. "I just know what they aren't."

After the burned-but-raw cattail pancakes and the blood, mud, moss, and child-neglect incident at dance class, I was feeling deeply discouraged. I had realized that while Hue had an almost encyclopedic knowledge of wild edibles, much of it was geared toward survival situations. Long after the grid went down and Safeways across the country had been picked clean, Hue would be fine, eating barbecued rodents and grubs. He'd told me grubs accounted for more than half of the diet of certain Australian Aborigines even well after contact with Europeans. Grubs were, in fact, one of his favorites.

I, on the other hand, had zero interest in eating grubs, no matter how nutritious and delicious Hue proclaimed them to be. I had not gone into this for survival training—I had thought that when eating wildly, I'd also be eating well. In terms of foraged food, however, this was certainly not where things were headed. I'd been ignoring the accumulating evidence that my stunt was not working out as intended. I might—might—be able to just barely survive consuming only wild edibles that I got myself. But after the cattail incident I had to admit that subsisting solely on food that I'd gotten with my own two hands was likely to be a very unpleasant experience, and even if I could succeed in pulling off the stunt I honestly didn't *want* to anymore. Not that I wanted to quit entirely. It was simply a matter of altering the rules of engagement.

Paula was all about getting free food from the woods that she liked to eat. I now had new respect for this approach. Even if her plant knowledge was less encyclopedic than Hue's, even if she didn't know her henbit from her deadnettle, I knew that anything I found with Paula would be not only edible but almost certainly appetizing as well. From now on, I resolved, if I was going to put this much work into getting something to eat, it had damned well better be something that actually tasted good. When Paula called me to go foraging with her again, I was in.

One bright spring day, the air so clear it almost felt carbonated, Paula and I met at Fletcher's and headed upriver into the woods along the Potomac. She pointed out the wisteria vines dangling from the sycamores like telephone wire. "You can make fritters from the flowers, but you can make fritters outta anything, you know what I mean? The seeds—it puts out these sorta knobby pods—are poisonous. I don't mess with them." We pushed on to a small stand of shin-high greenery, where Paula paused to rummage in her duffel. I asked if she knew the plants.

"Jesus, Heavey! They're stinging nettles. I already showed 'em to you once. Can't you remember anything?"

Evidently I couldn't. That was the problem with shopping outdoors. One little green plant looked pretty much like another and none of them were labeled. Paula pulled out a glove and silently harvested a plastic bag's worth, shaking her head as if marveling at my inability to retain information. "My favorite green," she murmured at one point. She'd chosen well. Some months later, when I went to hear Michael Pollan speak, he said that stinging nettles, along with purslane and lamb's quarters, were the three most nutritious plants in the world.

We came to a place where the woods got thicker and we either had to push through or go around. She must have wanted to show me something, because she tightened the chin strap of her Tilley hat and bashed onward. I balled up my fists at face level, like a boxer fending off punches, and followed. Suddenly we were at the water's edge, where an eddy slowly twirled in its bowl between two boulders poking their noses above the water. "I just like to check this place," she said. "Certain eddies, you know what you're gonna find there," she went on. "One'll be good for lost bobbers and lures, one'll be good for lumber, another one maybe gets coolers and canoe paddles. This one, though, you never know what's gonna wash up here." She told me that in nearly two decades along the river she had twice found, reported, and led the park police to "floaters." One of which she had found twirling in the current right here. "Nothing stinks like a human body, honey." She pulled her cigarette pack from its Baggie and lit one, then laughed at something. "You shoulda seen the cops when I led them here! They were tying orange tape every five feet like they were in the fuckin' wilderness instead of two hundred yards from Canal Road!"

She didn't tell me what she hoped to find in this spot, but she must not have found it, because after a while she said, in a tone that suggested a change of plan, "Let's see if we can find some goose eggs." I was momentarily bewildered, trying to square the two Paulas. Custodial Paula picked up park litter and reported deer poachers to the cops. Feral Paula wanted to steal and eat the unborn children of Canada geese, which, moral issues aside, is frowned upon by the authorities. Geese, as migratory birds, fall under federal, rather than state, jurisdiction. As we walked, she gave me an over-the-shoulder tutorial. Geese weren't God's smartest critters when it came to picking nesting sites. They tended to lay their eggs almost at water level, which meant the eggs often got wet, which meant they got cold, which meant they wouldn't hatch. "Sometimes they do hatch, which isn't necessarily good, because the babies end up like Jerry's Kids, if you know what I mean. The foxes get them pretty quick." There were too many Canada geese here, she said, many more than the area could support. This, as far as I knew, was true. There were geese everywhere along the tow-path of the canal, crapping all over the place. And they competed for food with ducks, whose numbers had been in decline for years. Paula never took duck eggs. Taking the odd goose egg, though, was to her completely ethical.

Suddenly she froze and held up a finger. "Hear that?" I didn't. I heard the never-ending procession of jets that use the river as their approach path to Reagan National Airport and the nearby rush of traffic. "There it is again," she said. And then I caught a faint birdcall, a liquid, rising, three-note call, tickety-tickety-tickety. "There he is." A tiny brown bird perched on a twig thirty feet away and about twenty feet up in a tree. "Wren, probably a Carolina," said Paula. "They don't migrate, and they don't do well in hard winters. Just not enough of a body to pack any reserves away." They made up for this, she said, by reproducing in large numbers when they got the chance. "You gotta give 'em credit, though. Lotta guts for such a little bird, you know what I mean?" I was struck again. She seemed to be toggling back and forth rapidly between the two Paulas. This was a rare glimpse of her tender side. (I would learn later that the pan lying in the driveway under Gordon's trailered boat wasn't to collect spilled oil. It was water Paula set out for the birds. When I asked about it, she became a little testy. "Well, there's no goddam water around here anymore," she said defensively. "All the streams they once had are in pipes under the street. What're they supposed to do?" I tried to tell her it was fine by me, but I think she was just miffed at having her sentimental side seen so openly.)

Walking along the river's edge at a place where little spits of ground jutted out into the main channel, we spooked a fox and watched it run off ahead. "He's doing the same thing we are," Paula said. "Huntin' eggs." I couldn't tell which was more striking, Paula's awareness of what was on the fox's mind, the notion that we suddenly found ourselves competing with animals for food, as our distant ancestors must have, or Paula's matter-of-fact tone, suggesting that competing with animals for food was an everyday dynamic that she viewed as anything but remarkable. By the time I'd formulated these thoughts, she'd put fifty more yards between us.

"Wait up!" I hollered. For once, she did. But only because she'd seen some nesting geese. When I caught up, she started toward them. The geese flushed, honking their protests and awkwardly hoisting themselves into the air when we were still sixty or seventy yards off. "If they flush that early, it means they're not sitting on eggs," she said. Had they been sitting on eggs, they'd have held out until we were much closer. A little farther on, she elbowed me and pointed to a Canada that had extended and lowered its long neck, the better to minimize its profile. "Bingo!" she cried. The goose held its ground until we were within ten yards, honking loudly as it left. There were two large, warm eggs in the nest, which was three feet from the water. Bits of goose down and droppings clung to them. "Must be a second lay for them," she sid. "She didn't defend it that hard, and usually a goose lays more eggs than two. If high water killed her first lay, she'll crank out another set. But her heart's not really in it, you know?" She explained that we needed to candle the eggs, hold them up to a light to see if they were still good. There was a kind of translucence to a good egg, whereas one too far along would look solid. Our only light source was the sun, so that's what she used. All of this was news to me, but the way she had explained it—the "as everybody but you knows" tone—made me reluctant, for once, to own up to the full extent of my ignorance. If you grow up buying eggs in the dairy case, you don't have any great incentive to learn to candle them. "Both look good," she announced. The egg she awarded me was, naturally, the one with more goose crap pasted to it. I was surprised by its size and heft. It was nearly the size of a grapefruit, and heavy. The difference between this and a hen's egg was amazing, like a rock and a soap bubble. The shell felt thick and tough, as if you could drop it from a fair height without breaking it. I did as Paula had, holding it up to the sun. It looked as solid as a bowling ball to me, but what did I know? Besides, I'd never gotten any further arguing with Paula than I have with Emma. So I didn't.

On the way back to the boathouse, Paula let out a little involuntary cry of surprise when she discovered a couple of morels—white-ribbed mushrooms three inches tall, looking exactly like the dead leaves they're surrounded by. She produced a knife and cut them off at the base, and then placed them in a paper sack she'd pulled out of the mysterious blue gym bag that always accompanies her and seems to hold whatever a situation requires.

Just short of the parking lot she stopped for nettles and dandelion greens, which, as usual, I didn't notice until I was standing on them. The distance from the printed page of my field guides to the real thing continued to confound me. It was a wonder that anyone ever identified an actual plant from its picture. Peterson's always showed plants in full flower, by which time virtually all wild edibles were too bitter—if not downright toxic—to eat.

Back at the boathouse, Paula told me how to prepare my egg. "Wash it real good before you crack it. That shit on the shell's full of salmonella and God knows what. And the shell itself is hard, calcium, the way an egg's supposed to be, you know what I'm saying? So you gotta really crack it." She said I had the makings of a nice omelet. I could sauté the dandelion in butter, or better yet, bacon fat. The nettles should be simmered a few minutes in just enough water to cover them. Simmering quickly neutralized their stinging properties. I could then mix the two greens together in the omelet. She gave me one of the morel mushrooms, explaining that I should slice it and sauté it slowly in butter. I could add it to the omelet as well, but she cautioned that its delicate flavor might be lost among the bitter greens so perhaps I should savor it on its own. And here I encountered another of the many contradictions of Paula. Although she dressed in the most worn and ill-fitting clothes and cussed like a sailor, she could sound like a Junior League luncheon hostess when she talked about food.

At home, with Emma tucking into a supper of Easy Mac and frozen peas, I found myself unexpectedly warming to my task. I was anticipating an omelet combining fresh and essential tastes: the richness of the goose egg, which I somehow imagined as substantial but not overpowering, paired with the earthiness and bitter tang of the dandelions and offset by some smoky bacon. I was careful not to overcook the greens. Heating a cast-iron pan, I added equal amounts of olive oil and butter so that the butter wouldn't burn. When it was sizzling, I rapped the egg smartly against the edge of the pan. The eggshell remained unscathed. I rapped harder. Jesus Christ, I wondered, did I need a nightstick to get into this thing? Finally, on the third attempt, I cracked the shell. And sliding out came a surprisingly small slurp of yellow yolk, followed by the blue-gray fetus—so fully formed that the face had an expression of Buddha-like equanimity—of an infant Canada goose.

I was horrified. The being was about three inches long and had two wings, two tiny webbed feet and a tiny unborn head. It was wet and blue and vivid and I had just fucking killed it. Maybe not—maybe it was already dead. Maybe it wouldn't have made it. I was in a state of near shock, and before I knew what I was doing, I was sliding it into the sink, out of sight, down the disposal, with the water running full blast as I groped for the switch to turn the motor on to grind it up and flush it away as if doing so fast enough would keep it from ever having existed in the first place. And it was essential that Emma not know, ever. Eyes averted, I hit the wrong switch, turning the kitchen lights off and then back on before I fumblingly found the right one and heard the lethal gargle of the disposal. I ran the water for a long time, until the disposal had long finished grinding and had resumed its normal hum for a full two minutes. Finally I shut it down. And then I staggered to a chair at the table. I was aflame with guilt and remorse. It took me a while to even question why this was affecting me so deeply. It was a goose egg that was further along than you thought, I told myself. You've killed geese before, as well as deer, fish, squirrels, wild pigs, elk, and God knows what else. It wasn't the Johnstown Flood. My daughter, also sitting at the table and picking at the last globs of powdered cheese as if they were the world's greatest delicacy, did not look up. For which I was thankful beyond all reckoning.

Half an hour later I called Paula to ask if she had eaten dinner. When she responded in the negative, I gave her the news. "Oh, no," she said. "Oh, you're killing me. Mine's probably the same. Ah, shit, I feel really bad about this." I couldn't think of anything to say. At last I asked, "So what are you going to do?"

There was a short silence. "Well, I killed it, so I gotta eat it," she said, her tone indicating no uncertainty whatsoever, an open-and-shut case. "I'll just hard-boil it and then slice it up thin so I can't see what I'm eating so clearly."

I was impressed when she said these words, and even more impressed as I pondered them afterward. Paula was an outsider—someone on the very fringes of society. I think that the possibility that she was crazy crossed my mind when I had first met her, however many years ago that was. And the longer I knew her, the harder she was to categorize. She wasn't big on the laws enacted by government, but she had a strong and codified sense about right and wrong. When told about the eggs, it hadn't even occurred to her to question the correct response. I realized what a rare thing this was—first, to have a code at all, and, second, to follow it so unflinchingly. Even when doing so meant eating something like a stillborn gosling.

I found that I was running a line from an old Dylan tune—"to live outside the law you must be honest"—through my head over and over. It had come unbidden and I had no idea why.

And then it hit me. The line had always baffled me. Before I had no context, no clear idea what it referred to. Now I knew. It referred to people like Paula.

CATTAIL PANCAKES

½ cup flour rendered from cattail rhizomes
1 egg
½ to ¾ cup of milk or water
2 tablespoons melted better or vegetable oil
1 tablespoon sugar (optional)

Salt (pinch)
¼ teaspoon baking powder
Maple syrup (for serving the pancakes)

Dig up 5 lbs cattail rhizomes. Rinse off blood.

Strip off the outer layers of each rhizome to reveal its core. In a bucket full of water, hold each core under the water and use your fingers to rip apart, shred, and "worry" the plant to separate the resident starch from the cattail root fibers. The starch will sink to the bottom. When you feel that you have worked all the starch from a given piece, discard and start on another rhizome.

Slowly and gently pour off the water, preserving the slurry of starch on the bottom of the bucket. Spread this out to dry on a tray or cookie sheet (either air dry over several days or speed things up by placing in a 200 degree oven overnight). This should give you approximately a cup of cattail flour. But it usually doesn't. Either mix in a little regular flour or suck it up and go with whatever you've got.

Mix ½ cup of the cattail flour with a pinch each of baking powder and sald, and the sugar if you're using it. Beat the egg with ½ cup milk, then add the melted butter or oil. Slowly stir this into the dry mixture until it's the consistency of pancake batter. Fry tablespoon-sized dollops of batter into silver dollar pancakes. You will have worked hard to arrive at this point and, understandably, will want to sample the finished product. Take a small bite, then toss in garbage pail. You have just proved that, should the grid go down, you could survive on foods like this. Go eat at your favorite restaurant and pray that this doesn't happen soon.

Chapter Five:
Enter the Girl, Sour Cherry Pie, and Five Bites of My Own Lawn

Even though I had given up on die-hard foraging, Hue didn't appear to hold this against me. Instead, we seemed to have become friends. He continued to visit almost weekly, usually coming after work. He would always pull up fifteen minutes early, his tie wadded up on the seat next to him like something he couldn't get rid of fast enough. His habit of arriving early baffled me until I recalled that my father, a former navy fighter pilot, had had the same tendency. In the military, being where you were supposed to be when you were supposed to be there wasn't a matter of courtesy. It was a matter of life and death. And the only way to make sure you were on time was to arrive early. Military service drilled that into you until it was reflexive.

We still went foraging, though now we'd often spend more time having a beer and talking than actively hunting plants. Hue and I did finally escape my yard, but not before he had identified seventeen edible plants and given me the full rundown on each—the what, when, and how of harvesting, processing, and cooking. One of our first off-site discoveries was a redbud tree near the bike path. We ate its flowers one week and young seedpods the next. Both were lemony and faintly sweet but seemed to lack calories. To me, eating redbud seemed more of a parlor trick—something you did to show off to others—than anything else. Hue quickly set me straight. I was correct about the calorie count, but that wasn't the whole story. The Indians and early settlers had counted on redbud both as one of the earliest spring edibles and as a needed dose of of vitamins, essential fatty acids, and antioxidants after the long winter. He also said redbud was a good way to "punch up" a salad, which seemed an incongruous manner of speaking for a former infantryman. But Hue was like that, part warrior, part aesthete.

My favorite discovery with Hue was pokeweed, the young shoots of which he said tasted like asparagus, only better. It grew abundantly along fences and alleys in my neighborhood. The drawback to pokeweed is that only the very early shoots are edible; the roots, seeds, and mature stems and leaves are all "dangerously poisonous," according to Peterson's.

I did some more research to find out what exactly kind of poison we were talking about before I ate any of the stuff. I found a webpage by an associate professor of botany at Palomar College that detailed the toxic compounds in pokeweed: an alkaloid (phytolaccine), a resin (phytolaccatoxin), and a saponin (phytolaccigenin). I don't know what these are, but they sound like ingredients in "RoundUp Shiva: Destroyer of Weeds." But the most serious hazard, it claimed, comes from a very toxic plant protein called lectin, which is also found in the castor bean (*Ricinus communis*) and prayer bead (*Abrus precatorius*)—the world's deadliest plants. These lectins happen to be the active ingredient in ricin, the biochemical warfare agent. Yum.

The new shoots of pokeweed, however, have not yet developed these toxins, and the books emphasized that only shoots newly emerged from the ground, less than six inches tall, were to be eaten. Even so you were supposed to boil them in at least two changes of water for twenty to thirty minutes each. After that much boiling they were safe to eat—and also unappetizingly colorless and slimy. I collected some with Hue one day and cooked them later. I did the two changes of water, but couldn't bear to see their crisp greenness turning to gray mush and pulled them out after fifteen minutes. With a little butter and salt, they were wonderful, similar to asparagus but with a deeper taste. I felt fine.

A few days later, I picked, cooked and served some to my mother. It happened that my sister had bought asparagus at the grocery store, so our dinner had a built-in competition between the two vegetables. After sampling each, Mom voted with her fork, helping herself to most of what I had cooked. "They're delicious," she said. "Such a 'green' taste." It is a wonderful thing to have someone appreciate a plant you've found, picked, and cooked yourself. I decided to spare her the fine print about the dangers of poke. Otherwise, symptoms or not, my mother would have insisted on going to the hospital.

After I had gathered and enjoyed poke this way three or four times, the weather warmed, the plants shot up overnight, and I had trouble finding "safe" shoots under six inches tall. So I began to push the envelope. After all, the stuff had once been a staple vegetable throughout the American South, where poke "salet" (from the Middle English, for salad, which itself derives from the Vulgar Latin verb "salare," "to salt") was traditionally savored as one of the first fresh greens after a winter of salt pork, beans, and corn bread. I bumped the Peterson's six-inch-maximum rule for shoots to seven inches, then eight. Once again I suffered no ill effects. But that was it. For once, I decided to quit while I was ahead. Eventually I learned it was a good thing I had: a friend described having seen impoverished southerners with what is colloquially known as "poke mouth"—lip sores caused by exposure to the toxic compounds in overly mature poke shoots and leaves.

One day, Hue mentioned that the previous weekend he'd attended a wild plant walk led by a woman in Baltimore. He thought I should meet her. "She knows a lot about wild edibles and writes a blog about food." She was also active in Baltimore Food Makers, a group of mostly younger people interested in growing and making their own food, as well as in eating locally and sustainably. He gave me her name and e-mail address, but I was pretty busy at the time. I was still manic about getting the last of the herring before they left the river. When I wasn't fishing, I was busy screwing up my vegetable garden.

I made all the standard rookie gardening mistakes, of course. I overwatered, overfertilized, and crowded plants together in the novice's misguided zeal for maximum production. But I took screwing up more seriously than other beginners. It was as if I had an aptitude for it, an impressively intuitive misunderstanding of gardening. I had, for example, somehow arrived at the opposite of "companion planting," which is the practice of siting herbs and vegetables that benefit each other side by side. Beans and squash complement each other, for example, because they require different nutrients. Beans have shallow roots, while squash has deep ones, another good combination. And squash tends to crowd out the weeds that frequently bedevil beans. I learned all this afterward. In the meantime, I had unknowingly hit upon "antagonistic gardening," a concept yet to be recognized in botanical literature. I planted my potatoes next to my beans, in effect inviting them to duke it out for the nutrients both crave. I planted cucumbers and squash next to each other, delighting every pickleworm in the tristate area, who came for the side-by-side convenience of their two favorite vegetables. I was accustomed to the natural world's vast capacity for indifference, but this was something else entirely. It was as if I'd actively pissed the old girl off. Great patches of my garden seemed to lose hope and went moribund, neither dead nor alive.

Meanwhile Hue, low-key but insistent, kept after me to call the plant woman. "I just think she'd be a good resource for you," he said. He mentioned something about her having two small boys and going through a particularly difficult divorce.

Almost as an afterthought, he added, "She's a peach."

Within the hour, I had e-mailed Michelle Gienow. I took the short and breezy route, a quick note describing my attempt to close the distance between me and what I ate and bemoaning the trying-to-drink-from-a-fire-hose overload of information faced by the novice forager. I closed by saying that Hue—who was a guy I didn't know particularly well but who obviously knew his plants and had been hugely generous with his time—had suggested I get in touch. A couple of days later, a reply came saying it was nice to hear from a "fellow forager" and that she'd met Hue only a month earlier herself. She was also a fellow freelancer, in both writing and photography. "My main beat is local food and sustainable agriculture," she wrote, "plus a healthy side order of DIY homesteading stuff." She had been foraging since early childhood, thanks to a Polish grandmother who had introduced her to wild foods. She wrote that she was committed—on behalf of herself and her two boys—to eating as sustainably, locally, and wildly as possible. Michelle tried to live off the grid to the extent she could, but felt that she'd largely failed at this. She did drive a biodiesel car and tried to shop for clothing for the boys— they were three and seven—in thrift stores and at yard sales, recycling someone else's still-usable clothing rather than buying new. She said she was "sympathetic" to my project and wanted to know more.

My first reaction to this was to feel intimidated. I've never been particularly committed to anything that smacked of the greater good and I have usually been either mystified by or downright suspicious of those who are. Here was a woman of limited means raising two kids who was still committed to her ideals, and—worse—talking about it in a disarmingly open and unironic way. I had worked hard to come by my cynicism and this woman was undermining it before we'd even met. I shopped at thrift stores and yard sales, too, but it was because I was cheap, not because doing so conserved the natural resources consumed or reduced the pollution created in the manufacture of new clothing. I had always more or less gone my own way and figured the planet could do the same. Someone like Michelle might uncover the weak spots in my alienation, requiring that I rethink all kinds of assumptions I had no interest in examining. And what exactly did a biodiesel car burn? Salad dressing? The french fry grease from fast-food outlets? This was unknown territory. Besides, what could she possibly know about plants that Hue didn't? All of that argued against meeting. And Baltimore was not only fifty miles away, but fifty miles through some of the heaviest traffic in the country. "Rush hour" in the D.C. area was pretty much anytime between 5 a.m. and midnight. Baltimore was a long haul for either business or social reasons. But then I realized that I was getting ahead of myself. E-mails didn't obligate me to anything. I wrote back, saying I envied her having a foraging grandmother. I confessed to being a child of the suburbs whose prior plant experience had consisted of collecting blueberries at Camp Yonahnoka in North Carolina. We picked them from low bushes that grew atop the local "mountain," which was only several hundred feet high but a long walk from camp nonetheless. The ladies who worked in the kitchen would make you a pie if you brought them enough berries. I related my discovery of smoked herring and that I'd begun sneaking a few wild edibles into Emma's food when she wasn't paying attention.

In return, Michelle sent me a list of what she was gathering and eating—and apparently feeding to her boys. It included dandelion greens, which she and the boys ate "almost daily." I couldn't quite wrap my head around someone picking and eating the weed that nearly everybody else in America went to considerable pains to exterminate. I'd tried to sneak some sautéed dandelion greens onto Emma's plate one night. She wouldn't touch them. When I urged her to give them a try, she crossed her arms and declared, "No! I hate nature food!"

Michelle was also eating a lot of garlic mustard—an invasive with a two-year growth cycle. Hue had several times tried to explain the concept of a two-year growth cycle, but I never understood it. Michelle not only understood biannuals, but explained them in a way I could follow. The garlic mustard in flower now, she wrote, was already too bitter for most palates. But beneath each mature one I could find the tender shoots of the second-year growth, the new plant. These little guys were choice now. They, too, would become bitter later in the year. "But once the first frost hits, they become really delicious again and stay green—and edible—all winter, even under the snow. That's why they were brought over from Europe."

Michelle expressed interest in my smoked herring and, saying she made a mean strawberry-rhubarb preserve, indicated a willingness to barter. In my response, I said I was game, but warned that smoked herring was pretty much all I had to offer. Actually, I wrote, suddenly remembering another, I was reasonably proficient at knife-sharpening. I explained that one of my beats for *Field & Stream* was the acquisition of a particular subset of manly skills, namely the ones that men are widely assumed to possess but that, in most cases, don't. Among these were carving a turkey, fixing toilets, and sharpening knives. Mastery of this last had, for some reason, seemed a particularly worthy goal. After reading up on it, interviewing various experts, and trying a multitude of stones and gadgets, I'd been forced to admit that I had no natural aptitude whatsoever. Sharpening was simple—you held the blade at a constant angle as you moved it across a stone—but not easy. I had at last become semi-proficient at it, mostly because I was unable to accept the thought of being defeated by something so basic. I'd kept at it long after a less insecure man would have given up. In any case, fish and knife-sharpening were the entire contents of my trade basket.

There followed nearly a month of sporadic communication—Michelle was an engaging writer—before we settled on my driving to Baltimore to meet her at Druid Hill Park, a large old tract in northwest Baltimore. She needed to scout the place for an "urban wild edibles" class she wanted to lead there. Her last e-mail included the note she'd made in her planner: "Meet strange man in secluded park. Bring knives."

I got lost, of course. MapQuest routed me right through downtown Baltimore and extensive road reconstruction. I was nearly an hour late before I even found Druid Hill Park, which turned out to be the size of Dulles Airport, and then spent another twenty minutes crisscrossing its many roads before Michelle guided me her way via text messages.

No single man with a pulse is capable of meeting an attractive single woman without immediately sizing her up as a potential mate. Within the first five seconds of laying eyes on Michelle, I had taken in the slender, lithe young woman in maroon corduroy jeans. I had registered the blue eyes, strawberry blond hair, fair skin, and absence of makeup. In her facial features and gaze I recorded a kind of intelligence and self-possession, neither arrogant nor meek. Above all else, I'd registered the specific meaning of the cordial but decisively noncommittal smile she sent my way. By the passing of the sixth second, all this neurochemical activity had created an executive summary in word form, the better to share it with the conscious brain.

The summary read as follows: *Total babe. Thinks you are too old for her.*

I pasted on the best smile I could muster and greeted her as if I, too, had always seen this as nothing more than a cordial business encounter. We moved immediately to small talk. She confessed to having flown out of the house without her strawberry-rhubarb preserves, and she seemed truly embarrassed about this. I sat on my side of the picnic table where she had a basket and backpack and offered her a herring. She said it was really good. "Wow," she said, chewing slowly now, tasting it more deeply, "I mean, this is *really* good." Although the herring was tasty, it was apparently the DIY angle—that I'd caught, filleted, brined, and smoked it myself—that impressed her the most. That, she noted, was "pretty hard core." I smiled and tried to give the shrug of a guy for whom pretty hard core was the norm.

Michelle struck me as someone combining traits not usually found growing in the same soil. There was something direct, open, and friendly about her—she was not the least bit coy. She seemed comfortable in her own skin, a state of being I've always found intimidating mostly because it's so unfamiliar to me. I knew she was genuinely this way because I spent so much time and effort affecting the appearance of low-key confidence that I would have recognized the machinery at work. She didn't have any of it running. And yet you felt that she wasn't giving away anything about herself. The openness and transparency went only so far and then stopped. It wasn't a wall. It just stopped. I figured her for a smart woman who took in more information than she let on. That was as far as I could get.

The next thing I knew we were up, walking and looking for edibles in the tightly mowed park. There wasn't much—"Dang, I was hoping we'd beaten the park department's annual spring close shave," she said—and the few we found happened to be ones I knew. Michelle explained that the Baltimore Zoo was in this park, which dated from 1860. As it expanded into modern captive animal "environments" the zoo had closed off its oldest areas, including its Victorian-era black iron cages. A lot of the fenced-off areas we were passing were decommissioned zoo exhibits, cages, and support buildings. She was curious about what might have grown up inside since then but said she didn't think there was any way in. The fence was pretty formidable, chain link topped with razor wire.

"Oh, there's always a way in," I said. You don't hang out with Paula Smith without learning a few things about fences. The master trespasser had taught me that any place worth fencing people out of invariably motivated some of those very people to create a way in. People who cut fences prized discretion, preferring sites where they were least likely to be observed, usually a low point, topographically speaking. Sure enough, the second ravine I tried had a torso-sized opening at the lowest point of the fence, the jagged wire-ends bent back with care to spare skin and clothing. "After you," I said. Then I squeezed through and we began exploring.

Michelle lamented that invasive nonnative plants—Japanese honeysuckle, kudzu, and some grass whose name I missed—had crowded out nearly everything else. I found some deer trails with signs of fresh use and pointed them out. "Mmm," she said, noncommittally. She was obviously more into wild edible plants than wild edible animals. We weren't finding much for her plant walk, but it was an interesting place all the same, ruins of buildings and iron bars from old enclosures slowly being reclaimed by the earth. She'd been right here countless times as a child. The hippo house had stood here; over there had been the elephant yard. We topped a slight rise where I pointed out oval depressions in the grass, saying that they were fresh deer beds. "Really?" she said, a rising inflection that combined requisite polite interest with obvious skepticism. I asked her to wait a moment, bent over one of the beds, and looked until I found a deer hair, which I held out to her. "Deer hair," I said, handing it over. "This one's a light color, so it came from its belly."

"Okay," she said. "I'm officially impressed." I knew instantly that she didn't really mean these words. She didn't give a damn about deer. And yet, I would argue, there is not a man breathing who does not delight at the mere prospect of impressing an attractive woman. I, for example, was ridiculously happy to have the words aimed at me, sincere or not. (Even as I lapped up this praise, I have to admit that another part of me was rolling its eyes, thinking, Good Lord, has there ever been a simpler, more easily manipulated thing than the male ego? It makes the toothpick look complicated by comparison.) We descended that hill and went up another. We'd arrived at the monkey house, a long brick structure that looked mostly unused. The occasional human voice and rumble of an electrically powered zoo vehicle could be heard. The sounds were fairly close but their sources weren't visible. Michelle seemed excited to be at this place. She confessed that she'd always wanted to break into the monkey house. It occurred to me that this woman had taken me for a pretty vanilla sort of guy, which is, after all, how I looked. She perked up when I noted that all we needed to do was find one unlocked window. The thing was, they were all casement windows, not easily opened from the outside. I found one that was barely cracked open and pulled out my pocketknife to see if I could pry it any farther. I worked on the window for a minute but couldn't get it to budge.

It would be months before she would tell me that trying to break into the monkey house had been the moment when she started to think I might be interesting after all. "Ninety-nine people out of a hundred think 'No Trespassing' means what it says," she would eventually tell me. "Not you. That totally got to me."

We gave up on the monkey house after a while and retraced our steps. At a picnic table near our vehicles we sat for a few minutes, having iced tea and her home-made granola bars. If something in her had shifted as a result of the monkey house, I wasn't aware of it. I was still operating under the rules implicit in her initial smile, but I had relaxed a bit. If I was too old, I could still sit and enjoy a conversation with a pretty woman. And if—as seemed to be the case—there was something about her I couldn't get a handle on, there was no great need to figure it out. After a few more minutes I said I'd better get going if I hoped to beat rush hour traffic. We said the normal things, I smiled, turned, and walked to my car. And that was that. We hadn't even shaken hands, coming or going. I drove home utterly unaware of how this woman would upend my life.

Meanwhile, the other woman in my life continued to charm me with the grace she brought even to small, everyday rituals. When Paula Smith called on the phone, for example, she didn't identify herself, ask how you were doing, or even say hello. You knew it was Paula because she was already well into a one-sided conversation, which, for all you knew, had started half an hour earlier. One hot morning in early June, a few weeks after meeting Michelle, I picked up the phone to hear a tobacco-cured rasp asking, "You like cherry pie?" This question was clearly rhetorical. "Gordon and I had the best sour cherry pie last night," she continued. "You gotta use sour cherries for a pie, you know. The sweet ones won't work. But they don't sell sour cherries in stores anymore. And you wanna know why? 'Cause *nobody fucking makes pies anymore, that's why*! But I've got the best sour cherry tree in town. I already hit it three times this year, but I think it's got one more pick left in it if you wanna try."

"Just fine, thanks," I said cheerily, "How are you, Paula?"

"Okay, I forgot, sorry," she said. One thing you had to give Paula: when she was in the wrong, she usually didn't hesitate to apologize. And she usually meant it, too. On the other hand, it didn't divert her from whatever was on her mind. "So what do you think about the tree?"

"Go today, you mean?" I said, trying to parse her meaning.

"Hell yeah, today," she sputtered, as if I were intentionally antagonizing her. "You think I meant next month? They're ripe *now*."

Of course I wanted to go. I'd never even had a sour cherry that I knew of. I did know that excursions with Paula had a way of putting you in unlikely places and that it was wise to determine where you were going before she got into the car. Because once she was in, you'd be going wherever she said. This was another of Paula's strange and inexplicable skills. It was your car. You were driving. And yet, somehow, she always ended up in charge. Actually, she started off in charge. You were merely quicker or slower in recognizing this.

"So where exactly is this tree?" I asked.

"Up past Adams Morgan," she said, still purposely vague. On general principle, a forager resists sharing the locations of favored trees and patches. On the other hand, as I pointed out to her, since I was driving us there I would eventually know the location anyway. She seemed not to have considered this fact closely, and evidently needed a moment to chew on it. I waited, determined that for once she be the one to break the silence.

"Okay, it's on one of the major streets," she said finally, as if under torture.

"So . . . a major street in major downtown D.C. Why don't we just ask Obama if we can take a look around his yard? Hey, his wife has a vegetable garden. Gotta be some interesting stuff in there, don't you think?"

She was growing irritated with me. "Listen, you in or not?"

Of course I was in. "Yeah. Twenty minutes," I said, and hung up. I got my blickey, which is any kind of basket you tie around your waist, leaving both hands free to pick. Mine was an old Tupperware container, about the size of a loaf of bread. I'd punched holes in it and tied it with paracord. I threw it and a bottle of water into the car and set off.

It should be noted that although Paula would go almost anywhere if she thought the place held shed antlers, old bottles, or edibles, she had a great aversion to being yelled at by landowners or other authorities. (This always struck me as odd, given that her social sensitivity, generally, was right up there that of a subway turnstile.) She timed her visits accordingly. Weekends were unpredictable. Generally, they were bad for residential sites but good for public ones: campuses, state and local agencies, businesses, etc. She once called on a bleak Sunday in January just after a winter weather advisory had been issued. It was sleeting heavily, and radio and TV forecasters were urging people to get off the roads. The excitement in her voice was palpable. "I got a place I been dying to go," she said. "The—." (She here named the facility, which was governmental and which she has, quite sensibly, forbidden me to name.) "C'mon!" she urged. "They just stopped bus service. With weather like this, it might as well be open house day. And the Redskins are playing. This is as good as it gets! The guards'll never even leave the fuckin' shack. It's *heated*." She sounded like an astronomer who had just been invited to watch the transit of Venus from a secret observatory in the Azores. I actually felt guilty at not aiding and abetting her in breaking federal law. But there was no way I was driving crosstown over roads best navigated on a Zamboni.

On cherry day, Paula was waiting for me when I drove up. She stubbed out a cigarette and put the butt back into the pack for later, and we drove into town on the coattails of morning rush hour traffic. "You want to head up 16th Street," she said. The fact that Paula knew the name of the street was itself surprising. Paula has never had a driver's license and gets around mainly by bus or commandeering rides from acquaintances. She usually referred to a given area by the bus number she took to get there, and this often made it impossible for us to communicate in the rare event she would tell me where she'd found things. We passed through downtown D.C., then up a hill. Office buildings gradually gave way to a neighborhood of churches and slightly shabby two-story row houses. "Park anywhere you can," she said abruptly. "It's in this block." I parked, but saw nothing that looked like a fruit tree. "Now listen," she said, as she led me across the street, "Just act like you know what you're doing. Used to belong to a Hispanic guy, never home, a lawyer or something. But I don't know if he still lives here."

Then she pointed out her sour cherry. It was not a tree. It was a bush, not much taller than I was, and spindly looking. The cherry grew out of the short, steep, untended bank of dirt between the street and the stairs leading up to the front door. With a folding pruning saw, I could have cut the thing down and carried it away under one arm. "Not a whole lot to it, is there?" I said, tying on my blickey and trying to tamp down my disappointment. It was impossible to imagine a more unremarkable shrub. Nor, for that matter, did I see many cherries on it, at least not at first. Paula ignored me. She was already on her knees and picking the lower branches. I heard the gentle thwap of the first cherries hitting the bottom of the paper grocery bag.

As I studied the bush, though, I started to see the fruit. There were actually quite a few cherries, if you looked closely. And if you squatted so that you were looking up at the underside of a given branch rather than the other way around, you saw even more. I was soon engrossed in picking from this position, digging in my heels to keep from sliding down the hill. It was a posture that engaged certain lower back muscles I'd never used before. You almost needed to be a circus contortionist to get at some of the higher-up fruit, though. At one point, standing to stretch my back again, I realized that there might be just enough room for me to squeeze in next to the one open spot near the trunk and pick from the inside. Folding and unfolding myself between the branches, I finally arrived at this place. The view from here was one of amazing abundance. There were cherries in every direction. The problem was that I could barely move. I snaked one hand up and bent the topmost branch down gently, then stood on tiptoe to get every last cherry. Frequently I would reach for a cherry and grab only air. The cherry was actually a foot nearer or farther than it appeared. The optical illusion, I finally realized, was because the place was so crowded with branches and fruit that often only one eye had a clear view of what I was after.

The cherries were deep red, almost purple. They felt soft and juicy. I put one into my mouth and winced at the tartness. There's a forager's joke about bitter edibles to the effect that "the second one tastes better than the first," meaning that once your palate gets past the initial shock of a new tart or bitter taste, you quickly acclimate and begin to taste "past" that to the other, more subtle flavors. That was the deal here. After the first few, the taste improved considerably. I wasn't entirely sure I liked it. On the other hand, I kept wanting more. The things were astringent, no question, but also dark and concentrated, a taste that seemed the very essence of cherries. I forced myself to stop eating, realizing that I really did want enough for a pie.

The idea of my first pie had begun to grow in my head. I'd never made a pie, had never had even the faintest desire to make one, and questioned the wisdom of those who did. But I seemed to be edging up sidewise to the notion, as was my fashion. Now that I thought about it, I realized I'd never seen sour cherries in a store or restaurant. And yet I was already beginning to think of myself as a connoisseur of the fruit. There were substantial variations in taste among the cherries even on this one tree, some more watery, others more concentrated. There were even variations among cherries of matching color from a single tree. Wow, I thought, you're turning into one of the very people whose preciousness you detest. Keep this up and pretty soon you'll turn into one of those whack jobs who can't stop talking about the time they tasted hand-harvested, unfiltered olive oil in Italy that had been pressed by eunuchs between two pieces of marble stolen from the Colosseum in the fifth century.

Picking keeps your hands busy. And even as part of my mind was already lost to abundance mania—focused on the next cherry and the next and the next—another part was wandering in the wider world of cherries. Consider supermarket cherries. I had no idea how far they might have to travel or what kind of shelf life was required in the produce aisle, but it stood to reason that a grower would have plenty of incentive to breed fruit that would ship well—that didn't bruise or collapse easily and that remained firm, if not exactly "ripe," for extended periods—and little reason to breed for flavor. These cherries seemed like the very opposite of the fruit required to make money on a large scale. They were pure cherry, succulent meat from skin to stone. They felt fragile in the hand, as if the weight of even three or four would crush the one beneath. I began to feel for the cherries at the bottom of my blickey. I worried that the guys on the bottom might not be doing so well.

But I consoled myself with the thought that they were all headed for the oven. This fruit, I realized, was at absolute peak ripeness. I had no idea how long these cherries would stay that way, but my sense was that it was likely measured in hours rather than days. I'd seen wineberries that weren't ready one day turn overripe the next. It seemed plausible that this fruit might yet last a day or two on the tree—and equally plausible that it wouldn't last even that long.

"Wow," I murmured to Paula as I caught myself eating another one, "These are intense." She was still picking the outside, stepping back now and then to look for areas that still had fruit. "Like I said," she replied, paying only marginal attention to anything outside the endless physical mantra of reaching and picking; "best fuckin' sour cherry in the city. You get all the high ones? There were a bunch I couldn't reach." I assured her the high ones had been plucked. I was getting everything I could reach, and pulling myself up to get as many others as possible.

At last, even Paula was satisfied. "I think we've picked this baby about as clean as we can," she said. "You good to go?" I was. I had about a blickey and a half of cherries in a plastic bag. Paula assured me it was plenty for a pie.

On the way home, feeling expansive from my little epiphany, I confessed to Paula how surprised I was by the tree's productivity, by its location, and that it nonetheless remained more or less unknown. "You know how many people walk by this tree every day and never think to pick a cherry?" she said, her voice rising with indignation. "Gotta be hundreds, maybe thousands. Because nobody gives a fuck. They want fruit from Bolivia or someplace that's grown in monkey shit and handled by people with God knows what diseases. But if it looks nice in the supermarket they're happy. You could take fucking crabgrass to the produce section, arrange it all nice and pretty, and as long as it's under those fluorescent lights and those things, whattya call 'em, that spray water in your face when—"

"Misters," I say.

"—Yeah, fucking misters. And all they do is make the shit that much heavier so they can charge you more for it. But as long as it's all nice and laid out like that, people will buy it."

We drove on in rare silence for a few moments. Then she asked if I even knew how to make a pie. I resented her for assuming that I'd never made a pie. And I specifically resented her for being right. I knew more about Ethiopian import restrictions on fennel than I did about making pies. "Okay, listen to me," she said. "First, don't rinse these cherries when you get home. The only fruit you rinse and scrub is apples. Besides, we've had tons of rain recently. You don't think that's cleaned them off? And if there's a bug in them, so what? You're cooking the damn thing, aren't you?"

She asked if I owned a copy of *The Joy of Cooking*. As a matter of fact I did. It was a long-ago Christmas gift from my mother back when she still hoped I might learn to cook. It was also the only cookbook I owned. No points from Paula, though. "Is it before 1978?" she asked. It was from 1992, I said. "Too bad. They changed 'em after that. Maybe it was 1979. Anyway, they took out all the good stuff: how to skin and stew a squirrel or a possum, how to cook a raccoon, all that stuff." Paula had eaten raccoon, of course, but it wasn't something she'd go out of her way for. "Anyway, *The Joy of Cooking* is what you want. Follow the recipe for the fresh cherry pie." She proceeded as if my pie education had somehow fallen to her. Which, in fact, it had.

Once Paula shouldered a responsibility—regardless of how it had devolved to her—she took it seriously. Part of instructing me in making pie evidently included describing all the ways I could screw it up. It was clear she didn't think it would help much. It was more a question of her having a clean conscience after the train wreck.

"Okay, when you start mixing in the fruit, sugar, and tapioca? The tapioca box has a little note on it that says, 'Shake before using.' They mean that. Don't ask me why, but you gotta do it.

"If they give you a range of sugar to use, say one and a quarter to one and a half, cups always go for the larger amount. I'm not a sweet tooth kind of person. It just makes the thing taste better." (This, incidentally, is completely false. Paula's pies were a dentist's dream. But the filing cabinet of Paula's mind had peculiar divisions. Liking sweet pies was, by her lights, very different from "having a sweet tooth." One was a matter of personal taste, while the other was a character flaw.)

"Buy the premade piecrusts. Everybody will tell you that they're easy to make. That's bullshit. Trust me.

"Now, look, you start the pie hot, at 450, to brown the crust. Then, after fifteen minutes, you cut the oven down to 350 for the rest of the time. And when you put the pie in the oven, you gotta crimp tinfoil over the edges of the crust. Otherwise it gets burned, which you do not want."

By this time, I was beginning to understand why no one made pies anymore. What a huge pain in the ass! I had loved picking cherries, but by this time my desire to make a pie had vanished. It was, however, too late. If I backed out now I'd never hear the end of it.

Paula had fallen silent, leading me to think our little talk was over. It wasn't. She was just reviewing to see if she'd left anything out. "Always put a cookie sheet underneath the pie," she said. "The thing bubbles over and then you have to clean the whole fucking oven. By the way, when the filling bubbles up, it's done. Take it out and let it cool."

I felt oddly like a soldier on the last day of basic training, my drill sergeant imparting her final words before I headed off to war. Having passed on the essential facts about pies, Paula again fell quiet. This lasted nearly a minute. Then, out of the blue, she told me with some adamancy that I should give the pie to my mother. "Mothers like that," she said. "She cooked for you her whole life. Now you return the favor." This was odd. There was a whole iceberg submerged in there, and this was just the tip of it, but my attempts to get her to amplify went nowhere. "I just think you should give it to your mother," she said. "But do what you want." And with that we were at Gordon's and she got out. I thanked her for showing me the tree. I meant it. She took very few people into her confidence, and doing so clearly made her uncomfortable. "Yeah, yeah," she said impatiently, flitting away acknowledgement as if it were a swarm of gnats. Then she leaned in and said, "Listen, don't forget about the cookie sheet."

After picking Emma up at school, I tried to pitch the pie as an adventure we would undertake together. To my surprise, Em was eager to help in the first step, pitting the fruit. I had her stand on a stool so we could work side by side at the sink, expelling the pits into a small bowl, the cherries into a large one. It was pleasant to be doing this together. It was nice, for once, not being the Homework Monster or the Bedtime Enforcer. I was a dad making something with his daughter.

110

This daddy-daughter domestic arts quality time lasted for all of ninety seconds, about five cherries each. One side effect of the process was the occasional wayward squirt of juice. By pure chance, Emma's first squirt went straight up into her face. "Gross!" she wailed, as if she'd been slimed by a giant oyster, and fled the kitchen. I sighed, the all-too-familiar feeling of not knowing what the hell to do enveloping me. I could have forced her to pit cherries, but that would just have made her resentful. I could think of nothing more constructive than to let her be for the moment and continue on my own.

Two quarts of cherries had looked like a lot. Pitted, the fruit looked sort of crestfallen and reduced, barely filling a nine-inch pie pan. I poured the fruit-sugar-flour-tapioca mixture into the store-bought piecrust. (In between dropping off Paula and picking up Emma, I had made three trips to the store to find the right kind of crust. This was because I fell prey—twice—to the various types of imposter graham cracker crust lurking in the baking aisle. I had reasoned, mistakenly, that all the piecrusts would cohabitate in a single supermarket aisle. Finally, I called Paula from the store. "The real piecrusts are in the refrigerated section for Chrissake. Usually right next to the butter. Didn't your mother teach you anything?" I bought two of the only kind of real piecrusts I saw, which were already in nine-inch foil pie plates.)

After adding the fruit mixture to one crust-plate, I attempted to ease the second crust from its dish to make the top. This did not go well. The more gingerly I handled it, the faster it disintegrated. I was soon holding the pastry equivalent of Stanley Kowalski's T-shirt. Finally I lost it, ripped the rest of the crust out with my bare hands, and molded it into a lumpy globe of aromatic Play-Doh. Which I then realized that I would need to flatten again. It was at this point that I discovered I didn't own a rolling pin. There had been no particular reason to think that I did, other than the fact that I own a great many kitchen utensils that I never use and whose functions elude me. Anyway, there was no rolling pin in the drawer that serves as the Tomb of Unknown Utensils. I had, however, heard somewhere that a wine bottle made an acceptable substitute, and wine bottles were something I always had on hand. Sprinkling flour onto my big plastic cutting board, I attempted the bottle trick. After a while I realized that you also had to flour the wine bottle. Even so, the thinnest I could uniformly roll the dough resulted in something still thick enough to chock the wheel of a farm tractor. I was approaching the end of my tether. There was flour all over the kitchen which, after an hour of preheating the oven, was very warm. It was seven p.m. I'd been at it for two hours, still had no pie in the oven, and had yet to consider what I would feed my child for supper.

In desperation, I went to my next-door neighbor's house and borrowed a rolling pin. This made no difference whatsoever. I opened the floury bottle of wine, poured a large glass, and considered the fact that despite the laborsaving use of premade crusts, I wanted to break things. Ugly as the situation had gotten, I was determined to see this through. I began lifting the rolling pin and pressing it down in different spots, which gave the crust a sort of oceany effect: little wind-raised waves chasing each other over its surface. And yet it did result in a thinner crust. At least in some places.

I had noted the "lattice" crusts while reading the other parts in *Joy* about pies and had thought maybe I'd try it. Now, reading the actual process involved, I realized that they required you to literally weave the fucking crust over and under itself as if you were caning a chair. Soon as Jesus comes back, I thought, and decided instead to "float" the large pancake of dough atop the filling. I then spent twenty minutes and five yards of tinfoil trying to get the tinfoil to adhere to the edges of the goddamn crust. In the end, I finally got part of the crust on one half of the pie covered and slammed it into the oven.

Emma and I dined at Burger King that night. "You should make pie again," she said.

An hour and twenty minutes after entering the oven, my first-ever pie emerged, the filling heaving slowly with volcanic purple bubbles. Amazingly, the crust had not burned. The pancake was golden brown. I was delighted. An hour later, the pie having cooled to a safe temperature, Emma and I sampled it. My child judged it too tart, although she gladly accepted the ice cream that went with it. As for me, I was amazed at my handiwork. It was wonderful. The crust was a little thick but intact. And the pie itself had a tantalizing tartness that perfectly offset the vanilla ice cream. I felt . . . "Promethean" is the word. I had stolen pie from the gods. It wasn't the world's first pie, but it was my first. Damn but I was proud. Was it not I who had purloined the fruit and pitted it? Was it not I who had initiated the chemical changes by which raw dough and fruit and sugar and well-shaken tapioca coalesced into a completely new thing—a pie? I am not ashamed to say that I polished off half the sucker in the first sitting, along with a pint of vanilla ice cream. I loved my mother, but she would have to wait. This was my pie. Then I decided to call Paula. "Made a pie with those cherries," I said when she answered, appropriating her preemptive conversational style. As if prearranged, a burp began to form in my throat. "I'll try to save you a piece," I said, and then let the burp out loudly. "But I'm not promising anything."

I hung up just as Paula began either laughing or cursing. Maybe both.

After my success making sour cherry pie, I began to feel I was getting somewhere. I had proved that it was possible not only for a theoretical person, but for a real one—me, for example—to go out, gather wild food, bring it home, and turn it not just into something edible but into something that you would actually want to pig out on while watching TV. (Not that I could do this, in the case of sour cherries, without butter, flour, sugar, tapioca, and salt. Almost everybody serving "wild food"—with the exception of really hard-core foragers like Sam Thayer—combines wild with non-wild ingredients.) Still, the notion that a dish based on wild food could in fact be a guilty pleasure, one not incompatible with sin generally and with gluttony in particular, was a breakthrough moment for me. It opened new vistas of hope and degradation. It restored some of the romance that Hue, with the best of intentions, had so thoroughly dashed when he pointed out that nearly every weed sprouting from the cracks in the sidewalk was a wild edible. Romance and guilty pleasure, at least in my mind, went hand in glove. And there were few pleasures, gustatorial or otherwise, as fully satisfying as guilty ones. They were the id's delight. If McCormick's lab people ever managed to synthesize guilty pleasure, imagine the condiment it would make. You'd be able to eat anything and enjoy it if you could just smother it with Guilty Pleasure. Although Guilty Pleasure Low Sodium and Guilty Pleasure Lite would inevitably follow.

During the time of cherry picking and pie making, I had more or less been thinking continually about Michelle, someone for whom it was routine to include foraged ingredients in daily cooking. I pictured her standing in her kitchen—with several pots on the stove and two boys rumpusing in the next room—and ducking outside for thirty seconds to grab a handful of dandelion greens or daylily buds, either as an addition to something or as a dish by itself. That someone I knew did this—reflexively, without the slightest interest in impressing anyone else or making "a statement"—seemed extraordinary. And very cool. The images of her doing this were more vivid than I wanted. I was increasingly having trouble separating this culinary mind-set—that the use of wild plants in daily cooking needn't be a solemn, weighty act but could rather be a kind of everyday magic—from the only person I knew who practiced it. Whenever I tried to picture myself cooking this way, the image that came wasn't me but Michelle. I always saw her backlit by slanting evening light, standing before a stove, pans crackling with just-picked greens, absently tucking a loose lock of strawberry blond hair behind an ear. She was fully engaged in her work and there was no doubt in my mind that she was good at it.

One morning, as I looked over my notes from outings with Hue and reread the list of edibles he had found on my property, it occurred to me that I could make a salad of them. Most were weeds growing right in my grass. I could still hear Paula's diatribe about how people happily ate produce from South America grown in God knows what as long as it was displayed under the consecrating fluorescent lights and misters of a grocery store. She was right. A lawn salad might be thought of as one man's act of defiance. The truth was that people who dropped phrases like "the politics of food" into everyday conversation always struck me as people who didn't have enough to occupy themselves. But if my salad was seen as one principled man's rejection of the industrial food system and I became a folk hero, that was cool, too. What really got me off the dime was the fact that making the thing supplied an excuse to stay in touch with Michelle. My motives, I could plausibly claim, were purely professional. This was a total lie, of course. But the important thing was that it gave me deniability on the older-man-hitting-on-a-younger-woman front, which was exactly where I was headed. In my dreams, at least.

The prospect of using my lawn the way other people used the produce section seemed safe enough. Not a speck of seed, fertilizer, or pesticide—organic, inorganic, or extraterrestrial—had hit my lawn since I had moved in three years ago. I felt I deserved a good conduct medal just for mowing the damn grass occasionally. I e-mailed Michelle, explaining my plan and asking for a feasibility assessment. She wrote back saying it was totally doable and described the contents of her own yard, which she suspected of being similar to mine. Hers, she wrote, was "roughly 20 percent grass, 70 percent weeds, 3 percent mushrooms, and 7 percent dog turds. But in aggregate the yard is green, so to me it's an acceptable lawn; I never have understood our national lawn fetish." (I was right on her wavelength about the lawn fetish, which, let's be frank, is nothing short of a national brainwashing.) In fact, she went on, one untampered-with lawn was so like the next that she was pretty confident that she could list the edible weeds in mine, despite the distance and the fact that she had never seen it. Which she proceeded to do. "The weeds, more or less in descending order of prevalence, are white clover, broadleaf plantain, buckhorn plantain, violets, wild alliums (onions and garlic), henbit, chickweed, sorrel, dandelions, and Indian strawberry. You didn't share the species list you are working from but I suspect your lawn is pretty similar, though with a higher percentage of dandelions, since I've been eating ours steadily since moving in here a decade ago." I was simultaneously encouraged and abashed by her response. It was fantastic that she was writing back to me so quickly and unguardedly. On the other hand, I was intimidated by her level of plant knowledge. She took this stuff seriously. Also, something else was now clear. What had begun as an idle thought—Hey, what if I make a salad out of the weird stuff I forgot to kill in my lawn?—was now something I couldn't back out of.

Unfortunately, she continued, the short period in early spring when nearly all of these were putting out their new shoots and leaves and were therefore at peak edibility was months past. Most had grown tougher since then and were now pumping out bitter chemicals of one sort or another. They did this to discourage animals—including us—from eating them. "Now, alas, they are more like goat fodder; won't hurt you but, since you lack multiple stomachs and/or a rumen, will be hell to masticate and digest." I was not entirely doomed, however, she went on. Most of these plants hadn't stopped growing altogether; it's just that by this time they were putting only a tiny fraction of their energy into new growth, apparently as insurance. In the event of some catastrophic early summer event—drought being the most likely—these guys would still have had a shot at starting over. The tiny leaves of this new growth, Michelle said, would be the most tender and least bitter. They grew at the very center of the plant.

So it wouldn't be a big salad. I was okay with that. It was more about variety and showing that the weeds we've been trained to kill as if they threatened the foundations of the Republic were actually nutritious. I was also intrigued by the notion that plants, like people, tended to get tougher and more bitter as time passed.

Armed with my Peterson's *Edible Wild Plants,* Hue's list, a printout of Michelle's e-mail, and images from the online Weed Identification Guide of Virginia Tech, I stepped out of my air-conditioned porch office and into one of those D.C. summer days that plasters your shirt to your back in three minutes whether you're moving or not. Michelle had nailed my yard, plantwise. I'd never really noticed before, but a multitude of white clover flowerheads stretched before me all the way to the back fence. I stopped short at the second sentence of the Peterson's "Uses" entry for white clover: "Although not among the choicest of wild foods . . ." I'd been around the block a few times by this point. "Not among the choicest" was code for "Tastes so bad you'll wish it were poisonous." I opted to go light on white clover flowerheads, which actually had a faintly sweet odor, and dropped only a few into my paper sack.

Broadleaf and buckthorn plantain were also easy to spot, especially once I got down on their level. Eyeballing my lawn while prone, I was struck by how little actual grass there was. It was nearly all green weeds of one kind or another. If I had used weed-killing fertilizer, my yard would have looked as though I were receiving a federal grant to grow dirt. Each plantain grew in a circular pattern known as a "basal rosette," a common structure among edibles. Kneeling, my face tickled by plaintain stalks, I carefully peeled back the outer leaves until I found the tiny leaves at the center of some of these rosettes. After an hour, I was soaked. I had grass stains everywhere. And a stiff back. For my pains I had nearly a forkful of greens. In short, my salad was coming along splendidly.

It was an absurd little project, yet I found myself strangely buoyed rather than frustrated by this. I had a bit of momentum and meant to harness it. I struck out on violets, which I still believe were there but were unidentifiable, at least to me, now that they had lost their telltale blue flowers. The heart-shaped leaves of the plant were everywhere, but there were any number of unremarkable plants with heart-shaped leaves in my Peterson's, including—I was reasonably sure—a few that would lay you out in no time.

Nor, armed as I was with descriptions and color printouts of the plant, could I find henbit. I knew that I had some; Hue had several times pointed it out. But I didn't see it now. Nor did I see purple deadnettle, its alluringly named cousin in the mint family, which he'd found growing in a crack in my front steps. I returned to the site but found only dandelions there. Those were edible, of course, so I went down on my knees to find the tiniest leaves of their basal rosettes. The heat was infernal by now. A passing car slowed to a crawl, apparently curious about the religion that led a man to prostrate himself before his own front steps during the most sweltering part of the day.

Next on the list were wild onions, a patch of which had taken up residence in the seriously overgrown flower bed by the air-conditioning compressor. At least I think it was wild onion. Since it was not in flower either, it might also have been wild garlic. Or possibly field garlic. Whatever it was, it thrived in the microclimate of hot wind forcefully discharged by the compressor. And since all three were edible, it didn't really matter. I dug up a few bulbs, peeled off the dirt and outer layers, and added them to the mix.

Now that I looked, the unpromising flower bed—sun-baked clay as hard as cement—had more varieties of weeds than any other spot in the yard. Here I found chickweed as well as wood sorrel, usually the first (sometimes only) edible plant that children learn, easily known by its clover-like leaves and agreeably sour taste. I took some of both plants, as well as a few Indian, or false, strawberries. These are the only kind of wild strawberry I have ever found, although virtually all wild edibles books assured you that the true (and delicious) wild strawberry was everywhere waiting to be found in some sunny or partially sunny location with poor, low-nitrogen soil that also happened to be both well-drained and moist. Indian strawberries had all the taste of Styrofoam packing material but made up for it by being eminently easy to find. Still, they were a vivid red and, since the eye-stomach nexus was not to be overlooked, I picked a few as a garnish. I later learned from Michelle that they are extremely nutritious.

At last, after three or four hours spent shopping my lawn, I retreated inside and set to washing, rinsing, and finally chopping my harvest. The greens barely covered the bottom of a small salad plate. It looked pretty and had an interesting variety of leaves and stems. But it would never have passed muster in a restaurant as any sort of "salad." Up until this moment my life experience had taught me that salad came from one of three sources: someone else's wooden salad bowl, a waiter, or a plastic bag. Mine was unmediated by any of these. With a sense of misgiving—Michelle had warned me that it would be fibrous—I mixed up the vinaigrette for which Michelle had sent a recipe and dressed it.

My first bite was . . . not bad. I realize that's a cop-out, but it was true. It was agreeably crunchy at first bite, after which I settled in for a prolonged period of mastication. She had nailed the fibrous part. I chewed until I felt as though the muscles on the sides of my head were actually increasing in size. I'd overdressed the salad—out of fear, mostly. I think I hoped that vinaigrette might have medicinal properties. This turned out to be a good move for entirely different reasons. Basically, the extra liquid made swallowing the partially chewed salad—which was as chewed as this salad could ever be—easier. If I had insisted on chewing until the plants had been properly broken down, I think I'd still be there now.

But below that first crunch and the vinaigrette I could taste the sour kick of the sorrel, an agreeable bitterness coming from another leaf—chickweed? dandelion?—and something else, something elusive that registered on my taste buds only as a state of being: it tasted alive. I had the pronounced sensation of eating raw things. This seemed strange, in that every salad I've ever eaten consisted of raw things. But these plants were a different kind of raw. They had just been separated from their roots and were not yet dead. They were the salad equivalent of a raw oyster. Vividly, stubbornly raw. The sensation was singular yet elusive. You couldn't put your tongue on any particular part that nailed down the taste. There was actually a moment when it tasted like dirt, but good dirt, working, purposeful dirt. Then I remembered that outing with Paula when I'd eaten the wild watercress. This salad had that same insistent vitality. And in five very chewy bites, long before I'd had time to sort the tastes any further, it was over. I was trying to pretend otherwise, but I felt a tad disappointed. I'd eaten my yard, but the act hadn't changed me. Except that I was now a guy who had eaten his yard. Which was not exactly a great conversation starter.

A few minutes later, thanks to a large burp, I was able to revisit the salad. What I remember tasting was the sharp tang of wild garlic. Garlic always seems to get the last word.

Not long after, I wrote to Michelle, saying I'd succeeded in collecting and eating a salad of lawn weeds, which weren't bad, although she had been correct about the goat-fodder part. All in all, I wrote, I wasn't sure how to feel about the whole thing. I was proud that I'd done what I set out to do. On the other hand, the more I thought about it, the less it seemed to amount to. It was like a man setting out to make himself a suit out of dryer lint. Even if he succeeded, what could he really claimed to have accomplished?

A couple of days later I received an e-mail from Michelle saying she was proud of me. Her memory of the event, I later found, was quite different from mine. "You sounded so proud of yourself when you wrote me about it," she would say. "I thought that was adorable." No man is entirely comfortable with that particular compliment. We'd much rather be thought of as hard-core or fearless or tough. But if I'd known adorable what was Michelle was after, I'd have done whatever it took to be that.

SOUR CHERRY PIE

(Adapted from *The Joy of Cooking,* 1975 edition, by Marion Rombauer Becker)

2 packaged prepared pie crusts (from the supermarket dairy case)
4 cups fresh sour cherries (Good sour cherries invariably involve crime. I obtain them by theft. If you succeed in finding ones for sale, the price will make you feel as if you've been robbed.)
2 tablespoons plus 2 teaspoons quick-cooking tapioca
$1^1/_3$ cups sugar
2 tablespoons Kirsch or Amaretto liqueur (optional)
2 tablespoons butter cut into small pieces

Do not rinse wild cherries or Paula Smith will come after you. Don't ask me why, but she's adamant on the subject. Instead, pit the fruit and place into a bowl. Mix tapioca and sugar, and then gently fold into the cherries. Sprinkle on liqueur, if using. Let stand for 15 minutes. Okay, 10 minutes is good enough.

Meanwhile, preheat oven to 450 degrees F. Pat out one pie crust into pie pan to form the bottom crust, making sure edges cover the rim of the pie pan. (Skip this step if you're using the kind that comes in its own aluminum pie plate). Pour the fruit into the shell. Dot with butter. Place second crust on top of pie, crimp edges, then prick all over with fork. Crimp tinfoil over the edges of the crust to keep it from burning. Good luck with this.

Don't forget to put the pie on a goddamn cookie sheet. Bake for 10 minutes at 450 degrees F, then reduce oven to 350 degrees F and bake for about 40–45 more minutes until the filling is bubbling. (Check the pie about 10–15 minutes after lowering the oven temp. By now the crust will be half-burned because the foil didn't stay in place. Take the pie out and use whatever you can devise— toothpicks, finishing nails, velcro—to try to reposition the foil.)

Let pie cool for much longer than it should require, 45 minutes to 1 hour. Eat at one sitting with a half-gallon of vanilla ice cream.

Chapter Six:
Among the Cajuns

A Cajun man named Jody Meche and I were bombing down the river into wind that was reshaping the frames of my glasses and sending over the bow an occasional splash of spray that stung like buckshot. Despite a good set of foul weather gear, I was wet, cold, and getting pounded like a piece of cube steak. After about ten minutes of this, during which I found myself thinking of a story Paula had once told me, I decided to turn and face aft. I was immediately much more comfortable. Paula's story concerned a possum she'd caught in the Havahart trap she'd set for the raccoons raiding her garden. Not having any use for the possum, she'd opened the rear of the trap and come back three hours later, only to find that the animal hadn't budged. Possums, as is widely known, aren't God's brightest creatures. Facing forward and seeing nothing but cage, this one had been so convinced of its captivity that it saw no reason to turn around. Paula had forced it to freedom at the point of a sharp stick. Thinking of this, I smiled. I might not be the smartest of men. But I was one up on that possum.

Technically, the water we were on was the Atchafalaya River, only that's not what it's called here. This part—a powerful fourteen-mile chute, dug 1,000 feet wide and dredged to a depth of 100 feet by the U.S. Army Corps of Engineers—is called the Whiskey Bay Pilot Channel. When the Mississippi floods, it endangers downstream population centers like Baton Rouge and New Orleans. When that happens, a series of massive flood control gates upriver can be opened, dispersing some of the excess elsewhere. One of those places is into the Whiskey

Bay Pilot Channel, which empties into the sparsely populated Atcha-falaya Basin, the largest swamp in the United States, roughly 3,000 square miles of swamplands, bayous, black-water lakes, and bottom-land hardwood forest.

Even on a normal day, the channel's current was swift and dangerous. Jody's eyes, I noticed, never stopped moving. He continually adjusted the tiller to minimize pounding on his boat and as he swept the water ahead for hazards to navigation. These ranged from the inconvenient (old fishing line and floating vegetation that could foul a propellor) to the catastrophic (huge old cypress logs floating just under the surface). The Basin's cypress trees, some of which were 1,000 years old when cut, had been pretty much logged out by the 1900s. But the same density that made the wood so desirable also made it prone to sinking when wet. Nobody knew how many big logs had sunk during the logging boom. What everyone knew now, a century later, was that the scouring action of the channel's swift current regularly dislodged such logs. When one of these ancient "sinkers" came back to life, it often floated just beneath the surface of the water, almost invisible until it was too late.

"You hit something like that and it jerks the tiller handle right outta your hand," Jody said. He was a happy fireplug of a man—five-foot-eight and 230 pounds, built like the football lineman he'd been for the six weeks he spent at college, which was all the time he needed to decide he'd rather be back catching crawfish in the Basin. The boat would turn sharply, he explained, and if it turned too sharply, the hull could bite the water in such a way that it actually propelled the craft downward. "Then you got a hundred fifty horses driving the boat right toward the bottom," Jody said. "A cavitation I guess you'd call it. The boat just buries itself." He had lost a friend in this very stretch of water not long ago and believed that's exactly what happened. The boat popped up and was recovered the next day. What was left of his friend's body—identifiable by his dental records—was found weeks later, fifty miles downriver. The guy had been a childhood friend. Jody missed him. "But he liked big motors and liked to run too fast," Jody said. He shrugged.

123

The Atchafalaya Basin, roughly twenty miles wide and 150 miles long, has long been and remains one of the wildest and most forbidding places in the country. Early travelers wrote of "birds and reptiles, alligators, enormous bullfrogs, night owls, anhingas, herons whose dwellings were in the mud of the swamp, or on its leaky roof . . . their voices bellowing, hooting, shrieking, and groaning." Today, environmentalists defending the Basin against various threats point to its role as the most productive land in the country, its 300 bird species, 100 species of fish, crawfish, crabs, and shrimp, and its forty species of mammals. Half of the nation's migratory waterfowl depend on it. One thing that has never thrived here, however, is forgiveness.

While Jody never stopped watching for danger, he was also busy doing one of the things he most enjoys in life, which was to scan the water for critters, pointing out the ones he spotted, and telling me how good each was to eat. And it seemed that each was better eating than the last. There were gators, of course, sunning on the banks and reluctantly sliding into the muddy water when the boat was still 100 yards off. "All good eating except for the biggest ones," Jody called over the motor's din. "That reddish-tinged meat's too strong." He flicked a finger as we passed stout fishing lines tied off to bushes along the shore, different owners apparently marking their lines with different flagging tape of different colors. "Set lines. Catfish, most likely." A minute later we scared up two coots, ungainly black birds that ran on top of the water for forty yards—looking more like cartoon birds than the real thing—before they finally attained liftoff speed. Even after liftoff, it took another forty yards of frantic flapping just inches off the water before they gained sufficient airspeed to climb. All I knew about coots was what I'd been told by duck hunters, who unanimously despised them. They referred to coots as "mud hens" and "the duck you'll only eat once." Jody actually looked both surprised and somewhat hurt by that assessment, which was nonsense. Coots were fine eating, particularly in a gumbo. "It's the fat and the skin that are fishy," he shouted. "You breast 'em out soon as you kill 'em, get rid a' that fat and skin, and they're delicious." Coots made Jody think of garfish, another fine meat that got a bad rap outside Cajun country. Gar are ugly, primordial fish, with an elongated body and a long jaw lined with sharp teeth. Their scales are so thick that some Indian tribes used them as arrowheads. In my world, if you happened to hook and land a gar, you had someone snap your picture with it, then threw it back into the river or into a garbage can, whichever was closer. Jody maintained that gar patties were delicious. Again, it was a question of knowing what to do with the animal. "It's got these sorta ligaments that you have to cut around. And you need to scrape the meat from the skin with a spoon and let it soften up in the fridge for a day or two. But mix that meat up with some breadcrumbs, dip it in milk and egg, then dredge it in seasoned flour, and fry it up? Hoo! Best thing you ever ate." The very thought brought a smile to his face.

His view about the superiority of gar patties as table fare held until he spotted a group of turtles sunning on a log. A couple were as big as any freshwater turtles I'd ever seen, nearly the size of trash can lids. I'd had sea turtle eggs years ago in Nicaragua but had never knowingly eaten turtle or knew anyone else who had. "Oh, you *gotta* love turtle, Bill!" Jody called, his tone almost worried, as if whoever had been charged with my upbringing had neglected his duty. "See 'em? See that big snapper, that big peaked shell? Now, snapper's good, but that other one there? We call 'em yellow bellies. That's the best. Smother 'em in a brown gravy, or brown 'em in a pot with some onion and make a sauce piquant? Talk about some good! Hoo, son! Shoot, you got light, dark, every kind of meat you could ask for is on a turtle." When next I looked, Jody had his head cocked ever so slightly to one side and I realized that for once he wasn't scanning the river for the next wild thing. He appeared to be savoring some distant memory. I couldn't be sure, of course, but I'd have bet money that it included people he loved and a large platter of yellow-belly turtle.

Having collected and eaten a salad of plants growing in my own lawn, I felt I'd taken personal locavorism about as far as I could. In addition to realizing the primacy of garlic in any dish it graces, I'd discovered just how much time and trouble it took for a child of the suburbs to close the gap between himself and what he ate. Which made me wonder if there were still people in America for whom it was *not* a time-consuming stunt, but something they just did. Were there people who had no need to rediscover the old ways because they'd never given them up in the first place? People who got their sustenance with their own hands as naturally as I selected a shopping cart from the parking lot corral and shoved it toward the motion-activated doors of my supermarket?

The circuitous path that led me to Jody Meche had begun with the old saying, "A Cajun'll eat anything that doesn't eat him first." At least I'd thought it was an old saying. Maybe it wasn't. Maybe I'd seen it on a bumper sticker. Whatever its origin, I couldn't get it out of my head. It might even be an apt motto for the whole human species. I'd been seeing a recent spate of stories in the media about new discoveries of humanlike species or subspecies with whom we'd apparently shared the planet for thousands of years. There were the Denisovians, discovered in Siberia in 2010, the Red Deer People in east Asia (so-called because of their evident fondness for venison), and a hobbit-like race discovered on an island midway between Asia and Australia. The discovery of these cousins had been a mind-bender. Like most people, I'd grown up thinking that our only competitors were the Neanderthals, the Hummer of humanoids—large, powerful, and doomed. Now it seemed that every week brought the discovery of a new shoot of the family tree. All of which made our survival that much more remarkable. We—*Homo sapiens sapiens*—had somehow beaten all comers and won the evolutionary Hunger Games. These discoveries were so recent that anthropologists had yet to advance theories about them, although those were sure to come soon. It was our bigger brain, some would argue. We'd schemed our way to the top. It was our constant horniness, others would say, the ability—and desire—to mate irrespective of the season. We'd sexually outhustled the competition, swarming them with superior numbers. I wasn't likely to be asked my opinion, which was infinitely more elegant. What if our forebears were proto-Cajuns? What if we'd prevailed because we'd eaten everything that didn't eat us first?

I started making phone calls and one contact led to another. Eventually, I talked to a woman named Toni Deboisier, who at the time worked for the Louisiana Department of Agriculture and Forestry. Unprompted, she actually quoted "A Cajun'll eat anything." Better yet, she knew some Cajuns who still got a good portion of their food from the Atchafalaya Basin. She gave me some background information about the place that I hadn't known. I was correct, she said, in that it had always been wild and sparsely populated. The few people who lived there gathered together in small towns—settlements, really—often consisting of just a few families and a store. These people got their living from fishing, hunting, trapping, and collecting Spanish moss, which was used as mattress stuffing and even in car seats until the early 1900s. Until well into the latter half of the twentieth century, when the market for fur collapsed, Louisiana had led the nation in the production of furs, well ahead of its closest competitor, Alaska. Most of its trapping took place in the Atchafalaya Basin.

If one were to identify a turning point, it was 1927, the year that the most destructive river flood in U.S. history came. It is hard to imagine the scale of this disaster. The Mississippi breached its levee system in 145 places and flooded 27,000 square miles of land, some of it to a depth of thirty feet. The flood affected seven states and killed 245 people. When it was all over, Congress gave the U.S. Army Corps of Engineers the responsibility of making sure such an event never happened again. And so the Whiskey Bay Pilot Channel was dug. As with most large-scale fine-tunings of nature, there were a few unforeseen consequences. The faster river carried more volume and dropped vastly more silt. Some parts of the Basin that had been swamp and marsh, suddenly receiving more water, became less productive. On the other hand, other watery places—bayous, swamps, and lakes—got silted up and turned into bottomland. A good number of houses in the Basin were literally underwater, while in other areas, siltation was turning once-navigable waters into bottomland forests. Towns that had kept in touch with neighboring towns by boat found themselves cut off. Fishermen found some of their best areas dry. With houses either washed away or isolated by the silt, people had no choice but to leave. One by one, the settlements withered. A centuries-old way of life came to an end.

Not completely, however. What happened in many cases—including Jody's, as I was to discover—was that while the family relocated to towns outside the Basin, the men either commuted to the Basin to ply their trades or built small camps where they could stay for days if the fish were running. And some of the children of these men still made their living by trapping wild crawfish in the Basin. Toni had come to know some of these people, who were about the only ones left making a living inside the Basin itself and who still got a lot of their food there.

She knew them because a group of crawfishermen had formed an organization to assert their rights against the oil and gas companies whose pipelines crossed the area and which leased drilling rights to areas in the Basin. In theory, under such leases the area itself was supposed to remain open to the public. In fact, the companies usually posted "No Trespassing" signs, put up fences, and closed off waterways. And they enforced their claims with armed guards. After decades of such treatment, the notoriously independent crawfishermen had finally banded together to take their fight to the courts. The group they founded was the Louisiana Crawfish Producers Association.

Toni offered to make some calls on my behalf but warned me that historically, outsiders had been viewed with suspicion by "swampers," as they called themselves. The first outsiders coming to the area had been game wardens. They were not welcomed with open arms. Swampers had never been much on paperwork, calendars, or limits. They took what the swamp gave when it gave it. Toni recounted a recent conversation with a man on the Monday after the Saturday squirrel season opener. "I asked how he'd done and he said, 'Real good, Toni. I got ninety-eight.'" When she had tactfully noted that the limit was twelve squirrels per day, the fellow had replied, "Hell, Toni! Gotta get 'em while you can!"

The one thing working in my favor, she said, was that the people knew they were a vanishing breed and wanted the old ways recorded before they were gone entirely. A few days later she called to give me the number of Mike Bienvenu, the president of LCPA-West.

When I got Mike on the phone, he didn't exactly rush to make me feel comfortable. After a few minutes of talking about nothing in particular, he said he was willing to tell me what I wanted to know, but there was something that I needed to understand before we went any further. I told him I was all ears. "Bill, the level of corruption in Louisiana surpasses anything else in the nation. Anything you've ever seen or heard or imagined. Because the oil and gas companies run everything here. Everything here exists to further their interests." He paused to make sure his words were registering. "Do you understand what I'm telling you, Bill?" I said that I understood. When you're a writer trying to gain the confidence of someone who wants to talk, you let him talk.

"They own every living politician in this state," Mike went on, his voice rising as he cataloged the bribery, extortion, and fraud. "Every sheriff in every parish. Every judge. They own the same state officials who are charged with seeing that they obey environmental laws. They pay these state officials more *not* to do their jobs than the state does to do them. Do you see what I'm telling you, Bill? So, if the police are called to a dispute between a crawfisherman and an oil company guard, who you think they're going to arrest? Our members. And, of course, the oil and gas boys are going to break every environmental law in the book when they dig their work canals and drill and build their pipelines. They're going to pile that spoil right next to where they dig it, which stops the natural flow of water in the Basin and kills all the fish because there's no oxygen left in the water. Because that's the cheapest, easiest way to do it and because they know nobody is going to come and tell them they can't."

The more he talked, the less Mike sounded like someone trying to sell me something. He sounded instead like a guy embittered by the corruption and injustice all around him, like a man trying to relieve himself of a burden by talking about it. It's a strange phenomenon, but not all silences are equal. I think Mike sensed that I was really listening. "Lemme ask you something," he said abruptly. "You think you would have heard about that oil spill"—the BP spill of 2010, when an oil platform exploded, killing eleven men outright, wounding many more, and releasing nearly 5 million barrels of oil into the Gulf—"if those fellas hadn't been killed?" His voice slipped into that of a befuddled oil company man who had just had a reporter's microphone shoved in his face. " 'Oil spill? What oil spill? I don't see no oil spill.' Hell no, you wouldn't have heard of it. You wouldn't have heard a peep. See, that's what I'm trying to tell you. Where you come from, corruption is a—whatchamacallit—an 'unfortunate aspect' of life or business or politics. Down here, corruption is not an unfortunate aspect of life. It's all there is. It's the way of life itself."

Mike said he had started crawfishing right after he graduated from high school in 1973. In those days, he said, he often caught 2,000 pounds of crawfish a day. Now he was lucky, "really lucky," if he got half that, though he was one of the few trappers still out there trying. These days, he said, very few people cared to venture any deeper into the swamp than they could while still keeping some outside reference point—a boat or a bridge piling—in sight. "The swamp is a scary place if you don't know your way around it," he said, describing the endless maze of bayous, swamps, and marshes. "You get turned around and it all looks the same unless you know it by heart." The wild crawfish trappers, who set and checked 200 to 400 traps a day, were about the only ones who ventured deep into the Basin regularly. They were the only ones who saw firsthand what the oil and gas companies did out there. "We're what you'd call 'inconvenient witnesses' to the oil and gas boys," Mike said. "We know what the areas they're ruining looked like five or ten or fifteen years ago, before they laid their pipelines and illegally mismanaged the spoil so that it made the water stagnate and the fish die. So of course they're doing everything they can to throw us out."

At a certain moment, I blurted out what I was really thinking, which was that all this sounded so deeply and hopelessly fucked up that I didn't think that I'd have had the stomach to keep fighting back. I asked point-blank how he kept from giving up. There followed the longest pause yet in our forty-five-minute conversation. I thought I heard him exhale and was for some reason sure he had been smoking the whole time. "Bill," he said in a subdued voice. "This is our life. This is all we got. I'll fight those sons a bitches till the day I die."

And then he invited me to come see the swamp for myself.

A few months later, I flew to Lafayette, rented a car, and drove an hour east to the house of Mike and Alice Bienvenu in the hamlet of Saint Martinville. A few minutes later, I was following their truck down LA 352, the Henderson Levee Road, a gravel road that sometimes ran parallel to the levee and sometimes atop it. The levee itself was a rounded hump forty to fifty feet high that looked as if it had been there for at least a century. Henderson Levee forms the western boundary of the Atchafalaya Basin and runs for many miles. After half an hour, Mike turned off the levee and descended to a boat ramp, where his skiff was waiting. Five minutes later, we tied up to the houseboat, which was moored semipermanently along the bank of a canal. It was essentially a barge, fifty feet long and twenty feet wide, with an open porch at either end and walkways on both sides of the "house" part, which took up less than half the available space. Three other skiffs were tied up, and four or five adults and as many children were aboard. The adults were taking it easy and the kids were fishing from the boat, running ashore into the woods and back again, shouting and playing.

I was immediately hit by a wave of hospitality unlike anything I'd ever experienced, one that rendered all resistance futile. I'm not inexperienced in southern hospitality. I was born in Birmingham into an old southern family. This, though, was hospitality of a different magnitude, as if it came from a different place and time. I was immediately plied with food and drink, of course, despite having eaten barbecue on the hour drive from the Lafayette airport. Then, within minutes of meeting me, almost all the people on the boat were offering me the use of their homes whether they were there or not. They told me where they hid their spare keys, and urged me to help myself to anything and everything I wanted. A couple of men offered to take me duck hunting. Another offered to take me fishing. One offered to do both. These were people I'd known for twenty minutes.

When the conversation turned to setlining for catfish, I had but to express an interest before Alice grabbed an umbrella-like net that happened to be handy and threw it over the side. Two minutes later she pulled up a quivering load of little grass shrimp, one of her favorite catfish baits. We were soon running down the bayou in her skiff, stopping where she had tied baited hooks to overhanging branches or poles she had stuck deep in the mud. If the pole was bent and wobbled at the boat's approach, it meant there was a catfish on. If so, Alice grabbed and unhooked it, threw it into the bottom of the boat, and rebaited the hook with deft, practiced movements. If the pole wasn't moving, she inspected the hook, rebaiting the bare ones and those whose bait she deemed too old. She didn't use regular fishing line; her line was waxed black twine that looked stout enough to hoist 200 pounds. One piece, severed a few inches above the water, swung slightly in the breeze. "Gator," Alice said.

Alice's swamp pedigree was impressive. Her daddy's side had lived in the swamp for more generations than any of them could reckon. He had fished and hunted the family's food all his life. "In those days, nobody thought of anything as 'poaching,'" she told me. "It was just how you did." A standing joke among Mike and Alice's friends was how when they were first dating, Mike had invited Alice to go deer hunting. She'd agreed and asked what time he'd be coming. When he said an hour before sunup the next morning, Alice had said, "You want to go deer hunting during the *daytime?*"

For the next three days, I was shown crawfishing traps, shrimp traps, and duck and deer blinds. I was lent a .270 and guided before first light to the best deer stand, where I sat for a couple of mornings without seeing anything. I was given boat rides and four-wheeler tours and fed constantly. There were hot pork cracklings with just the right amount of too much fat, salt, and crunch. There were stews of duck and squirrel in brown gravy over rice. Fried catfish. Hush puppies.

Gumbo and étouffée so complex, with flavors so unbelievably nuanced they would make Emeril slap his mama.

After seventy-two hours, however, Mike decided that what I needed was to go deeper into the Basin. "You need to go duck hunting with Jody Meche," he announced one morning. "It's too tame out here to really give you a good idea of the swamp. He'll take you down to the hunting camp they built after his daddy's fishing grounds silted in and he had to move the family to Henderson." It didn't matter that I had no idea who Jody Meche was or even how he knew these people. When a Cajun takes it upon himself to show you a good time, you don't have a great deal of say in the matter. The arrangements had already been made. Mike's nephew, Casey Bedoin, would meet us at the boat ramp and drive me to Jody's house in Henderson, half an hour away. I had long since given up resisting whatever my hosts had in mind. I had been showered with attention and goodwill to the point that I was a little bit nuts. Had they tied me to a chair, wrapped an anchor chain around my legs, and pushed me off the houseboat, my last thought would have been, Well, this was awfully thoughtful of them.

Jody Meche was sitting in his truck with an aluminum skiff riding on the trailer behind when we pulled up. He greeted me warmly and talked about hunting with Casey for a bit (it had been too warm lately for much activity by either ducks or deer), and then off we drove to a put-in. All Mike had told me about Jody was that he was a crawfisherman and a fourth-generation swamper. Then I remember that Jody was the guy Mike told a story about one evening. The tale began with Jody and two of his sons, who had been out catching frogs one night on Lake Rycade, a body of water off the channel of the Atchafalaya River. It was a place where Jody had fished, frogged, and hunted all his life. But a hunting club believed it had leased exclusive rights to the area from an oil or gas company that "owned" the land and water, and one of its members, seeing the light of an outsider's boat on "his" water, didn't particularly care for a trespasser. Jody heard the crack of a deer rifle, followed by the sound of the bullet ricocheting off the water near his boat, and then saw ripples caused by the bullet. "If it'd been me, I'd have gotten the hell out," Mike said. "But Jody's different." Mike said Jody, who was unarmed, told his boys to lie down in the boat, cranked the motor and, at full speed, headed straight for the dock by the light. According to Mike, only a floating log between the boat and the dock prevented Jody from jumping out and "wrapping that boy's rifle around his neck."

One look at Jody and you could imagine the scenario. He was a jovial man with an easy manner and a wide smile. But you sensed that there wasn't much of anything he feared. There are certain men who project a kind of natural physical authority. Jody was one of these. As we drove to the put-in, he told me the crawfish hadn't run the way he'd hoped last year but that he was expecting better this year.

He was married, with three sons. "I want them to know how to crawfish," he told me. "It's a good skill to have if hard times come. But I don't want them to do it for a living. Between the degradation of the Basin by the oil and gas guys and the way they're trying to keep us off public water, it's too hard and uncertain a way to make a living." I asked why he did it and his smile went wide again. "Because I'm stubborn, I guess. And because I love it too much to quit." He told me he was skilled at "bending pipe" and could make better money working on oil and gas rigs and other facilities. But he didn't like working indoors and preferred to be his own boss.

After half an hour, we drove through the gate of a private boat ramp off I-10 and Jody backed the trailer into the water until the boat floated off. Which was how I ended up getting Jody Meche's high-speed tour of the Whiskey Bay Pilot Channel on the way to hunting camp. After showing me the critters and making a trip of half an hour or so, Jody drove the skiff up onto the muddy bank and tied it off to a tree. The spot looked no different from a hundred others we'd passed. The red mud banks extended a good ten feet above the waterline. Once you climbed up, it was all thick bottomland forest, mostly cypress and tupelo. Only a narrow four-wheeler track, invisible until you were looking down at it, hinted at anything beyond. Two hundreds yards down this trail, however, was a large clearing where sat a dozen or more ramshackle buildings of the hunting camp. They included a shed to house the big diesel generator that supplied electricity, another for the dozen or more four-wheelers that members kept here, others for machines I couldn't even identify. There was a scaffold made from what looked like industrial-grade stainless steel with hoists that looked capable of handling three or four deer at a time, an outdoor fish-cleaning station with a sink and running water, and another station to dress waterfowl that had an electric plucker, a sort of wheel studded with fingerlike rubber "paddles" to remove feathers. Trailers of various sizes—some in use, some long abandoned—stood in the long grass. The main building looked like nothing I'd ever seen. It wasn't just that the original structure had been added onto nearly a dozen times over the years. It was the way each addition leaned drunkenly against the one before it—a conga line of bunk rooms, with every fourth or fifth room full of chairs and card tables. There was even an overgrown plot that had once been a garden. "That was mama's," Jody said. He told me that she had worked that plot right up until she died three years ago. "She was the best cook you ever saw," Jody said. "She'd come up to camp and make a big breakfast for everybody after the morning hunt during deer season. Got so that guys would come to camp just for her cooking. Wouldn't even go out to hunt some mornings. Word got out, some of their wives got pretty hot about it." He smiled at the trouble his mama's cooking had caused. You got the feeling that a Cajun wife would sooner forgive a man who strayed for sex than a man who strayed for another woman's cooking.

Over a dinner of fried venison, fried mushrooms, and fried potatoes, Jody told me about his family. His father and grandfather lived in Upper Grand River, a settlement that had amounted to eight or ten families at its height. His grandfather ran a small general store there, the site of dances on Saturday nights. "My father could cut across Whiskey Bay—it was a big, shallow lake then—to Lower Grand River to Henderson, to his fishing grounds, anywhere he needed to go. There was a school boat that my older brothers took to and from the little school over at Butte La Rose. This was all before I was born, late 1950s, early 1960s. But once the Corps dredged the channel, Whiskey Bay got so silted in that you couldn't get a boat through it, so Daddy moved us to Henderson. He still had to fish, though, so he built a shack right down by the river near here. And he probably slept more nights there than he did with us in Henderson."

Jody's father, like his grandfather, his great-grandfather, and maybe further back than that, made his living by the seasons of the swamp. He set nets and trotlines for catfish, gaspergou (freshwater drum), choupique (bowfin), buffalo (a kind of carp), gar, sac au lait (literally, "sack of milk," a mellifluous word that is somewhat more appetizing than the name by which the rest of the world knows the fish, "crappie"), turtles, and crawfish. "But crawfish wasn't a big part of his catch. Wasn't much market for them in those days. Crawfish was bait, you know what I'm saying? He got three cents a pound for 'em. He kept his catch alive in cypress boxes set in the river, and sold it to a buyer's boat that passed by twice a week, once on its way out and once on its way back to Henderson. That's where they had an icehouse and a little processing plant and the railroad to take it to market." (Henderson still numbers just 1,500 people and boasts the highest concentration of French-speaking residents of any county or parish in the country.)

I was trying to imagine life in the lost world of a place like Upper Grand River, where your groceries were primarily what you grew, trapped, netted, or shot yourself. I asked Jody how much of his family's food he brought home himself. He thought for a moment. "About half," he said. He thought some more. "Maybe seventy percent if you don't count vegetables. I can't keep up with gardening and hunt and fish." So, I ventured, what was in his freezer back home at the moment? Well, first of all, he needed two freezers because it wouldn't fit into one. "Right now, I got four squirrels, about a dozen ducks, some rabbits, some leftover wild turkey we deep-fried a while back. Five pounds each or so of deer sausage, smoked deer sausage, and ground venison. I think that's it. Oh, and some shrimp. Tracy—that's my wife—likes to eat shrimp year-round." He sounded almost apologetic at the paucity on hand. It was because the family preferred to "eat fresh," he said. They usually ate crawfish twice a week when the mudbugs were in season. "Oh, and fourteen frogs," he added. "They're for gifts. Everybody loves frog."

Frank and Loretta Meche had eight children, four boys and four girls, of which Jody was the youngest boy. "Mama used to tell the story of the first time Daddy brought her home to meet his parents. She was fourteen and he was nineteen. And Daddy's family wasn't wealthy by any means, you understand, but they were well off compared with Mama's folks. In her family, the kids only got one pair of shoes a year, you know what I'm saying? Anyway, when Daddy's mother served the family dinner, she put a whole French duck—what you call a mallard—on that girl's plate. And Daddy's mama said that girl just sat there and hardly said a word. After they got married, she told Mama that she'd looked at that whole duck on her plate thinking, 'My, these people must be rich!' Ain't that something?"

In the winter, Frank Meche trapped mink, otter, muskrat, raccoon, and nutria. Jody, more than any of his siblings, always wanted to go along. His father taught him to hang a piece of fish from a pole and to place the pole so that anything jumping up after it would land a foot in the trap. He carried a hammer to dispatch the animals without damaging their pelts. "He really didn't like killing," Jody said. "You could see how it pained him. But that was part of his living so that's what he had to do." The only time Jody remembered his father disciplining him was when he got his first BB gun and, as boys do, began shooting at songbirds. "He took me aside and he told me he didn't like to see me doing that. Not mad or anything, but he told me it's a sin to kill anything you're not going to use. And he loved cardinals. Loved to see those little red birds. They were special to him."

I had seen this seeming contradiction before. People who lived close to animals were accustomed both to adopting them as pets and to killing them without remorse. Paula happily ate rabbit while leaving apples and vegetables for wild bunnies in the yard. She had one tamed to the point that it would almost let her touch it. She took me outside to see it in its spot under a bush but gave strict instructions that I was to look at it only out of the corner of my eye. A direct look would mark me as a predator and scare the little bunny. I knew by her tone that I wouldn't be easily forgiven for scaring it. I'd followed her outside, expecting the animal to be hidden deep within the bush. It was sitting several feet into the lawn, contentedly nibbling something. I walked within a few feet of it. Later, she told me she thought the fox that lived in the park across the street had gotten it because she hadn't seen it in a while. When it turned up a few days later, she was so excited she called me up and said, "My bunny came back!" She sounded like an eight-year-old.

Dark and early the next morning, Jody put me on a four-wheeler and I tried to keep up as he raced down paths that felt more like tunnels bored through the big woods. When he abruptly stopped at a spot of no particular significance, I thought he just needed to pee. Instead, he shut his ATV down and hauled out an overturned canoe from beneath a bush. He kept a number of such craft stashed throughout his hunting grounds, he said, the better to access his secret spots for deer, turkey, waterfowl, and squirrels. We launched the canoe into the shallow water, using our paddles as push poles until the water got deep enough to paddle in. At every turn, our headlamps lit up the paired red embers of gator eyes. Sometimes they sank slowly into the water and disappeared at our approach, other times they didn't budge. "Rule of thumb is a foot of length for every inch between the eyes," Jody said. He said there were a few ten- and twelve-footers in these waters. But cagey old gators that size rarely showed themselves. This suited me fine. A ten-foot gator could kill and eat an adult deer. I was in no hurry to meet one.

Just as the darkness started to lift, we reached what felt like a more open area. Jody paddled toward what became a huge cypress stump. Just as I was about to brace for the collision, I saw the cutout in the trunk just above the waterline. Jody told me to duck and the canoe slid into the cutout. I stood up and unloaded the guns and ammo. At the waterline, he had laid a rough floor of two-by-fours, on which sat two folding chairs. The trunk was seven or eight feet across and had been cut off three feet above the water. There were still holes where the logger had inserted pegs and laid a board across them to stand on while he cut the tree. I wondered how long it must have taken a man to topple a 150-foot cypress that had stood for somewhere between 500 and 1,000 years.

Jody, wearing chest waders, had hidden the canoe beneath a bush and waded back. He pulled himself up into the blind and sat. As the light grew, I could see that we were in a long, narrow "lake" of open water that bulged to about eighty yards at its widest. I suddenly real- ized that we were in the midst of an entire flock of ducks already on the water and whispered, "Jody!" But he had seen me tense and now tried not to laugh. "Those are my dekes, Bill," he said. The place was so remote that Jody did something no duck hunter from my world ever did on public water: he'd left his spread of decoys out. "Nobody comes here," he said. "The only people who know about it are friends who wouldn't come here without me. Daddy started bringing me here when I was a little kid. His daddy probably did the same."

With legal light upon us, we each loaded three 12-gauge shells and scanned the sky for ducks. "Got some behind us, Bill!" Jody whispered loudly. "Don't move!" He began blowing furiously into one of the calls hanging around his neck and pulling a string at his feet tied to one of the decoys. Dekes on the water are good, but actively feeding ducks, ones sending ripples across the water as they bobbed and fed, were better. I kept my head down. By the time ducks had made it from their summer grounds in the upper Midwest to Louisiana, they'd been shot at plenty of times and were on the lookout for human faces. Jody's blood was up. He called, yanked, and repeatedly hissed at me not to move, although I hadn't shifted a muscle. The eight or nine ducks made a circular pass over the decoys, then another, lower. They flew around again and seemed to hesitate, widening the circle as they debated whether to keep moving or land. I was rolling my eyeballs hard to try to see what was going on without showing my face. Jody redoubled his calling and jerked that string for all he was worth. At last the birds committed. Waterfowl are at their slowest and most vulnerable in the moment when they set their wings and go into a stall just before settling onto the water. It's at this moment that the hunter designated to call the shots—and at this moment I realized that duck hunting must have been the source of the idiom—gives the command, which has probably been the same for centuries. "Take 'em," Jody said.

We rose at the same moment, but by the time the butt of my gun reached my shoulder, Jody's had fired three shots. I remember seeing two of the ejected shells still tumbling end-over-end in midair in my peripheral vision. Two birds had already fallen and the third hit the water an instant after the third shell. The remaining ducks had flared to the sides and were gone before I thought to aim. Jody immediately apologized for his inhuman speed and lethality. "I'm sorry, Bill. I just get so excited when they coming in purty like that. Did you see 'em when they set their wings? Man, those were some purty ducks." I told him they were indeed pretty and not to worry. The scenario repeated itself a few minutes later and quickly became the norm. Jody saw the ducks first, told me to be still despite my not having moved, yanked and called like a man possessed, and then shot. It was as if he and the ducks had reached an understanding long ago. He shot, they fell. I have been around some good waterfowl shooters, and even a well-shot duck often struggles to stay aloft for a few last wing beats before it falls. A duck thus wounded often flew in a manner similar to the damaged fighter planes you see in clips of actual combat from World War II, the pilot coaxing the last bits of flight from his doomed aircraft. But Jody didn't so much shoot ducks down as expunge them. He erased them from the sky. One second they were flying along fine, the next they were plummeting down like the inanimate objects they had just become. And then Jody would apologize once more for having taken all the ducks. After five or six times, we had a limit. I think I might have put a few pellets into one or two birds, but they were probably ones that Jody had already killed and were on their way down.

We were on our way out of the swamp by ten o'clock. As we paddled around a bend in the trail through the reeds, a harsh squawk rent the air and a big yellow-crowned night heron helicoptered itself awkwardly up from a low branch. "Gros bec, Bill!" Jody blurted, and caught himself, gun halfway to his shoulder. He stopped, shook his head, grimaced, and finally grinned as he watched the bird disappear. "Federally protected," he said with a rueful shake of his head. "It's a $450 fine to shoot that bird, and I'm on the town council now. But I tell you what: I grew up on 'em. Best-tasting bird you ever had."

Was he serious? I'd never even heard of anybody eating a heron. For starters, the bird looked to be nothing but beak, sinew, and bone. There couldn't be much meat on one, and what little there was would be stringy. Worse, herons were fish-eaters, a trait generally associated with game birds you didn't want to eat. But Jody was adamant. "Oh, no, Bill," he said. "They're delicious. All they eat is crawfish, you know. Better 'n any duck. Hoo!"

It was November, and I was anxious to get home for deer season. But I felt that I'd just scratched the surface of this world. I asked Jody if I could come back and see what crawfishing was like when he started up in the spring. "You're welcome anytime, Bill," he said. "Come 'bout the end of March and I'll take you frogging, too."

I did want to get back for deer season, but deer weren't all I was interested in. I also wanted to get back to Michelle. I'd been thinking about her a good deal since that day at Druid Hill Park and our e-mails about my lawn salad. We'd been e-mailing regularly since, and with each new one she sent, I had a growing feeling that maybe the age gap wasn't as big a deal as I'd thought. Or maybe that I'd finally reached the point when being immature for your age had an upside. When I got home there was an e-mail from Michelle saying that she was teaching foraging classes the next weekend at a primitive skills gathering. She'd have her boys—Luke, eight; and Adam, four—with her. She had committed to teaching one three-hour class per day and we wouldn't have much, if any, time to ourselves. But she thought I might enjoy it. I said I'd be delighted to come. And the truth was that I liked the idea of seeing her with her boys and other people around. I was in no particular hurry. I wanted to get to know her, and seeing her in this setting would, in its way, be more relaxed than seeing each other one-on-one.

I hadn't expected the event to be so big. There were several hundred people at the summer camp that had been rented for the occasion. And she had been right about our having limited time alone. We never managed more than a few minutes at a time. And yet, looking back, I'd date the start of our relationship from that weekend. It hadn't seemed that way the time. In hindsight, I saw that what I'd really been doing that weekend was courting her indirectly, at one cool remove, mostly by hanging out with her boys. Adam, the younger, was a force of nature, a law unto himself, a stranger to the notion of self-doubt. If he wanted to wade into the shallow pond after a butterfly on a lily pad, he went, and Michelle patiently waded in after him. She wanted to be close for safety's sake but otherwise let the boys discover the world on their own. If you told Adam "no" and he didn't want to hear it, he had a way of looking right through you. He liked me for his own solid reasons: I made good paper airplanes and would swing him around in circles like an airplane. My initial take was that he was very intelligent, charismatic, and intentional. I thought he would either end up running General Motors or in jail.

Luke reminded me of myself at that age. He was smart and too sensitive for his own good. At eight, he already worried a lot and became discouraged if he couldn't do something perfectly the first time. Maybe I was projecting, but I saw a boy carrying burdens he wouldn't be aware of for many years. Michelle had told me little of her breakup other than to say that she'd stayed as long as she could for the boys' sake before realizing the situation was hopeless. Her ex had kept the house, cut her off financially, and, she feared, said things to the boys no child should ever have to hear. Luke, like any child, was confused by the split and felt responsibility for it. The vibe I got was that he wanted to like me but feared being a disloyal son. I knew too well the responsibilities often borne by the oldest boy in a troubled family. My parents actually had a good marriage, but there had been strong disagreements about how the children were to be brought up, and my sister and I both rebelled in our own ways. My father had been an army brat who idolized his father but didn't see that much of him. He believed in discipline and saw the world as a place where something was either right or wrong. My mother was nearly the opposite and there were times when she considered leaving him. If Luke was anything like the boy I'd been, it had fallen to him to be his parents' conciliator, the loyal son, the glue that held things together. Such expectations are never articulated. They don't need to be. I wanted to tell Luke that he was the one who got to decide whether he liked me or not, and that it would be all right if he didn't. But you can't say something like that to a boy you've just met. All you can do is let him know that you're available and interested and wait for him to make the first move.

There was, however, a rather large chink in Luke's armor, which I intended to exploit. Luke had never caught a fish but was convinced, as only a boy can be, that there was one swimming around down there with his name on it. Michelle, knowing nothing of fishing but wanting to encourage her son, had picked up a fishing outfit at Walmart on the way there to use in the little pond behind the shower house. I asked to see the outfit. She pulled out a purple Dora the Explorer combo, with a banana-yellow push-button reel shaped like a chocolate egg. The thing was still in its plastic clamshell, along with an assortment of tiny bobbers and hooks. The rod was thirty inches long and would break the first time you snagged your hook on a bush and gave it a good tug. The bright yellow reel was absurd, with a functional life unlikely to exceed fifteen minutes. There were actual stickers on the rod and reel: daisies, the ever-smiling Dora herself, as well as Boots, her beloved blue monkey.

"Good God, woman," I sputtered. "Are you afraid your son might *not* turn out to be a homosexual?" Michelle flushed, momentarily looked as if she might kill me, but eventually decided that I might just be yanking her chain, and wordlessly ascended the steps into her cabin, the screen door slamming softly behind her.

With Mom out of the way, I motioned Luke over for a man-to-man. I got down on one knee so we were at eye level with each other. "Luke," I said with utmost seriousness, "we don't need Dora the Explorer.

We're gonna make our own rods. And tonight, after dinner, you and I are gonna catch you a fish. Okay?" His eyes got big and he froze for a moment. He nodded once, solemnly, just the downward part of the nod. Then he ran away.

I am painfully aware of my limitations as a parent. I frequently hear myself being overly demanding and critical with Emma and it stings. I know that I'm replicating the very same behavior that I resented in my own parents and vowed I would never inflict on a child of my own. And yet, more often than I care to admit, I find myself unable to *not* do it. On the other hand, I wasn't entirely blind. I recognized that getting the chance to put a boy onto his first fish was as great a privilege and trust as a man is vouchsafed in this life. And it was something I knew how to do.

The primitive skills movement, not surprisingly, draws more men than women. An attractive, friendly woman like Michelle got lots of attention in the camp's mess hall. I spied her talking to a guy in a cowboy hat and red kerchief. He was smiling and leaning in a little more than he needed to be. I approached and tapped her on the shoulder. "Ready to eat?" I asked brightly. She later said she'd felt that I had given the guy a pretty obvious hands-off signal. "You think?" I answered. "I was afraid I was being too discreet."

After dinner, I found a plastic half-gallon milk bottle from the trash, sliced the bottom off with my knife, and gave it to Luke. "You're in charge of getting bait, bud," I said. I told him that I'd seen some damp ground by a seep just below the pond. "I bet if you dig around under those leaves, you'll find plenty of worms." I retrieved some loose hooks from the Dora the Explorer clamshell. The outfit must have spent time in a hot container somewhere between China and the Walmart, because the monofilament line on the reel broke at nothing more than a good tug. In the parking lot I had seen a number of pickup trucks with fishing gear in the back. I told Michelle to find one of these. "We need about fourteen feet of line. Flirt with the owner if he's around. Steal it if he isn't. You got a knife?" She didn't, so I gave her mine. I retrieved a multi-tool from the glove compartment of my car and went looking for the nearest bamboo. I had long ago come to believe that a man should always know where the nearest bamboo is. I'd used lengths of it to retrieve Frisbees from roofs and trees, to drape Christmas lights, and to knock down all manner of fruits and chestnuts from trees. I found a stand sixty yards from the pond and cut a ten-foot length, then stripped the branches off.

By the time I got to the pond, Luke was proudly holding the jug, which now contained a great deal of dirt and a few worms. Michelle presented the fishing line. It was ridiculously heavy stuff for our purposes, probably from a catfish angler, as it was at least forty-pound test. I had to shave the first foot of it thinner with my knife to be able to thread enough of it through the eye of the hook to tie a knot. We were just about ready.

"What about a bobber?" Luke asked anxiously. "Aren't you supposed to have a bobber?" It was clear that he had had a preconceived idea of how his fishing pole should look. And a bobber was most definitely part of the picture.

I again got down on one knee so we were eye-to-eye. "Luke," I said, "I'm going to tell you a secret. You'll catch more fish without a bobber. It stops the worm when it should be falling. That makes the fish suspicious. And suspicious fish don't bite." At last he nodded.

I threaded a worm onto the hook. As I handed him the rod, I realized it was too unwieldy for a boy his size. I'd been thinking about getting the bait out to where the fish were, not about how much rod Luke could handle. "We'll do this together, okay?" I said. Standing behind him, I put my arms and hands around his, and then, four-handedly, we swung the bait back and out into the watery world. The worm landed all of eight feet from the water's edge and had just begun its slow free fall through the water when a little bluegill darted out of nowhere and nailed it. Luke, as focused and spring-loaded as any first-fish boy I'd ever seen, yanked—hard. The fish exited the water like a missile, flew straight up and back over our heads and landed flapping in the grass behind us. And then were whooping and pumping our firsts like a couple of fools. I got the hook out and let Luke touch the fish before releasing it. We caught two more bluegills and one tiny largemouth bass before it began to get dark and they stopped biting for the night.

"You're a darn fishing *machine,* bud," I said after we called it a night. He beamed. Michelle looked at me with undisguised gratitude. "Thank you," she mouthed, not wanting Luke to hear. That was our most intimate moment together of the whole weekend. On Sunday afternoon, having loaded up my car, we said our good-byes and I gave her an awkward peck on the cheek.

Three days later, the phone rang. Michelle said she just wanted me to know that since Sunday, Luke had taken to telling everyone he met—including total strangers, like the cashier at the supermarket—that he was about to share a true secret about fishing with them. "If you're trying to catch a fish, you do *not* want to use a bobber."

I didn't know why or how, but those words ambushed me. They pierced some restricted area, someplace shuttered so long ago I'd forgotten it existed. I was stunned to find that tears were rolling down my cheeks and over my lips. I have since tried to parse that moment. Maybe in guiding Luke to that fish, I'd ministered to some wound of my own. Maybe it was awe at realizing how the depth of influence—for good or ill—a man could bring to bear on the soul of a boy. I did know one thing: something long locked inside me and in dire need of redemption had just received it.

"Are you still there?" Michelle said. I turned my head away from the phone and only then trusted myself to open my mouth. I tried to clear my throat.

"Yeah," I was finally able to say. "Truck just went by."

After the weekend at the primitive skills gathering, despite having hardly a private moment together, Michelle and I had begun thinking of ourselves as a couple. The following weekend, when neither of us had children, we made up for lost time. It was then that Michelle told me that she didn't know how I'd managed it but that I'd slipped through her defenses—the ones so deftly deployed that most people never knew they were there—as no one else ever had. I told her that the same went for me. For me, that moment had come weeks earlier, when, almost in passing, Michelle had mentioned my "anhedonia," a fancy word to describe people who have difficulty experiencing pleasure from the things that give most people pleasure. That stopped me cold. This recurring affliction—along with the depression and despair that occasionally overtook me, bleeding the colors out of life and leaving me stranded in the bleakest of places—was one of my deepest secrets. I'd been convinced that I hid it pretty well. Certainly no one else had ever remarked on it to me. That Michelle had noted it was both extraordinary and somewhat alarming. That she'd noted it so casually—something to be acknowledged rather than dwelled upon, as if it were just another feature of my personal landscape rather than its most salient fact—amazed me. Like everybody, I'd spent much of my life wanting to be seen for who I was and loved in spite of it. A much smaller percentage of humanity ever realizes that wish. To me falling in love with Michelle felt like the few times I've been thrown out of a boat in white water. It started with a loss of balance and then I was roiled by the hydraulics of fear and gratitude, anxiety and relief. I had never met anyone like Michelle. The last time I had felt so alive and vivid was when, as a child, I had had the most powerful squirt gun of any kid on the block. This was even better.

I decided that it was time to tell Michelle about the other woman in my life. I said that Paula and I shared a love of the outdoors, a fascination with deer, a deep affection for fishing, and a core belief that "No Trespassing" signs didn't apply to us. On the other hand, I said, she was also a bit eccentric. She habitually dressed in men's clothing, had a morbid fear of being stuck in rush hour traffic even though she didn't drive, and was incapable of refraining from graphic profanity even when around children. This close friend also considered me essentially incompetent except when it came to making smoked herring. I also mentioned that she shared a house with Gordon, twenty years her senior. Theirs was an unusual arrangement by societal standards, but it was hard to imagine having any other kind with somebody like Paula. They seemed to have arrived at a sort of campionable arrangement.

147

Both were boathouse regulars, liked the outdoors, and they often fished together. By this time, as a unit, they had become like family to me. I checked up on them every week or so whether I saw them or not, and they checked up on me. I had no idea of their relationship when they were alone and felt no need to know. But they were important people in my life and I wanted them to meet Michelle.

We invited them over for dinner at my house on Saturday night. I hadn't expected to be nervous and was surprised to realize that I was.

But Michelle and Paula seemed to hit it off within minutes. Shortly after I served drinks—sparkling cider for Paula, cocktails for the rest of us—the two of them were out back, where the barbecue was already going, so that Paula could smoke. Gordon and I talked as I dry-rubbed a venison tenderloin (salt, pepper, paprika, five-spice powder, garlic, onion, flaked cayenne, dried parsley, celery seed, and a bit of brown sugar). Meanwhile, I caught snatches of the girls' conversation through the screen door. It concerned the finer points of upright freezers versus chest freezers, which fruits and vegetables were better canned and which frozen, and which apples made the best pies. Paula, naturally, did most of the talking. A while later, as Paula realized that Michelle knew more about apples than she did, I actually heard Paula ask Michelle for information about a certain variety of apple. That was a first.

Dinner was a success. We started with a bruschetta. Michelle had made the topping using late-season tomatoes and basil from my garden. Paula and Gordon inhaled a bowlful of the stuff, which we ladled onto toasted bread drizzled with olive oil. They'd never had it before and were instant converts. While I wasn't unfamiliar with bruschetta, I'd never had any that was even in the ballpark with this stuff. The homegrown tomatoes and basil made a difference, of course, but so did Michelle's recipe. "You rough-chop the tomatoes," she'd said while she worked the knife, "add about twice as much fresh garlic as you think looks right, and throw in a bunch of minced basil. Then I add salt and a splash of good olive oil." You used a nonmetallic bowl so the acid in the tomatoes wouldn't react with the metal and add its flavors. And, while you could certainly use the topping immediately, she was of the opinion that letting it sit for an hour or so improved the taste. By the next day, however, the tomatoes would have broken down and the whole thing would be watery, at which point it was really good only in salsa or gazpacho. Bruschetta had always tasted to me as though vinaigrette was part of the mix, but Michelle shot me a look when I asked about this. "With subpar tomatoes, you might use a bit to amp the acidity. But with tomatoes like these, it's criminal." From her tone, I could tell that this was not the sort of crime that could be plea-bargained down to a misdemeanor.

Michelle's cooking and attitudes toward food had been formed during two years she spent living in Naples, Italy, right after she'd graduated from college. Her Neapolitan landlady, who was only four years older than Michelle but already had an eight-year-old child, had taken the young *ragazza* under her wing. The first thing she had done was introduce Michelle to all the shopkeepers on the block, telling them not to overcharge her—since overcharging was customary in dealing not only with clueless Americans but even with any Neapolitan foolish enough to frequent shopkeepers not on one's own block. Shocked that a twenty-two-year-old girl knew so little about cooking, she had begun Michelle's culinary education. Rule one: you bought vegetables fresh and used them the day you bought them. As for buying only what was in season, not only was that simple common sense, but doing otherwise was a kind of foolishness that wasn't even possible, since, with the exception of bananas and oranges, Neapolitan grocers sold only that which was ripe and regional. Another cardinal rule of cooking was that you interfered as little as possible between really good ingredients and the finished dish. You did not, for example, insert yourself between a good tomato and its natural acidity by adding vinegar.

After we had served dinner and cleared the table, I went out to extinguish the coals, where Paula stood alone, enjoying her after-dinner smoke. I was about to ask how she and Michelle had gotten along, when she spoke first. "She could be good for you," Paula said. I stopped for a moment, surprised, and was just starting to say something about how I agreed, when she held up her hand, silencing me. She took a drag and thought for a moment, as if weighing her words. This in and of itself was unusual. Paula generally shot from the hip. "She's smarter than you are," she continued, taking another drag.

"What do you mean, she's—" I sputtered, but she silenced me again, this time with the other hand, the one with the cigarette. I was, as usual, struck not only by her authority over me but also by her awareness of that authority.

"She's smarter than you," she continued. "She'll make you work, but you need that."

"Make me work how?" I asked. Paula again paused. Things were becoming stranger and more momentous with each pause. "Lemme put it this way: She's the kind of woman who, if she wants to get something done, it gets done."

I didn't know what to say to this. I must have stood there for fifteen seconds trying to take it all in. Finally, Michelle appeared at the screen door. "Who wants apple pie?" she asked.

"I do!" Paula said. She clapped her hands gleefully, carefully stubbed out her cigarette, put the butt back into the pack to finish later, and headed into the house. Leaving me alone in the backyard, still speechless, wondering what the hell had just happened.

In the days to come, the accuracy of all of Paula's observations would be verified. There have been times when, like the rest of the world, I questioned the tightrope she walks between eccentric and crazy. But I had to give her this: very little escaped her notice.

SAUTEED DANDELION GREENS

Dandelions are Michelle's favorite wild green, and this is her favorite way to enjoy them. The best time to collect is in the early spring, when the plants are the most tender and least bitter. But you can find dandelions almost year-round.

Get a colander and go outside to your yard. If you don't have a yard of your own, think of the laziest resident on your street and visit that guy's yard. Or go to a public park. What you're trying to do is to avoid herbicides. Generally speaking, healthy-looking dandelions are healthy dandelions. Avoid dead, brown, or suspiciously droopy ones.

Larger outer leaves will become tough and bitter as the year progresses. These are not fun to eat. Aim instead for the small new leaves, which grow from the center. You won't get as many per plant, but nature really doesn't give a damn about inconveniencing you, so get used to it. The newest, most delectable dandelion leaves have a delicate, almost elastic, feel when compared with the doughtier exterior leaves. Even the tenderest and newest dandelion greens have a sharp, acerbic flavor—imagine a cross between the bite of arugula or watercress and the bitterness of brussels sprouts. The taste won't appeal to all, but it does grow on you. While you grapple with the taste, bear in mind that dandelions are extremely nutritious, high in vitamins A, C, E, and K, as well as beta carotene, potassium, iron, and manganese.

The other big pain-in-the-ass factor is how drastically dandelion greens shrink when cooked. A colander-full shrinks to just a few forkfuls in the skillet. Pick about half a ton. Back home, rinse them in the sink and remove any non-dandelion-green items like pine needles and blades of grass and insects. Heat a skillet over medium-high flame and melt a couple of tablespoons of butter or bacon fat; when this starts to sizzle, toss in the damp dandelion greens. Stir a couple of times, then put a lid on and cook for about two minutes. Remove the lid and stir them around for another minute or two, until completely wilted and vastly reduced in volume. Season to taste with salt and pepper.

Chapter Seven:
Of Closet Carnivores and the Gospel
of Small Fish

In falling in love with Michelle I'd unwittingly fallen for a foodie, although of a kind hitherto unknown to me. My experience with foodies had revealed people with more money than imagination who were nonetheless intensely competitive. Food, eating well—these were just the playing field, not the thing itself. The real game was status. You gained status among other foodies by identifying the hottest, most exclusive new eatery; dining there; and then recounting the experience. You might, for example, describe in rapturous tones the perfection of a simple beet, carved to resemble a flower, set in a cucumber granita with the whipped llama bone marrow "snow." The most irritating thing about foodies was the self-congratulatory tone that invariably crept into their speech. The host of one food-oriented program on NPR was, to me, the embodiment of this. I'm sure the woman knows a great deal about food, but whenever I heard her gush about the pleasures of handpicked wild capers from the mountains of southern Tunisia packed in pink Himalayan sea salt, I was afraid she was headed for an on-air orgasm. This was not something I wanted to hear. But I made a point of tuning in whenever I felt the need to annoy myself.

Getting to know Michelle forced me to do something I abhor, which was to reassess my assumptions. We had met through foraging. She was comfortable in hiking boots and overalls, moving through fields and forests, either gathering wild edibles for herself or teaching others how. For me, the problem was that she was equally at ease in the mainstream food world of hip restaurants and air kisses. She wrote about food and restaurants for several newspapers and magazines in Baltimore. She knew about different cuisines, was up on current food trends, and was friends with a number of prominent Baltimore chefs. These were hard things for me to square.

Taking Michelle to a good restaurant for the first time was an eye-opener. The moment she walked in, her very aura shifted. She became more commanding, exuding a kind of authority I'd never seen. Maybe it was simply a gear she'd had all along but deployed only in certain situations. In any case, I watched, fascinated. She knew how to ask for—and get—a prime table. As we sat down, she was already scanning the floor and taking mental notes as to what the restaurant did well and what it didn't. We ordered the rabbit terrine appetizer and she perused the wine list for something appropriate. (Okay, she'd ordered it. Actually, I'd had a panicked instant of thinking "terrine" was the French word for "terrarium," but I knew that even Michelle wasn't going to order a glass box with a bunny in it.) The sommelier materialized, genie-like, at her side. He knew immediately that the lady was calling the shots. Hearing of the terrine, he suggested a certain bottle. Michelle replied that she knew and liked that wine but wanted "something a bit more tannin-forward." Tannin-forward? Was she serious? You could have knocked me over with a low-density polyethylene wine cork. "Tannin-forward" was the kind of thing I'd say if I were goofing with the guy. But she was quite serious. (I actually sometimes do goof with wine people in pretentious restaurants. It is my way of evening the playing field, and something everyone should try once. When the wine comes and the sommelier pours your trial sip, you take it in, swish for two seconds and then expel it—forcefully and without hesitation—back into the glass. In your best outraged voice, say "Do you honestly expect me to drink this swill?" The flustered attendant will wince and immediately offer to bring another bottle. At which point you smile and say, "No, this is fine. I was just hosing you." The wine steward almost certainly won't like this but will have to pretend that he appreciates your little joke. I guarantee that the waiters—who always resent wine stewards because they get paid so much more for doing so much less—will appreciate it. They will give excellent service for the rest of the meal.)

For me, the sticking point was not only that Michelle knew what tannin-forward meant but could also taste and appreciate it. That someone could do this and not be a jerk was totally outside my experience and confirmed that I really did need to reexamine my prejudices. Evidently, there was more to the foodie world than I had thought.

And yet Michelle was, at heart, anything but a conventional foodie. One of my nerdier foraging projects had been to create a "fruit and nut map" of twenty-three taped-together Google Maps pages noting the location and species of edible-yielding trees in my neighborhood. Upon seeing it, she had immediately insisted on a tour. There was the chestnut at the bottom of the street, which in some years produced wonderful nuts inside prickly husks like green sea urchins. If you waited until they fell by themselves you got empty husks, because the squirrels loved the nuts, too, and ate them while they were still on the tree. While I'd declared a moratorium on killing the rodents, my antipathy toward them was still very real. I cut myself a twenty-foot length of bamboo and knocked as many chestnuts off with that as possible. There were fig trees on a neighboring street, one of which I had permission to pick. (The only caveat here was that you had to move slowly and deliberately, because of the hornets. They were especially fond of the sweetest figs, which were the ones hidden and rotting in the tall grass. They buzzed around slowly, obviously drunk on fermenting sugars, but if you pissed one off it could still sting you good. You learned to test each step before committing weight to it.) But the thing that most impressed Michelle was the tall, spindly persimmon tree that stood, stranded and alone, in the asphalt sea of the United Methodist Church parking lot.

How the tree came to grow there and why it had been left standing were mysteries. I'd seen a circle of fallen fruit one day from my bike and had stopped to investigate. It must have been a domesticated tree, because it fruited months before the wild ones and yielded larger, sweeter persimmons. I'd never seen anyone picking it. The fruit just ripened, fell, and got flattened by car tires. As far as I knew, the local birds and I were the only creatures that ate it. There were already a good number of persimmons down when I showed it to Michelle. She picked one up, blew off the asphalt crumbs and dirt, and tasted. "Oh my God!" she cried. "This is the best persimmon I've ever had!" She ate another. It was true. They had always been good, but this year's were especially sweet. If you've ever eaten a wild persimmon, you know that it's a roll of the dice. A good one is wonderful, while an unripe persimmon gives new meaning to the word "astringent." Your mouth goes so dry and puckery that you want gallons of anything wet to allay the feeling, only to discover that liquids have no effect on this unpleasant sensation. The downside of wild persimmons can be enough to put you off the things entirely. But these were like little globules of persimmon jam, orange and wonderfully sweet and tasting faintly of apricots. We stood there eating fruit that had violated the five-second rule by a week or more, until a neighbor woman in a house dress started giving us the hairy eyeball from her front door. "Just as well," Michelle said, wiping her hands on her jeans. "We'd probably get sick if we ate any more. What's next?" And off we went.

The moment when I realized just how deeply my girlfriend could be moved by wild tastes came the weekend we drove to West Virginia to go trout fishing. We weren't having much luck, and eventually approached a guy who looked like local and, judging by the three trout hanging from the stringer tied to his waders, competent. We chatted with him, hoping to gain some trout intelligence. He kept fishing all the while, telling us that pretty much any eddy was likely to hold fish, although in water this high and fast such places weren't easy to find. Suddenly his spinning rod bent under the weight of a good fish. A minute later he hoisted a fat rainbow from the water. As he did this, the fish began to expel roe—a mini cascade of large, translucent orbs. Instantly and wordlessly Michelle fell to her knees and cupped her hands to catch the eggs, which she lifted and sucked into her mouth, then immediately re-cupped her hands to receive more of the still-falling

155

roe. I was surprised. But I had nothing on the angler, who looked like a man in fear for his life. It was an unlikely tableau: West Virginia trout fisherman in hip waders and, kneeling before him with her hands cupped at roughly crotch height and a look of bliss on her face, a very attractive woman. And standing three feet away, her boyfriend, trying desperately to look nonchalant. I felt for the guy. You could see the machinery turning in his head. But there was no way to connect these particular dots. He finally gave me a pleading "aren't you gonna help me out?" look. But I was a little startled myself. Meanwhile, Michelle, totally absorbed in the moment, either didn't notice us or didn't care. Food could do that to her. "Wow," she finally murmured under her breath, heedless of both of us.

"How's it taste?" I asked.

"It's so . . . clean," she said, still not looking up. "It's got a mineral taste, like spring water." She ate some more. "And then it sort of slowly blooms into a hint of ocean and salt." She poured some into my hand and I ate it. But she had already described the taste with such authority and specificity that my own taste buds sort of shut down. If asked my impression, I couldn't have managed anything more detailed than, "Fishy, but, you know, in a good way." By this point, the fisherman had decided to move upstream.

As it turned out, while she cared nothing for trendiness, Michelle was near the forefront of a food trend herself. She had helped found Baltimore Food Makers, a distinctly non-elitist group whose members were interested in traditional methods of producing and preserving food. The group served a forum where like-minded food geeks could connect to share skills, knowledge, and food resources, and also get together at monthly potlucks, which usually featured somebody teaching a skill of interest. The group's core principles included a commitment to sustainable, organic, local, and ethically produced food and the idea that, as Michelle put it, the "best distance between you and your food is no distance." She had become interested in learning where her own food originated after an early experience in her career as a photographer. She and a writer had somehow gained full access to the workings of Valley Proteins, a rendering plant that processed restaurant grease and offal in Baltimore. The pair had followed a rendering truck on its pickup route to restaurants to collect fryer grease, to slaughterhouses to get the animal parts that even slaughterhouses had no use for, and finally to the city animal pound, where open steel bins heaped with the carcasses of euthanized dogs and cats were dumped into the truck. Everything was delivered to Valley Proteins, where it was processed into various by-products, many used to make soap, cosmetics, fertilizer, and even feed for pets and livestock. Michelle was a woman of strong constitution but told me that what she saw while taking pictures had nearly made her sick on the spot. She kept it together mostly because the reporter did, and her professional pride wouldn't allow her to be the weak link in a team effort. But the experience had turned her against what she termed "the industrial food system," which turned out to include pretty much any meat most of us don't think twice about buying and eating everywhere. It also led her to grow or forage as much of her own food as she could. Anything else she tried to buy directly from whoever produced it.

Baltimore Food Makers was a big-tent bunch, ranging from orthodox Jewish earth mamas trying to feed a family of nine as cheaply and sustainably as possible to cheese geeks bent on inoculating and aging their own Camembert. Michelle dragged me along to a few of the monthly potlucks. One member demonstrated canning. Another described laying out an urban garden using vegetables I'd never even heard of. Food Makers was definitely tapping into some unfulfilled zeitgeist. There turned out to be quite a few Baltimore twenty- and thirtysomethings who, having been brought up in the age of supermarkets, knew almost nothing about what have come to be known as "homesteading" skills like growing and preserving food, keeping backyard chickens, and making soap. But they were eager to learn them. The group grew to 500 members in less than four years. It was as if these people were nostalgic for a past they'd never had. Their idea of a good weekend was packing a fermenting crock with vegetables they'd grown themselves from heirloom seeds, which, ideally, they had bartered some homemade kefir to obtain. I wondered if this was just some quirky Baltimore thing, but then I did some research. It wasn't. An intensively hands-on food revolution seemed to be sprouting all over the country.

My own food world, hitherto a reasonably straightforward place, was becoming more complicated by the minute. There were a lot of things going on that I'd never given a thought to. I'd just returned from Louisiana, from people who had learned their food skills from their parents, who had learned them from theirs. This unbroken chain made them exceptions to the norm. The people in Baltimore Food Makers were exceptional in a different way, in their desire to learn traditions of which they had no direct experience. For the most part, though, the urban homesteaders were focused on things like gardening, canning, and bread making—activities that, no matter how passionately pursued, still fell into the domestic arts category. Aside from Michelle, who was the unofficial foraging expert, there were few interested in the wilder side of food—foraging, hunting, and fishing. Maybe I was more hard core than I'd thought, because there was something pussified about their indoor orientation.

I knew I wasn't Food Makers material—home ec, no matter how hard-core, just didn't do it for me. As far as canning went, for example, I was in Paula's camp: "Life's too short, honey. Trust me." I'd actually made and canned my own tomato sauce the summer before. It had started swimmingly and I was feeling fairly smug—despite the infernal heat in the kitchen. This lasted until I watched 100 ounces of tomatoes slowly dissipate into tomato-scented water vapor. The shrinkage factor was crazy-making. In the end, those 100 ounces—representing God only knows how many actual tomatoes I had personally and painstakingly planted, raised, and wrested from my garden—yielded six ounces of tomato sauce. Not me, honey.

On the other hand, I'd known an unexpected sense of fulfilment in making a pie from foraged (okay, stolen) sour cherries, and in frying up white perch I'd caught and cleaned myself. And when I grilled the tenderloin of a deer that I had killed with a bow, and gutted and skinned and butchered myself—and that I was now eating with Michelle, who might contribute a sautéed a hen-of-the-woods mushroom she'd found or some dandelion greens—I had to admit that it felt pretty cool to have put really good food on my plate. The experience was so new that I'd only begun to parse it. I knew only that it was powerful and that the power went deep. I felt that I was starting to close the circle.

I wasn't the only one noticing the power of getting your food close to home. Every week I seemed to come across another locavore/foraging story in the press. In the highly competitive restaurant world, a trendy chef's trump card had long been to serve some obscure thing that none of his competitors offered. And that coup was both more powerful than ever and getting harder to pull off. Hand-harvested day boat scallops? Heirloom tomatoes grown on a biodynamic farm within shouting distance of the kitchen's back door? Any chef with a checkbook could get those. If you really wanted to wow folks, sooner or later you put wild edibles in front of them. The very existence of such plants set them apart. Other food had to be sown and cultivated. Wild edibles grew themselves, arising spontaneously from the earth. It didn't get more authentic than that. Celebrity chefs weren't just buying from foragers, they had begun putting foragers on retainer—and making sure that diners knew this by mentioning it on their menus. The hottest restaurant in the world for three years running had been René Redezepi's Noma, a twelve-table restaurant in Copenhagen that relied heavily on wild edibles.

Here—provided you could get a reservation—you could chomp down on wild sea buckthorn "leather" with wild rose hips pickled in apple vinegar while you sat wrapped in an actual bearskin robe. You might be served a flower pot in which entire baby radishes "grew" from the hazelnut "soil." You ate everything but the pot—the radishes, leaves and all, as well as the soil. You would be handed an authentic Nordic hunting knife for the meat course, slices of "summer venison" cooked rare and served along with the summer plants the deer fed on: chanterelles, chickweed, fiddlehead ferns, lettuce root, burnt wild asparagus, and wild grape leaves, the whole dish bathed in a woodruff sauce. The knife was an artful folly, since the meat was fork-tender. Then you might have—well, you really have to read the review itself to get a feel for the breathlessness of it all: "Then came one of the most ethereal food experiences we have ever had. This dish was a will-o'-the-wisp—it was there one minute and gone the next but the flavours lingered and the sheer perfection of the dish will stay with us for a long time. On the bottom was some incredibly thin herb toast—just thick enough to allow you to pick up the morsel but thin so that it dissolved instantly on eating. Then some vinegar powder, an emulson of smoked cod roe and then topped with a duck stock film created by drying out the skin that forms on the top of a rich stock. The whole dish was a study in lightness and flavour—it captured exactly what we crave in food—restraint, technical excellence, flavour, lightness—and above all deliciousness."

I didn't have the money to go to Noma. Fortunately, I didn't need to. So many "I went foraging with Redzepi" stories had been written that food blogs themselves had started making fun of them. As Michelle pointed out, the writers of such stories generally knew squat about foraging. They usually described epiphanies about common plants like yellow sorrel or purslane, as if these were incredibly exotic, when in fact they were the ones you learned in the first half hour of your first foraging walk.

Whether foraging was just having its fifteen minutes or was a genuine game changer in the food world had yet to be determined. I sure as hell didn't know. All the same, the notion that Paula Smith and, say, Alice Waters were both fans of foraged backyard sour cherries was an interesting thing to contemplate. The difference, of course, was that Paula was throwing hers into a store-bought piecrust and eating them while looking through a hunting magazine, while Waters was cooking hers in a compote over goat's milk panna cotta and charging fourteen dollars per serving. Fourteen bucks was about what Paula spent on her wardrobe over the course of a year.

Meanwhile, I kept coming across references to the food scene in San Francisco, which had led the trend in restaurants serving sustainable, locally sourced food and was now clearly leading the way with wild edibles. There was an outfit called forageSF that had been receiving lots of laudatory press, including two mentions in *The New York Times Magazine* in the same month. The group's goal, according to its website, was to "connect Bay dwellers to the wild food that is all around them." ForageSF was founded by Iso Rabins, a twentysomething entrepreneur who seemed to be going places.

Rabins sounded like the Patrick Henry of the foraging movement, a big-idea guy, a revolutionary willing to lead a charge. He sought, according to the group's website, nothing less than to form a "wild foods community" and to "rediscover a forgotten food system and reduce carbon miles." Through forageSF, he even hoped to make full-time foraging a "sustainable lifestyle"—aka a paying job. The group was described as offering a biweekly box of foraged edibles to subscribers—in effect, a foraging CSA—with half of the profits going directly to the forager. It held regular walks through the city to teach people about the wild edibles all around them, as well as a "wild sea-food walk." It put on monthly dinners where subscribers could enjoy an eight-course meal, each course built around a local and sustainably foraged ingredient. The group's most recent undertaking was its underground markets. These were a way for ordinary people—foragers, homesteaders, aspiring foodies—to sell their homemade kombucha and jalapeño–Meyer lemon marmalades and chocolate-covered smoked bacon to the general public.

In short, forageSF sounded like a hub of foraging zeal and chic. I wanted to meet these people. I wanted to rub up against them and see if some of this chic might stick to me. I wrote to the "contact" link on the website and said I wanted to come and visit. Things got weird rather quickly after that. The harder I tried to pin down forageSF and its "community," the more elusive it became. I was told that Iso was away indefinitely, traveling and foraging his way through Europe. I said that I regretted missing him but wanted to come anyway and had already picked a week during which three forageSF events were scheduled—a wild plant walk, a wild seafood walk, and one of its

"Wild Kitchen" underground dinners. In response, I received a note saying that it would be better if I could come at a time that was "less busy." This was passing strange. Seeing the group in action was the whole point. Covering a foraging group at a "less busy" time was like reviewing a canceled concert. Having already shelled out for a plane ticket and three events, I wasn't about to wait. I replied with a breezy e-mail saying that I was on my way and looking forward to it.

Once I got to San Francisco, it didn't take me long to realize that forageSF was not quite the hotbed of a foraging revolution I'd taken it for. For one thing, the underground markets were no longer operating. Actually, they'd been victims of their own success. But they had never really been about foraging anyway. Rabins had pitched them as "an incubator" for "beginning food entrepreneurs" to get their products to the public without "the cost and delay of myriad regulatory structures that has arisen around food production." The first one, held in a private house in 2009, attracted seven vendors and 200 attendees. Within a year, underground markets were being held monthly in warehouses Rabins rented and were attracting crowds in the thousands. Rabins would vet the sellers ahead of time, rent booth space to those selected, and charge customers five dollars a head for the privilege of entering. The events skirted the laws against selling food from noncommercial kitchens by billing itself as a private club whose members had signed up on the forageSF website, which claimed to have had "over 300 vendors and 50,000 attendees." People in lines several blocks long would often wait hours to gain entry. But it was hard to keep something that attracted such crowds "underground"—or at least off the radar of the Health Department, which eventually shut the operation down. (In July 2012, forageSF was able to restart its underground markets by, essentially, taking them aboveground—"Permits, inspections etc., we did it all. The health inspector came and hung out with us for what seemed like hours, making sure everything was legit," Rabins wrote in a blog posting.)

As for the foraging CSA's biweekly box of foraged edibles, that never even got off the ground. In the end I met only two expert foragers associated with forageSF, one of whom led the wild edibles walk I went on soon after arriving.

The e-mailed instructions for the wild plant walk told us to meet outside Buena Vista Park near Haight-Ashbury. I showed up on a Saturday afternoon to find a dozen or so people milling about. Eventually, via mutually raised eyebrows and tentative smiles, like strangers meeting for a blind date, we confirmed that we were all here for the same purpose. Eventually, an earnest, clean-shaven young man in his early thirties appeared and identified himself as "Feral Kevin," forageSF's manager of wild food walks. He had on a North Face shirt, a fanny pack, and Merrell hiking boots that looked cleaner than one would want in a serious forager. He was carrying a large book, *Chanterelle Dreams, Amanita Nightmares,* which doubled as writing surface on which each of us signed a release form.

Feral Kevin quickly showed himself to be a knowledgeable and experienced forager and eater of wild plants. By this point, I'd learned that there was no shortage of people who knew the basics of foraging and could lead a walk. The number of such people who regularly ate wild plants, however, was considerably lower. Kevin was among this elite. He not only knew the plants themselves but also gave detailed descriptions of the when and how of harvesting, processing, and preparing them. He described their flavor, and how he liked to cook them. He knew a fair bit about their nutritional value—information always difficult to come by, since nutritional value is compiled only if a plant is widely consumed by livestock. More often than not, he could even say something about the plants' importance in other cultures. He was, quite simply, as knowledgeable as any forager I'd ever met.

On the other hand, he sucked dry any hopes we might have had about foraging being fun. He started his talk by noting that foraging in city parks in San Francisco was a misdemeanor punishable by a fine of up to $500. "So if anybody—especially anybody in a uniform—asks, you are on a 'plant identification' walk, not a 'wild edibles' walk, okay?" But, he continued, you wouldn't have wanted to forage here anyway, because we all lived in "a poisoned world" and cities—such

163

as the sunny, beautiful one we were standing in at the moment—were "among its most poisoned places." You'd have thought that this pretty much covered the subject, but Feral Kevin was just getting warmed up. "One definition of a city, in fact," he said, "is any place that can only sustain itself by importing food grown outside it." He pointed to a robust-looking dandelion sprouting from a crack in the sidewalk. Its bright yellow flower, looking as if it had just opened, nodded in the breeze. "That can make you sick," he said. He warned us about lead in old paint and the dangers of foraging near old buildings. Roads were equally dangerous, as the lead in automobile exhaust from the days of leaded gasoline was still there in the soil. "I see people growing tomatoes in median strips and I'm like 'No!'" he told us, and the anguish in his voice was palpable. It was as if he had lost some of his best friends to the silent scourge of median strip tomatoes.

I wanted to like Kevin. He walked us through an impressive number of wild edibles and seemed genuinely interested in sharing his knowledge. But there was an air of gloom around him that was hard to get past. As he led us up a steep sidewalk skirting the park, someone asked why we had yet to enter the park itself. It was, he said, because you usually found more wild edibles on the edge of a park than inside. This was consistent with what I had learned from Paula about edibles and also with what I'd learned on my own while hunting deer. "Nature loves an edge" is how this phenomenon is often phrased. It's true. Edibles often thrive in the transition zone—often only a few yards wide—between woods and more open ground. Deer trails are usually deep enough in woods to provide cover but parallel to field edges. Urban or rural, edges are where the action is.

My brief moment of plant walk glory came a few yards later when he plucked a bright red berry from an evergreen shrub and asked if anyone knew what it was. "Yew?" I ventured. Paula had showed me yew bushes not two weeks before, saying that every part of the plant—including the seed inside the berry—was toxic to one degree or another, except for the berry itself. She maintained that yew berries had been shown to have anticancer properties, which was why she made a point of eating a few each year. "Wow," said Kevin, genuinely impressed, "you're the first person I've ever had get that one right." For a brief moment, I basked in the group's admiration. Had Kevin been struck dead by lightning at that moment, it was clear who would be the logical choice to replace him.

Any hopes that San Franciscans were more enthusiastic about learning to forage than other people, however, were dashed shortly into the walk. Though I'd been scribbling almost nonstop, I saw only two other people take any notes at all. Neither was in danger of running out of ink. On the whole, my fellow attendees looked more like people who'd happened to be in the area when the walk started—in the same way that one might listen in on someone else's guided tour of a museum—than folks who had shelled out thirty dollars apiece for a wild edibles walk. I couldn't imagine any of them picking and eating a wild anything.

The next afternoon I reported at the wild seafood walk along the city's waterfront, specifically the Saint Francis jetty near the Golden Gate Bridge. By now, I easily identified my fellow forageSF walk participants: we were the ones standing around looking sheepish and unsure of ourselves. It was a cool, blustery day. A number of nearby fishermen had their backs to us as they faced the water. When one of them looked around and, seeing us, braced his rod against his bucket and strode over, I figured him for our leader. The guy was in his early forties, tall, and wore chunky geek-hipster glasses and a porkpie hat. He held a pipe clenched between his teeth, the wind tearing wisps of smoke from it as he approached.

I had a sinking feeling. The pipe, glasses, and hat all pointed toward somebody trying a little too hard to be a "character." I pinned my hopes on two counterbalancing factors. The first was that he was wearing a baggy, well-worn pair of orange Gruden bibs, the foul weather gear of choice among commercial fishermen. Maybe he knew his stuff after all. The other thing was his walk. Oversize bibs aren't the easiest things to walk in. But rather than being slowed down by them, he galumphed happily along, taking long, enthusiastic strides, almost like a kid wearing fireman's boots. He introduced himself as Kirk Lombard or, as he referred to himself on his website—here his voice suddenly deepened to a dead-on caricature of an emcee—"Lombard of the Intertidal." He warned us that in the next two hours he was going to tell us more than we could possibly remember. But we could find it all and more on his blog, *The Monkeyface News*.

"When the apocalypse hits, remember: the closer to the Golden Gate Bridge and points west, the better the water," he said. "The inner harbor, it's pretty horrid what goes on in there. You got people cleaning their decks with Pine-Sol or dumping raw feces. There are regs against both, but they're pretty hard to enforce. This is your bay, folks. Don't think what happens here doesn't affect you."

Within two minutes, I realized that Kirk was charismatic and eccentric. He was a live wire, a loose cannon. If Feral Kevin saw a world on the brink of apocalypse and despaired, Lombard saw the same thing with a glint in his eye. Sure, he seemed to say, it's a drag we fucked it all up, but the good news is that there are going to be some awesome visuals before the lights go out. Kirk had the enthusiasm of an eleven-year-old boy, paired with an encyclopedic knowledge of the Bay area's marine life and its fishing history. But his real passion was chasing the buzz he got when directly connected to the natural world via a fish or any other sea creature. He confessed to being a lousy fisherman but didn't let that get in the way. (Shades of my own niche at *Field & Stream*!) Like Paula, he seemed incapable of editing his profanity-laden speech. Unlike Paula, he seemed incapable of embarrassment. I was captivated by the guy. As was everyone else. You couldn't help it. Before you were even aware of it, you were already living vicariously through him. Like all of us, Kirk was a walking collection of drives and impulses. Unlike most of us, he had no intention of inhibiting them. On the contrary, he was all about feeding them, keeping them satisfied, happy, and engaged. And if that entailed occasionally looking like a fool, who the hell cared?

The contradictions were glorious. He told us he was a lifelong city boy, the child of theater actors in New York City, and had grown up living in subsidized artists' housing in Manhattan. He had also been an obsessed angler since childhood. Seeing the looks on our faces as we grappled with a city boy and fishing addict, he turned the question back on us. "What's the surprise?" he asked rhetorically. Nature, after all, was the champ when it came to being resilient, resourceful, and "very, very sneaky." Sure, much had been lost. "But don't be fooled by all the concrete, cars, and people around you," he half-shouted as a fire truck blew down Marina Boulevard behind us. "There's still a lot of nature left in the city. You just have to know where to look." Kirk, of course, knew where. He told us he knew places where you could pull fish up through city sewer drains. If we didn't believe it, we could see videos of him doing exactly that on his website. (I looked that night. There were three such videos, all of them hilarious.)

His background was exactly what one would expect of an urban outdoorsman and naturalist. He'd worked as an art teacher with troubled teens, a street performer, a puppeteer, and a founding member of Rube Waddell, a band whose nearly unclassifiable mix of punk, rockabilly, Americana, and blues had earned it a cult following in San Francisco. (The group performed every Friday for years on the sidewalk outside Leeds Shoe Store, a gig known as "Live at Leeds.") For the last seven years, he'd worked for the Department of Fish and Game as a "catch monitor," doing surveys of recreational anglers. This job involved doing one of the things Kirk did best: talk. He interviewed thousands of anglers a year about their catch, and as a result he'd become familiar with every ethnic fishing subculture in this polyglot city. He began ticking the groups off. I scribbled, "Chinese, Korean, Cambodian, Mexican, Salvadoran, Ukrainian, Lithuanian, Portuguese" before I fell behind, but he named twice that number. He had even compiled two fish identification charts—"Common Baitfishes of Northern California" and "Common Surfperches of California"—that the department still published and distributed to the fishing public. And—get this—he'd done these on his own time. Talk about a fish nerd. Then, the previous Christmas day, he had received notice that the department, hard hit by budget cuts, was offering him a choice: take a 50 percent pay cut or quit. He quit.

Kirk spent a good bit of time writing addictively eclectic, stream-of-consciousness entries for his blog, *The Monkeyface News*, named after a local species of eel. The monkeyface eel was—like Kirk himself—a wild beast that thrived in urban environments. In fact, it was not a true eel at all but something called a "prickleback," a distinction he explained using scientific terms that lost all of us instantly. I did glean that the creature's genus, *Cebidicthys*, derived from the Greek word for the capuchin monkey. And this apparently suited it because, unlike most eels and eel-like creatures, the monkeyface has close-set, forward-facing eyes, very like our own. "Personally," Kirk said, "I think the average monkeyface looks more like Joseph Stalin than a monkey. But who gives a shit—sorry—what I think?"

"They're a locavore's dream," he said, ticking off the monkeyface's qualifications. "They're native, sustainable, abundant, underappreciated, and tasty, especially flash-fried or simmered in a pot with garlic and tomato sauce."

Monkeyface eels remained obscure, he said, because, even though they spent their lives just yards away from shore-dwelling humans, they holed up deep beneath the rocks of the intertidal zone. Thus, they were rarely seen, much more rarely caught, and even more rarely eaten. "They can breathe air for days if deprived of water," he told us. "And to kill one you basically pound on its head with a hammer until you feel you are an evil, evil man. Five minutes later, you look and the thing has jumped out of your bucket and is humping its way across the sidewalk toward the water." He smiled, as if to ask how anyone could fail to love a creature so devoted to life.

Somehow, there had never been a commercial monkeyface market. Even if you knew what the hell they were, because of their behavior and where they lived, large-scale fishing for them was impossible. They could be taken only singly. And the only practical way Kirk knew of to catch them was with a pokepole, an implement of aboriginal simplicity. He likened it to "fishing with a pool cue."

(Kirk was shortly to create a market for monkeyface eels almost single-handedly. He even supplied some for one of Chez Panisse's fortieth anniversary celebrations.)

Kirk's pokepole epiphany had come courtesy of a gentleman he referred to only as "Cambodian Stan." One day, he said, he'd been fishing from shore, as was his wont. More specifically, he'd been casting from atop a boulder at Muir Beach. After several hours, he had only a single small green rockfish to show for his efforts. "If you're a shore fisherman, you have this idea that the big fish are always just a little farther out than you can cast," he said. "So you live in a state of constant frustration." A man in a tattered wet suit appeared. He was carrying a satchel full of fish in one hand and some kind of stick in the other. The stick was a five-foot length of bamboo cane with fourteen inches of coat hanger wire duct-taped to the end. Attached to the wire was a three-inch length of heavy fishing line and a 2/0 octopus hook, baited with a small piece of squid. "So he sticks this thing under the very rock I've been standing on all day, and ten seconds later he's pulled out this fucking—sorry— huge eel! *From right under my feet.*" Kirk, naturally, asked about the implement. The man, who told Kirk his name, Cambodian Stan, said it was a pokepole. Kirk converted on the spot to this unorthodox manner of fishing and begged his new hero to teach him. Cambodian Stan assented, telling him to come back the next day. Kirk did. The lesson took all of two minutes. You inserted the baited hook into the rocks, probing the crevices for the holes in which monkeyface eels make their lairs. The flexible coat hanger wire was essential for this. It and it alone let you snake the bait deep into the rocks. When the eel took the bait, it was a tug-of-war, man against eel-like prickleback. His work done, like the Lone Ranger, Cambodian Stan then vanished. For keeps. Kirk knew every fishing spot in the Bay area and all of the regular anglers at each by sight if not by name. And he never saw Cambodian Stan again. You got the impression that he found the man's appearance and disappearance inexplicable, wondrous, and—somehow—apt.

In the meantime, he'd become a maniac for both the pokepole and the quarry it seemed to have been designed for, the monkeyface eel. "The books say that they're vegetarians, surviving primarily on sixty different species of algae, mostly reds and greens," Kirk told us. "Cut one open and that's what you find inside. Algae. Every time. And nothing else. But you know what? When you put a piece of squid in front of them, dude, they're going to nail it." He leaned forward and, in a stage whisper, continued, "Just like half of the vegetarians in San Francisco, monkeyface eels are *closet carnivores.*"

"Shit!" he exclaimed, smacking his forehead. "I forgot!" He jogged back to the fishing rod he'd been holding before the class began and began reeling in furiously. Whatever he had thrown out had gone a long way, because he was at it for a while. I found myself thinking that there was something winning about Lombard, something that suggested a very intelligent child trapped in the body of an adult. He was part John Belushi, part Huck Finn, and part Tom Waits. And you couldn't take your eyes off him. You had no idea what was coming next, but you sure as hell didn't want to miss it.

At last, Lombard must have seen the end of his line, because he stopped reeling and exulted, "Goddamn! Am I good or what?" And then he held in his hand a small steel cage that bristled with little loops of clear fishing line. It looked like some up-armored soap dish. Dangling from cinched-down loops of the fishing line were two big crabs, roughly equal in size, one with creamy-colored claws, the other's almost black. They hung there, apparently relaxed, as if awaiting the start a one-claw pull-up contest. The steel soap dish was actually a crab snare, Lombard explained. "You put your bait—I use squid but most people take a can of cat food and just punch holes in it—inside the cage. Close it up, throw it out. The crabs come to the bait, catch a claw in the loops as they go after it, and then the loop cinches down and snares them. And the beauty of the thing is that it's eco-friendly. It catches crabs but not fish."

The two types of crab, he said, were a lesson in the Bay's ecology and economy as well as the arbitrary nature of human food preferences. The creamy-clawed creature was a Dungeness crab, the aristocrat of local crustaceans, sold daily and dearly in nearby fish markets and restaurants. Dungeys were heavily fished, he said. They were strictly off-limits in the Bay itself, and you could keep a maximum of only six to ten per day (depending on where you were) in the areas where they were legal. "Get caught with a Dungey here and you're subject to a fine ranging from $350 to $1,500." He deftly unhooked and tossed the Dungeness back into the drink. "And you will get caught. I know most of the wardens around here. They like to watch through binoculars, wait until you've loaded the car and are about to head home. That's when they nail you."

For Kirk the main attraction was never the obvious one. It was the other crab that he wanted us to consider. The lowly dark-clawed one was a rock crab, a species ignored by nearly everyone. Most crabbers saw it as a nuisance, eating bait from the traps set for Dungeys. As a result, you could keep up to thirty-five rock crabs of legal size per day, even from where we were standing. They were, however, rarely eaten. "Ask anyone which crab they prefer," Kirk told us, "and the response is invariably, 'Dungeness.'" Lombard, naturally, questioned that preference, wondering whether it was grounded in fact or received knowledge. So, on a day when he was in possession of just-caught crabs of both types, he conducted a blind taste test among his friends. "And every person liked the rock crab better." He let his words hang in the air for a while, something that didn't happen frequently. Rock crabs' shells were a little thicker, he continued, so they were a bit more work to process. They didn't yield quite as much meat per pound of crab as Dungeness crabs. "But they're abundant, local, sustainable, and tasty. So the question is, Why don't we eat more of them?" He shrugged, tossed the rock crab back, and looked out to sea.

It was hard to say what the shrug meant, but I wanted to know. It could go either way. Either most people were such blind and gullible consumers that we wanted only what we'd been told we like, or maybe people could wake up to underappreciated resources and start enjoying them. He didn't say.

Instead, he led us down the seawall until we arrived at a place where the water gave way to a few feet of rocky beach. He swung a leg over the seawall and disappeared. A moment later he climbed back up holding a few dark shells which he had pried off the rocks. "California mussels," he said. "Go to any archaeological site around here and you'll see lots of these. Some anthropologists estimate that they made up to half of the diet of Native American tribes in this area. Mussels get big, but this size, three to five inches, is my favorite." He'd eat these, he said, but where we were standing was about as far down the Bay as he recommended going. "Raw shellfish from the Bay can contain fecal coloform bacteria," he says. "So you want to chuck any that open before you get home, because they're dead. But, generally, you'll be fine as long as you cook these fuckers. Sorry." He passed the shellfish around, then made sure all were returned to the beach intact.

"By the way," he said, "You can forget all that crap about eating shellfish only during the 'r' months. That rule dated back to seventeenth-century England and only applied to oysters anyway. But it was a tidy little rule, so we adopted it." What the modern mollusk collector in the Bay area should look for instead were cold water and the absence of algal blooms, aka "red tides." The thing about algal blooms was that they could release very nasty biotoxins, which were absorbed by filter-feeding shellfish like mussels. "You can get amnesiac shellfish poisoning from mussels. It basically wipes your hard drive clean. Or paralytic shellfish poisoning, which kills you." Kirk hastened to say that he didn't meant to scare us. In fact, the only shellfish-related fatality that he knew of happened nearly twenty years ago. This was reassuring. "The guy, a diver I think, ate a scallop. And ten minutes later he was dead." This was less so.

This was all interesting stuff, but we were standing on the shore of San Francisco Bay. Take a left and in one mile you'd be in the Pacific Ocean. Some impressive fish, big suckers, everything from salmon and rockfish to halibut and great white sharks, could be found nearby. I was wondering when we would hear about those guys. What came next was instead one of those moments when something you've always known but never stopped to think about suddenly bitch-slaps you.

"Life as a hunter-gatherer for me didn't start until I embraced small fish," he said. "I was just like everybody else. I wanted to eat big fish. There are four 'rock star' fish in the Bay, as far as recreational fishing: California halibut, stripers, salmon, and sturgeon. And, yes, you can keep up to three sturgeon a year, although I strongly recommend that you don't." For one thing, he said, local sturgeon spent the majority of their lives in the delta of the Sacramento River, a severely compromised ecosystem. "It's full of dioxin, PAHs, mercury, all kinds of good stuff. And sturgeon are basically bottom-feeders that can live up to a hundred twenty-six years. That's a long time to be bioaccumulating all that shit. Sorry."

"But the real point," he continued, lapsing into uncharacteristic sincerity, "is that we didn't *evolve* to eat only those fish. They're all apex predators, the top of the food chain. Eating them is like being a hunter and only eating mountain lions, bears, and eagles. It makes no sense, either for our personal health or for the health of the planet." And although ordering up a hunk of swordfish or tuna was something we did routinely, it was unprecedented in our history as a species. It was only with the relatively recent technologies of fast ships and refrigeration that we could catch and sell such fish.

"The Indians who lived here and our own ancestors for hundreds of thousands of years sure as hell didn't eat many of those fish. We all fed much further down the food chain."

As large predators ourselves, we ought to take a lesson from large predator fish. Instead of eating those apex predators, we might think about eating what they ate—little fish. The average apex predator fish, he explained, took a decade or more—if it survived that long—just to reach spawning age. Once it did, it reproduced only sporadically. Female sturgeon, for example, were thought to wait somewhere between two and nine years between spawnings. And—again assuming it hadn't been caught, stripped of its caviar, and cut into steaks—a sturgeon produced comparatively few offspring. In case we had ever wondered why the severely overfished populations of these big fish took so long to rebound, now we knew. They matured slowly and had few offspring. They were just like, well, us.

173

Now, he said, consider the little guys, the baitfish, which were very nearly the opposite: short-lived, usually hell-bent on spawning within a year of their birth, and reproducing in stupendous numbers. "Nature designed them to withstand massive predation and bounce back quickly. It's why they're called *baitfish*." He ticked off the advantages of consuming them: easy to catch, plentiful, nutritious, and—because they aren't around long enough to bio-accumulate toxins—better for you. "Gee," he asked rhetorically, "you think nature's trying to tell us something?"

He admitted that his was anything but an easy conversion. "Look, I didn't want to eat sardines and smelt. You ever see a top smelt? Or a jack smelt? They're not even true smelt! They're in the *Atherinidae* family, silversides, more like a grunion." It was clear that he detested jack smelt on a personal level. "They're long, sticky, stinky, and chock-full of worms and larval nematodes." His voice rose as he named each thing he hated about them. And he clearly wanted us to share his hatred of the fish. "I mean—Jesus!—just a horrifying fish to clean. Talk about a god-awful mess! You got black gunk dripping out of their guts, you got scales flying everywhere—it takes three days just to get them outta your hair—worms crawling all over you. And the meat! Jesus! Mealy, fishy-tasting, nasty, nasty stuff. And everybody says their grandmother knows some secret way of making them palatable. But you know what? That's *bullshit*! Never again, man. That and leopard shark ceviche. Count me out." He actually had to pause and catch his breath.

Damn. This was awesome. Kirk's rant put me in mind of someone like Paula, only with more library time. I didn't want him to stop. I would have stuck a quarter in his mouth and pumped his arm to keep him talking. I was dying to ask about leopard shark ceviche, hoping that might set him off again. But someone else had beaten me to it, only with a noninflammatory question that I couldn't hear. "Ah, well," he said. His knowledge of fish had come from exhaustive reading on the subject. Working for Fish and Game had involved endless hours waiting for party boats of anglers to return. But he wasn't allowed to screw off during working hours and his bosses checked on him regularly. He couldn't read, for example, unless the material related directly to his job. "So I spent thousands of hours reading up on fish and the history of fishing in the Bay area. My favorite book was *Probably More Than You Want to Know About the Fishes of the Pacific Coast*, written by Dr. Milton Love." In Kirk's view, it was the definitive work on the subject.

One woman in the group could stand it no longer. "Wait," she blurted out. "Are you BS-ing us or is that a real book?"

"Hell, yeah, it's a real book," Kirk said, affronted. It was impossible to know, of course, if he was truly insulted or just milking the moment. "He's a research biologist with the Marine Science Institute at Santa Barbara. And he's already working on the sequel, *Certainly More Than You Want to Know About the Fishes of the Pacific Coast: A Postmodern Experience*." He shook his head and smiled. "Milton Love is the man," he said.

I knew he was telling the truth. This was too preposterous to be a lie. "You think he's serious?" a guy near me inquired of his friend. "Like, one book is *Probably More Than You Want to Know* and the other one is *Certainly More Than You Want to Know*?" The crowd liked Kirk, but people were having trouble deciding what was shtick and what was real. I was having a little trouble myself. The difference was that I didn't care. Kirk's passion for fish and his joy when connected to them were the real deal. His unlikely environmentalism was the real deal. That was enough for me. I was hooked.

"I'm pretty sure he's serious," I told the guy in the crowd. "You can't make up stuff like that on the fly. Trust me, I'm a freelance writer." (Both titles turned out to be accurate. Milton Love is a respected marine biologist at the University of California and an authority on Pacific Coast fishing. And his books—with the titles Kirk mentioned—are a rare combination of heavy-duty research and deft humor.)

As for me, having already discovered the joys of smoked herring and white perch, I was halfway to being a convert already. I'd even started buying anchovies, which I'd realized had nearly vanished from contemporary cuisine. They were no longer found on lists of pizza toppings or in Caesar salads. But I'd never heard the argument for eating small fish laid out either so comprehensively or with Kirk's mix of eloquence and passion. It was bracing stuff. The way forward was a step back. We should eat the fish our species had eaten for thousands of years, the ones that were easy to catch, the little fish. Kirk was such a character you could almost miss the fact that he was also a man on a mission.

The tour continued for another hour. By the end, everyone seemed ready to embrace the Kirk Lombard Gospel of Small Fish. Afterward, I invited him out for a beer. "Sure," he said, "but there aren't any decent bars around here." We hopped into his little truck, which reeked of old bait and wet waders. Every time he took a turn, several pounds of sinkers beneath the seats rolled from one side to the other. We ended up at a wonderfully seedy bar in the Tenderloin. Kirk was about ten years my junior and, after the first beer, confessed that he'd been having a hard time finding employment since being laid off. It was hard because his wife was making a lot more money than he was. I asked about the tours for forageSF. "This is actually the first time I've done anything with them," he said. "This was my trial run." I asked if he was serious. He was. In that case, I said, he needn't worry. He knew his stuff, knew how to spin it in a singularly entertaining way, and clearly loved to perform. People would definitely come. (They did. Later that year, in fact, Kirk's wild seafood walks were named "Best Walking Tour" by SF Weekly, which dubbed him "guru of SF's seafood foraging scene.")

As we drank another beer, I mentioned the fish ID charts he'd done for the department. That was something only a geek's geek would have undertaken. "Oh, Jesus," he said, taking a long pull on his bottle. "That was an idea that got seriously out of hand." Basically, he'd seen the need. There were dozens of species of small fish in the Bay that people caught but couldn't identify. So he had decided to create the ID charts. He had easily caught and photographed most species. But there were some he knew about but couldn't find photos of. So he began driving up and down the coast trying to catch and photograph like the longjaw mudsucker, a fish he had a soft spot for because it had once been the preeminent bait in the Bay area. Its dominance was due to the fact that it stayed alive and kicking on an angler's hook long past the limit of other baitfish to endure. But few people used it anymore and no one knew where to catch one. So Kirk had spent days driving up and down the coast, visiting obscure places where people had reported catching them in the past. And once Kirk got obsessed, he stayed obsessed. He had spent between 400 and 500 hours of his own time ("At some point, it's better not to know, you feel me?") compiling the two charts.

Another beer later, Kirk invited me to go catch night smelt about twenty-five miles down the coast. He had only recently found out that the little buggers existed, let alone that that there were people who fished specifically for them. "Dude, a fishery that I didn't even know about? After the thousands of hours I've spent fishing and talking to fishermen around here?" He looked to see if I understood how unlikely that was. I did. I was, furthermore, realizing that Kirk's degree of local fish knowledge was even deeper than I had thought. It seemed endless.

The hidden nature of the night smelt fishery was understandable, he explained, given the particular fishermen who knew about it. "It was just these old Portuguese guys, all of whom are named Joe or Mike for some reason. Out of all the ethnic fishing communities, the Portuguese are the most secretive." So, I asked, how'd you get them to teach you? "They took pity on me," he said. "I was out there with a homemade dip net and didn't have the faintest idea what I was doing. But I kept at it, you know? I just kept going out and trying. And they liked that."

He said that the smelt laid their eggs only on coarse beach sand, roughly BB-size, only when the tide was near full and going out, and usually on days when the water was fairly clear. "In northern California, that's about ten percent of the time," he said. In short, he was inviting me along on a fool's errand. I said I was in.

First, though, I had to work forageSF's upcoming "Wild Kitchen" event. I had thought of the wild plant and seafood walks as steps toward this apex of my time in San Francisco, a dinner in this "roving underground supper club" featuring foraged wild foods. ForageSF hired a chef to put together the menu, but an unpaid army did the rest of the work required in pulling off such an ambitious event. Everything from helping with foraging and food preparation to greeting the guests as they arrived to waiting on them and busing their dirty dishes—it was all done by volunteers for no more remuneration than the chance to eat the same dinner for free, albeit in bites snatched in the kitchen between rounds of plate carrying. Wanting to see the Wild Kitchen from both sides, I had signed up both to attend and to work the event. I hoped to see how forageSF connected with the city's elite foodies, people for whom the pursuit of the edgiest eating approached a competitive sport.

For the paying diners, the deal was this. For $80—the price has since jumped to $100—forageSF offered a maximum of eighty diners (the number varied with the venue) an eight- or nine-course meal, each course "highlighting a sustainably foraged ingredient from the local landscape." To get around regulations—licensing, inspections, certifications, etc.— the enterprise billed itself as a "supper club" with a strict BYOB policy. Further, the location—typically an artist's studio in a slightly dodgy part of town—was revealed only by e-mail the day of the dinner. Taken singly, any of these factors might have been off-putting. Most people, I'd have wagered, prefer food prepared in professional kitchens that have been certified as sanitary. Most would also prefer to know ahead of time where the restaurant was and to avoid the rougher neighborhoods. Taken together, however, the factors produced some alchemy, making a Wild Kitchen dinner one of the most sought-after tickets in town. They offered exclusivity, secrecy, and a chance for well-off eaters to add to their eating résumés, do a little slumming, even have an exhilarating frisson of illegality. Whatever it was, the Wild Kitchen dinners tended to sell out almost as soon as they were announced.

The night before, I called Michelle from my tiny single room—if I stretched out my arms I could just about touch both sides at once—at the San Remo Hotel and confessed that I didn't really understand the appeal.

"It's San Francisco," she said.

"I know where it is," I said.

"You know where it is, but not what it means. San Franciscans are like"—she paused, apparently searching for a comparison that I could grasp—"the Navy SEALs of foodies. The trendiest of the trendy. And, you know, what's trendier than a little danger? Plus there's the grunge factor. I totally get it."

I told her I did, too. Even though I really didn't.

"Baby, this trip is kind of wasted on you," she said, not unsympathetically. "You're the opposite of most people. You don't do trendy. I mean, it makes you actively uncomfortable."

Damn. She'd nailed me again. We'd known each other only a few months, but Michelle already knew things about me that I didn't know. Or that I'd never brought into consciousness. Now that I thought of it, trend and I seldom crossed paths. Actually, we were more like opposing forces. On the few occasions I'd found myself surrounded by stylish, vivid achievers, my instinct had invariably been to flee. I left by the front door if possible, but I'd climbed a few back fences when that was the only escape. Like everyone, I had a deep hunger to be seen for who I was and loved in spite of that. It was wonderful to feel that with Michelle. It also scared the bejesus out of me. I realized then that I could never lie to Michelle. She would see through it even before I'd gotten the words out. I had fallen for a really hot polygraph.

At 12:30 the next day, six hours before the doors opened for dinner, I knocked at the gated front door of a two-story row house in the Mission District belonging to an artist who went by the name Chicken John. No one answered. I walked around the block, wondering if I'd come to the right place. Twenty minutes later, I rang again. No response. A few minutes after that, however, a big guy in full black leather backed a heavyset motorcycle to the curb, got off, and unlocked the door. He was Jordan Grosser, a classically trained chef and veteran of restaurants in Tucson and San Francisco. He also had his own cheese business, Flossa Creamery, and was the freelance chef in charge of tonight's dinner.

For the next six hours, I sliced, chopped, carried, and swept. I quartered platters of potatoes. He instructed me in handpicking Italian parsley. He wanted just the leaves—no stems—from three huge bunches of the stuff. After an hour of this tedious labor, I was handed another, slightly larger batch. I took a deep breath and dug back in. Other volunteers started drifting in. There were two young women and a subdued, purposeful guy in his early twenties, all of whom brought their own knives, the mark of a working cook or at least a serious amateur. There was a dance teacher. There was a handsome young Indian actor, currently starring in a production of *Julius Caesar*. He would work the front of the house, welcoming guests. I listened in as the actor talked about food events he was planning—hoping to make some quick money doing other kinds of onetime "by subscription only" and "underground" dinners—with another chef on the side. It was tricky, because he was timing those ventures so he could also be in Los Angeles for winter casting calls, when actors were chosen for the upcoming season of TV sitcoms and dramas. I was the old man in a group that mostly consisted of young people in a hurry. They volunteered here because it was fun and a good, free meal—and also, apparently, a good opportunity to network.

Grosser assigned tasks and periodically checked on the large hunk of wild boar that had been in the oven at 225 for fourteen hours. The boar was part of the main dish of the evening, the chef's take on poutine, the famously downscale Canadian dish of chipped potatoes with curd cheese and gravy. At one point, I was given a tray of astonishingly stinky yellow-orange ginkgo fruits. Imagine a malevolent cheese made from fermented diapers and you're in the olfactory ballpark. It was a powerful appetite suppressant. My job was to separate the fruit from the husks, each of which contained a tiny green nut. It probably took forty-five minutes, seemed much longer, and left me unable to smell or taste anything for a good while afterward. When finished, I had less than half a cup of these pea-sized suckers, which eventually were doled out like diamonds, one or two per plate, atop the dessert.

As the dinner hour approached, the pace quickened in the kitchen. At one point, I remarked on Grosser's calm. He shrugged.

"Would you feel better if I was nervous?" he asked. Absolutely, I told him. It would make for a much better story. He just smiled. Jordan was a veteran of high-pressure kitchens. This was a walk in the park. Also, I reminded myself, this was California. It was highly uncool to appear stressed out, even if you were. The diners began arriving. The popping of corks and buzz of conversation could be heard from the studio. The communal nature of the meal had been part of the pitch. What "communal" meant here was two long rows of wooden tables covered in what looked to be printing press paper with forty folding chairs pulled up to each row. When the menu, on unadorned printer paper, was distributed, the buzz of conversation increased.

Trout Crostini
with Pickled Nasturtium Seed Pods
and
Gleaned Apples

Wild Clam Tomato Chowder
with
Wild Nori

Braised Wild Mushrooms, Poached Farm Egg
Foraged Watercress
and
Crispy Potatoes

Flossa Creamery Goat Cheese
with
Pickled Gleaned Fruit
and
Roasted Boquerónes
with
Shisito Peppers, Foraged Grapes
and
Chorizo Lentil Vinaigrette

Wild Boar Poutine
with
Parmesan, Gremolata, and Pickled Shallots

Salad of Foraged Nasturtium Greens and Flowers
with
Candied Walnuts with an Orange Sage Vinaigrette

Pumpkin Panna Cotta
with
Bruléed Gleaned Fig
and
Wild Fennel Pollen Mascarpone Cream

Just before the first course went out, Grosser strode to the front of the room to address the guests. He seemed the picture of low-key self-possession, still wearing his apron as he popped the cap off a beer with the bottom of his lighter, a trick I've ruined any number of lighters trying to learn. He tapped a very large pocketknife against his beer bottle for quiet and then described what was coming, a procedure he would repeat before each course of the dinner. He spoke as if this were an impromptu dinner for eighty of his closest friends. In retrospect, I think that he knew full well what I then only vaguely suspected, which was that these diners had shown up ready and eager to be entertained, charmed, and even enthralled. One of the hallmark phrases of the anti–industrial food movement is "food with a story." Knowing how and where the animals and plants on your plate were raised was essential to the experience of eating them. The more you knew, the richer the story. By contrast, industrial food would most definitely prefer anonymity about those particulars. These diners were clearly eager for stories, and they were going to get them. Grosser apologized in advance for the fact that not all of the mushrooms served tonight were wild. He and some friends had driven up to Mendocino the day before in search of chanterelles and oyster mushrooms. They had found some, but not enough, so they augmented their haul with some store-bought chanterelles. The diners seemed just as charmed by this story of failed foraging as by the accounts of successes, maybe more. On cue, a parade of five or six of us waiters emerged to serve the trout crostini.

Having not worked as a waiter in thirty-five years, I was both surprised and pleased when the skill set came back instantly. There was the endorphin buzz of rushing to serve and pick up plates. There were the different kinds—micro and macro—of attention and focus required. As I served each diner, I also scanned the length of the table for anyone trying to catch my eye to replace a dropped utensil or refill a water glass. I had forgotten the pleasure of the dance of waiting tables, the sudden, nonverbal intimacy with strangers. Those of us who had worked in restaurants instantly recognized one another by the way we moved. We also recognized those who hadn't. Outgoing food, for example, always has the right of way. This is true everywhere, but it was especially important here at the bottleneck of the kitchen's swinging door. Experienced waiters knew how to make themselves small in such situations in a way others didn't. Some of us got to know each other well simply by the necessity of constantly reading and adjusting to each other's body language, the better to serve and bus tables more efficiently. A backward glance to another server while retreating with a tray laden with stacked dishes might translate as a call for help serving or clearing. A cock of the head might signal that although the server was carrying all he could, there were still more plates back there waiting to be taken away. There was a sheer physical pleasure to this work that I'd forgotten.

Before bringing out the goat cheese and "pickled gleaned fruit," Grosser had the room engrossed in the story of how the semi-successful mushroomers, returning after hours of foraging in the woods, had seen from the highway a just-picked vineyard with grapes still on the vines. They stopped, asked and received permission to glean the zinfandel grapes, and had brought home boxes of them. I'd seen the grapes. They were misshapen and tired-looking. You wouldn't have given them a second look in a store. But now they had a story. They had taken on the status of gleaned fruit, the same way that an artist picks up a discarded object and transforms it. It suddenly seemed improbably strange that "gleaned" fruit carried such cachet. Historically, all the way back to Ruth in the Old Testament, gleaning was the province of the poorest of the poor. Jean-François Millet's 1857 painting, *The Gleaners,* was famous—and famously derided by critics of the time—for its sympathetic depiction of the lowest ranks of French rural society. I once spent a couple of days working on a small organic farm in upstate New York, and the farmer's wife told me how one fall they'd opened their harvested fields to gleaners. They'd given the matter little thought. After all, they were done with their work. The next thing they knew, she said, they had been inundated with people they'd never laid eyes on. There were hundreds of people parked along the field roads. "You ever see gleaners?" she asked, shaking her head. "Half of them—I'm serious—just looked like they were crazy."

Grosser had probably "pickled" the grapes that graced the goat cheese as much to disguise their condition as anything else. But the diners ate it up—both food and story. Most chewed in rapt silence, their expressions suggesting that they had never paid true attention to grapes before, regretted it, and were now bent on atoning that sin of omission.

But it was an earlier course—one that replaced a planned dish of wild sardines that Kirk Lombard, an unnamed contributor to the dinner, had attempted to obtain—that prompted the greatest reaction. ("Hey, man, sardines are hit or miss, you know? And the little fuckers just weren't running," Kirk had explained to me.) And the reaction started before the first bite, at Grosser's description of the dish. Lacking sardines, he had substituted "boquerónes" (a term I later looked up to discover it was the Spanish word for fresh anchovies) marinated in vinegar, garlic, and parsley and served over Shisito peppers that he had just "blistered" in the oven, along with a "chorizo, green lentil, chive, and lemon zest relish." At the description of the relish, one woman moaned audibly with pleasure. After a second, a round of applause quickly erupted. It was the most bizarre thing. The seemingly involuntary moan had something in it that was decidedly *not* involuntary—a subdued but distinct note of self-congratulation. It was as if by her outburst, the woman were staking her claim to having—even among devoted foodies—a passion for food that was more profound and heartfelt than anyone else's. The subsequent applause seemed, to my ear at least, almost involuntary, a collective gag reflex. It was the hasty applause of people who'd just realized they'd better join in quick or risk not being part of the club. In the end, I couldn't have told you what they were applauding—the chef's imagination, the woman's appreciation of the chef's imagination, or the fact that they had all snagged seats at the hippest meal in the city that evening. Whatever it was didn't matter, except that this was the moment when I realized I did not and would never belong among these people. If this was trendy, you could include me out.

The courses and wine kept coming. At a certain point I realized that half the room was smashed. While uncorking a guest's bottle of wine, I found myself almost involuntarily caricaturing a waiter in a pretentious restaurant. Draping a clean towel over my left forearm, I poured a sip into the woman's glass and bent forward attentively, the better to receive her reaction, as if she had the option of sending back her own bottle. I thought she would get the joke. I was wrong. She took the proffered glass, swished the wine around for a test drive, then swallowed and murmured, "That'll be fine." I bowed as I filled her glass, somehow unable to break character. It was only when I was a few steps away that I allowed myself to wonder what parallel universe the woman was living in.

Late in the evening, we split the tips the diners had left us. They'd evidently enjoyed themselves, for they'd tipped well. We pocketed more than fifty bucks apiece. I did some math before leaving San Francisco. This wild dinner alone ran for three nights, on each of which eighty people were served. Eighty people at $80 each times three is $19,200. I didn't know what Rabins's overhead was, but it couldn't have cost anything close to that to get the food, rent the space, and pay the chef for the evening. ForageSF, for all its talk of rediscovering a forgotten food system and building a wild foods community, was one slick little business machine.

I never did meet Iso Rabins, although I spoke with him once very briefly on the phone and e-mailed him a few times. Over the phone he told me that after college he had sold mushrooms for a while, had worked as a line cook at ten bucks an hour, but had "always been business-minded" and that he thought "everyone could start their own business and make money from what they're passionate about." At one point, I proposed coming back to watch him and Grosser get the food together for another Wild Kitchen dinner, especially if we could hunt boar together. I never heard back.

Iso was probably smart to avoid me. He was an entrepreneur, a mover and shaker. My interest and sympathies lay further down the economic food chain, with the guys who actually foraged, the people he hired to give forageSF legitimacy. Both Kevin and Kirk, I learned, were paid flat fees. Kirk characterized his as "not much." He had never heard of Iso until Iso called after reading about him in the local press. Nonetheless, later, when Kirk tried to branch out, offering his own private walks and fishing classes in addition to his forageSF work, Iso was displeased. Feral Kevin seemed caught in the same bind. When I spoke with him privately, he complained that he was paid "very little" for the walks he ran, even though he also did all the administrative work—scheduling, registering attendees, collecting the money. As with Kirk, Iso had made the first move, contacting Kevin, who said he'd taken Iso out a few times and showed him where to find various edibles. Kevin, a self-described hermit, wasn't as entrepreneurial as Kirk, and had never gone out on his own. So he accepted the deal.

It wasn't at all clear to me that forageSF was succeeding in its stated goal of making foraging "a sustainable lifestyle," though through the Wild Kitchen it was certainly getting people to pay for it.

The typical piece about Rabins—and there were a lot of pieces, not just in food magazines and blogs but also in the national press—described him more or less the way Lettuce Eat Kale's Sarah Henry did: "The frequently plaid-clad Iso Rabins is a king of inner-city cool and in high demand in culinary circles." They praised the follow-your-bliss principle he applied as a businessman and his savvy in keeping his ventures "light"—i.e., free of capital-intensive outlays—so that forageSF could be responsive and flexible. Most articles included what I came to think of as the "when he's not foraging" clause, which listed all the things Iso also managed to cram into his busy life: the occasional column for *chow,* blogging, speaking at food panels, working on a book of wild food recipes. The problem with this is that I never found any evidence that Iso had ever been either particularly skilled or passionate about foraging itself. When we spoke on the phone, he told me he foraged "one day a week at most." I suspected it was actually less than that. What he was indisputably successful at was finding a way to build his brand and to monetize foraging and underground food cachet.

It was possible that what Iso was doing really was a form of genius. After all, nobody else at the time had managed to bring foraging anywhere as close to the mainstream as he had. And in founding forageSF he had at least helped bring the whole world of wild edibles to a wider audience. But if I had gone to San Francisco in search of the center of a potential wild foods revolution, I hadn't found one. Iso, I decided, was a guy looking for business opportunities. He wasn't a wild edibles revolutionary. He was a guy who had found ways to make money from the revolution.

Wild Kitchen duties done, I was happy to go smelt fishing with Kirk. I'd already told him about my experience working the wild dinner. What I had learned there, I told him solemnly, was that it didn't matter whether we actually caught smelt. It was that our food should have a story. He repeated his warning that this was likely to be a futile quest. With that settled, we headed north along the coast. Kirk pulled over at the first overlook to gauge water conditions. He came back to the truck and said, "There's like four fucking sets out there. And it's pretty crunchy." I had no idea what any of this meant, but the tone was not hopeful. I could feel him mentally rifling through possible fallback plans. "What the hell," he finally said. "Let's keep going." A few miles later we stopped at another overlook, a little lot where fishermen and surfers parked before descending a steep, treacherous-looking path to the water. I was struck by the coastline. I was used to the wide, flat beaches of the mid-Atlantic coastal plain and their small, orderly waves. The coastline here was one of the cliffs and mountains that tumbled into the Pacific Ocean. Ninety percent, maybe more, of the shore was inaccessible, sheer cliffs. If you ever found your way to the edge, it was one step and several hundred feet to the ocean, where big waves pounded the rocks senseless. It was as if the ocean had a grudge against the land, one so old that it could no longer remember why it was beating it up but kept on anyway. Sometimes there was a tiny piece of beach way down there, but mostly the waves just crashed against the rocks in discrete, incredibly loud claps. It actually did sound like cannons firing. Lombard was used to that. He was focused on what was happening farther out. "Water's a little better out there," he said. "But those gulls facing away from the water?" He pointed to a short, steep beach a few hundred yards off. I could barely make out the white dots against the khaki sand. "Means nothing's happening." Back at the truck, a knot of about twenty other seagulls screamed hoarsely as they fought over a fish head by a Dumpster. One bird would grab the head and attempt to fly away, whereupon it was assaulted from all sides. It was as if the purpose wasn't so much to get the fish head yourself as to make sure nobody else did. We watched for a moment. "Gulls," Lombard said absently. "They're such haters." The observation struck me. It wasn't just that it was so casually apt— although it was. It was the casualness with which he said it. It bespoke someone who with an intimate knowledge of gulls, someone who had spent a long time observing them.

At our target beach—which Lombard absolutely forbade me to name—he finally smiled. "Goddamn," he said. "We just might get lucky here." I told him I didn't understand. There were gulls at this beach, just like the last. I could see them several hundred yards off.

"Yeah, but look closer," he said. "They're facing the water, which means there's at least the possibility of food there. And look, they're following the waves in and out." I could just make them out. They were following the forward lip of each wave as it lapped up the beach and slid back into the sea. Kirk had lent me a pair of waders to wear in the cold water, but he was going to fish—I finally learned that you threw a cast net to catch surf smelt—in a swimsuit. We walked down a long set of wooden stairs set into the hillside and headed for the gulls. At a certain moment, without saying a word, he took off at a jog. I could see some other birds, which looked like cormorants, diving and swimming a few yards from where the gulls were following the waves. In any case, it was more than Kirk could stand. I could hear the plastic bucket containing his gear thump against his leg as he ran. I quickened my pace to try to catch up. But as soon as I did, the bucket was thumping at double time. I'd seen a piece of black driftwood being pushed around by the surf. Now I realized that it was a sea lion. Even I knew that had to be significant. Maybe that was why he'd taken off. I'll be damned, I thought. Evidently, the planets had aligned.

Kirk had already made a couple of throws with the cast net by the time I arrived. He had caught a few smelt and was keeping them in the bucket filled with seawater. They were inside a yellow mesh bag, which had handles like a purse. This, he said, was to deter the fucking seagulls, which would otherwise pluck them right out of the bucket. The smelt were sleek, silvery things, five or six inches long. They were handsome fish, with clean, sculpted bodies. As they lay suspended motionless in the bucket, to my eye they looked like nothing so much as really expensive fishing lures. Kirk, barefoot, would wait for the wave to break and flatten out before he threw the weighted circular net just behind the lip. The water he was targeting couldn't have been more than twelve to eighteen inches deep. I watched as I struggled into the waders trying to see how it was done. He stopped to give me a two-minute tutorial on throwing the net. The process was too complex to explain here, involving draping the net over one arm, holding the weighted edges in your mouth and both hands, and spinning the thing as you threw. It was one of those things that is essentially quite simple when done correctly, but could also go wrong in any number of ways, most of which I explored in depth. When this is done correctly, the net blossoms into a circle and sinks. My blossoms were long and narrow, but Kirk said I was doing fine. I knew this was a lie. He just wanted to get back to casting himself. I was grateful for it anyway. I figured I'd improve with practice. "This is called 'blind tossing,'" he said. "The Portuguese guys would laugh their asses off at us. They don't throw unless they can see the fish. But in dirty surf, it's this or nothing."

My first two throws came back fishless, but the third yielded three or four glistening, flapping surf smelt. As they spilled from my net, I fell to my knees, cupping each against the sand before waves or gulls—both quite close—could take it away. The beach itself was short and steep, and with a powerful undertow. Fighting the blow and suck of the waves—even in water only eighteen inches deep—was surprisingly hard work. The waders were just that much more surface area for the water to work with. I figured I'd be better off without them. I hadn't brought a bathing suit; I had only my jeans. And I wasn't going to wet my only pair of pants. "I'm gonna strip down to my shorts," I told Kirk.

"Dude, don't," he said urgently. "I know people here." The unembarrassable Lombard looked abashed. But it was too late. For one thing, there was nobody else in sight. For another, I figured that anybody who did see us would do so from a good distance, at which my plaid boxers would look like swim trunks. The undertow was a little less forceful, but my feet went numb within minutes from the cold water. The sea lion, often just yards away, ignored us, confident of its protected status. He was a big boy, longer than I was and a good 400 pounds, possibly more.

"Make sure that rope's not looped around your wrist," Kirk called. "Snag that guy and it'll be your last ride. You feel me?" Wow, I thought. I hadn't considered this. The animal looked calm and probably was. But I'd mistaken "calm" for "tame," and this large marine mammal was anything but. A toss that landed on any part of him would undoubtedly set him off. I'd heard of anglers getting an arm caught in a loop of fishing line when fighting a big fish—a marlin or tuna—and being dragged down hundreds of feet to their death. I increased my distance from the beast and slid the loop off my wrist.

I made a particularly sloppy throw that must have hit a school, because my net was alive with fish when I pulled it in. "Holy shit!" Kirk shouted, running over to help. I counted forty-one surf smelt as I slid them into the mesh bag and back into the bucket. Within a couple of hours, we had a quarter of a bucket—maybe seven or eight pounds, more than enough for dinner. Kirk hoisted the mesh bag and told me, "Smell." I did and inhaled the clean and unmistakable scent of fresh cucumber. "Weird, huh? People usually don't believe it when I tell them smelt smell like cucumber. They think I'm being poetic or something." It was amazing. I'd sniffed actual cucumbers that smelled less, well, cucumbery than these little fish.

At the truck I changed back into my pants, ditching my wet shorts under the front seat. We drove back into the city, to the apartment where Kirk and his wife, Camilla, live. Within an hour we had cleaned the fish, dredged them in egg and seasoned breadcrumbs, and fried them up. They were delicious. We were both pumped. Every so often a one-in-ten shot—Kirk's assessment of our chances when he suggested the trip—pays off. I couldn't help picturing the smelt served as a forty-dollar entrée in one of San Francisco's upscale restaurants. The chef at any one of these, I was certain, would have paid top dollar for those fish—as obscure, fresh, local, and difficult to obtain as food got. The fact that we were eating them at Kirk's kitchen table with a couple beers and the stereo playing old Slim Harpo blues in the background made them taste that much better.

I had come to San Francisco hoping to find a young but promising wild foods movement. Over the past five years or so, there seemed to be a growing collective awareness of the disconnect between people and food, accompanied by a sense that the industrial food juggernaut, which had been humming along on autopilot for decades, was due for an overhaul. More people were wondering if cheap chicken justified searing the birds' beaks off so they could be raised in closer quarters, or breeding them to have breasts so heavy their legs wouldn't support them. San Franciscans were leaders in this kind of thinking. Given the rise of forageSF and the current wild edibles craze in the restaurants here, it seemed that if there was going to be a foraging movement coming together anywhere, it would be San Francisco. I'd expected to find at least a few people who, like me, were interested in learning to forage, fish, and hunt. It hadn't happened. People here valued food that had come directly from the wild, especially if it was fresh and local and came with a story. But they seemed to want merely to consume such food, not to be part of the story. Bottom line, the act of getting the food yourself didn't seem to have any more traction here than it did at home.

It was weird. Many people I'd talked to genuinely desired to shorten the distance between themselves and their edibles. But they seldom took it further than voicing that desire. Maybe it was the steep learning curve. One of the cardinal rules in foraging is to eat nothing your first year unless and until it has been confirmed as safe by someone with years of experience. As Michelle told me the very first time we met, when I had asked what percentage of her family's food she got through foraging and her answer—20 to 30 percent, depending on the season—had obviously disappointed me: "Hey, agriculture arose for a reason."

But maybe there was something else going on. Sure, foraging was difficult. So was learning to sail or to identify birds or to climb vertical expanses of rock. And plenty of people took up those activities. Was it simply that most people just didn't want to get their hands dirty? That, while they liked the cachet of wild food, buying it was easier than getting it themselves.

I flashed on a moment in June when Paula had called to say that the wineberries were ready. She was headed out and asked if I'd wanted to come. I was on deadline and couldn't. But, chained to my computer, I was suddenly desperate for some wineberries, a nonnative raspberry that has become naturalized all over the eastern United States. A bit tarter than regular raspberries, wineberries are fantastic mashed into vanilla ice cream until the whole thing turns a deep pink. Soon I was dying for some. It wasn't merely the fruit itself, good as that was. I also wanted in on the connection to the annual cycle that the berries were part of. Paula loved wineberries above almost all the other fruits she collected—more than pawpaws or blackberries or apples, peaches, pears, and figs. She counted the days until they were ready, usually in late June. They were almost always done by the Fourth of July. Being there to pick during that brief window of ripeness was a kind of sacrament for her. The more I thought about this, both the thing itself and what it meant, the more I craved wineberries. Finally, I tried something I'd never done. I called her back, caught her just as she was leaving, and offered to pay if she'd bring me some. I was hoping for a quart, but I'd have gladly taken a pint. I hadn't even pegged a price point. I was willing to pay pretty much whatever she asked. Paula just laughed her gravelly laugh and turned me down. Her refusal implied that my request was as outlandish as a child asking for a pony. "Honey, you couldn't pay me enough to pick wineberries for you or anybody else," she said. Then she hung up.

This might not have been completely true. For fifteen or twenty bucks a pound, I bet she might have been willing. But I didn't make that offer, and not because of the money alone. It was because I felt rebuffed by her larger point, which she didn't address directly but which I felt nonetheless. I'd been struck by the fact that Paula hadn't had to think at all before refusing. I took that to mean that wild, seasonal, ephemeral things like wineberries and the everyday world of commerce were never meant to go together. Maybe foraging wasn't meant to be a profession. It was something that appealed to outliers—the eccentrics, the weirdos, the people who liked difficult paths. To get wineberries, you first of all had to know they existed, and this criterion cut out 95 percent or more of the population right off the bat. Then you had to know where to find them—not an easy task—and when they ripened. And then there was the arduous, tedious picking of the berries themselves. It was hot work. Wineberries grew at the edges of woods, often along highways. They grew in dense thickets and, though not terribly prickly themselves, were frequently entwined with the aggressively thorny multiflora rosebushes. That usually meant you could pick only the outside edges. And even then you wanted long sleeves and pants that could stand up to the thorns. The good wineberries I knew grew along thoroughfares where pedestrians weren't allowed. Paula had been hassled by a Park Service cop the previous season for trying to pick in one of these abundant but off-limits areas. The guy had warned her once, passing by again forty-five minutes later to make sure she'd obeyed. Paula had simply dropped into the brush and waited until he left to resume picking. That an officer of the law would devote that much time and energy to hassling a woman picking berries speaks to the inherently subversive nature of foraging.

I'd never really thought about how much trouble wineberries were until I tried to get someone else to pick me some. No wonder there was no grassroots wild foods movement gathering steam. It was too much work for most people. I was okay with that. It meant more wineberries for me. If I could ever get the hell out there to pick.

It wasn't long after I returned from San Francisco that Paula called. "You want some fresh pawpaw?" Sure, I said. "Well," she said, "They're in, and I got a bunch. Good year for 'em. Better get over before I eat 'em all myself," and hung up. Gordon, I knew, didn't particularly care for them, but Paula was a connoisseur of pawpaws.

It was unusually thoughtful of Paula to alert me to pawpaws' moment, much less offer to share her haul—it must have been a truly bountiful year. When I asked where she'd gotten them, she said, "Why the fuck should I tell you?" I tried to think of a reason. I couldn't. Paula then told me about a story the *Washington Post* had run several years earlier on pawpaws. It had listed places where the fruit might be found, including one that happened to be Paula's favorite spot. "Boy, did that fuck things up," she said. "All the yuppies came out to gather the next weekend. And what happened? I get there and half my trees are broken down from these idiots. *They're breaking the tree to get the fruit!* I mean, how shortsighted can you get? That's why I never tell people where I get things. As soon as the public knows they fuck it up.

Every time. They have no respect for the natural world. They don't take what they can eat, they take as much as they can carry, you know?"

In fact, Paula had first showed me flowering pawpaw trees in the woods the day we had found the goose eggs. The slender, spindly trees were common in the fertile floodplains along the Potomac, although I'd never paid them any attention until she pointed them out. Paula said that they needed sufficient rain at just the right time if the trees were to bear fruit. According to her, about half the time that didn't happen. When they did fruit, however, pawpaws, along with wineberries, were at the top of her list of favorites. At the time of our walk, I'd yet to taste one and I didn't encounter the fruit until the next year. Shortly after I'd begun foraging in earnest, I was fishing for smallmouth one Saturday near Harpers Ferry, where the Potomac and Shenandoah rivers converge. As I walked back toward my car along the C&O Canal towpath, I encountered a man coming the other way. He had two fishing rods in one hand and plastic bucket full of green, kidney-shaped fruit in the other: pawpaws. Catching his eye, I pointed with my chin at the bucket. "Gotta show the young-uns," he said. "They'll never even know what's out here unless somebody does." He smiled and went his way.

I entered the next thicket of woods and found a stand of pawpaw trees. The leaves are distinctive, large and widening toward the tip ("obovate," in language of tree ID books). The trees require shade for their first several years, so they start life as an understory tree. I remembered Paula telling me that you harvested pawpaw by shaking the trees—but gently, because they're easily damaged. It wasn't until I shook the third one that a succession of dull thuds announced that half a dozen had hit the forest floor. The last one down, medium-sized, bonked me right in the head. I was lucky. Pawpaws are the largest edible fruit native to the United States, occasionally attaining a weight of two pounds. Fortunately, the one that hit me was a half pounder. It's also fortunate that the things are faily soft when ripe.

I peeled one with my pocketknife and tasted. The flesh was sweet and luscious, fantastic. I tasted bananas, mangoes, and a hint of apple. No wonder its nicknames include "custard apple" and "Michigan banana." It really baffled me that a fruit like this—tropical-tasting, utterly different from any other native fruit I'd ever eaten—grew *here*. And that something so delicious was so utterly unknown.

It turns out that pawpaws, which range from northern Florida to southern Ontario and as far west as eastern Nebraska, were much better known 100 years ago than they are today. The historical record dates to 1541, when Hernando de Soto noted their use among the Indians of the Mississippi Valley. The journals of Lewis and Clark record how pawpaws helped save the explorers from starvation. Interest in them as a commercial crop started in the early 1900s but then waned, and pawpaws more or less disappeared from our culinary radar. The problem was transportability and shelf life. They bruise easily and can go from underripe to rotten in a few days. Pawpaws were a locavore's dream and a fruit wholesaler's nightmare. In short, they had no place in the industrial food economy.

That previous season in Harpers Ferry I had found only a few pawpaws and had eaten each as soon as I found it. With juice dribbling down my chin I pondered my luck in stumbling upon them at precisely the right time. The moment was charged with an odd and surprising power. I'd been foraging long enough to have mistimed almost everything I'd come across, arriving too soon and too late. I'd definitely been late to the party, for example, when it came to making my lawn salad. By the same token, my searches for wineberries, mulberries, figs, and other fruits and nuts often turned up those that were not yet ripe. The berries would be hard and colorless; the nuts, when hulled, green and thin. I'd also had the experience of finding immature fruit, then returning a day or so later to find it past ripe and starting to rot. It had taken me any number of such experiences to truly grasp the merciless speed with which things in nature went from inedibly immature to inedibly old. I'd grown up in a world of supermarket fruit, where all things were uniformly and perpetually ripe. In the wild, the tyranny and contrariness of ripeness were stunning. Maturity took its time arriving, then was gone almost before you could say hello. And there wasn't a damn thing you could do about it except hope to hit it right twelve months later. Shakespeare had nailed it. Ripeness is all.

Now pawpaw season had come back around. Determined to find some on my own, I went prospecting. The woods along the river above Fletcher's were full of the trees, but, once again, I was unfashionably late to the party. Except this time it was other people, rather than nature, that had beaten me to it. I shook but nothing fell. Then I noticed the bent trees and boot prints in the soft dirt. Paula and I obviously weren't the only pawpaw lovers in these parts. The prints were too big to have been hers. I ventured farther upriver, where I managed to shake down a few. But only a few.

The pawpaws I got that day were good all by themselves, especially chilled. But the best way to appreciate them, as far as I was concerned, was the same way I liked wineberries—thoroughly mashed into a bowl of vanilla ice cream. Pawpaws and good vanilla ice cream are made for each other. When I tried substituting them in a recipe for banana bread, though, the result was disappointing. The bread wasn't bad; it just completely lacked flavor. I consulted Paula, who gave me the lowdown. "Cooking destroys the flavor. Completely. Don't ask me why, but it does. Some people say you can freeze 'em, but it's never worked for me. The best thing you can do is just eat 'em, you know?" I told her I'd been looking hard but finding only a few. "Yeah, I know. There's an Oriental guy starts down in Georgetown and goes all the way up the river picking every one he can get. Takes way more than he could ever eat. He's gotta be selling them in a Chinese market somewhere." She asked where I had been looking. When I told her, all she said was to try farther up. Coming from someone as secretive as Paula, this was an act of considerable goodwill.

The next day, following her advice, I stumbled upon a paradise of pawpaws. The trees tend to grow in stands, and once inside the woods I saw stand after stand of virgin trees—no bent branches, no footprints. I shook one of the trees, and half a dozen pawpaws hit the ground, a wave of thuds like someone taking short punches to the stomach. I shook another tree. More thuds. I gathered the pawpaws up and could tell by the smell alone that they were ripe. I ate one on the spot, not even peeling it, just breaking it open and sucking the flesh away from the skin and spitting out the seeds. It was delicious. Abundance mania kicked in, just as it had while I was picking ripe sour cherries or catching perch when they were biting. This was it, the blind hog jackpot, the Pawpaw Convergence. I texted Michelle that I'd just stumbled upon the mother lode. "We could fill a wheelbarrow," I tapped. While I was texting, greed kicked in. In addition to the intensification of consciousness that ripeness and abundance always produced in me, there was, I suddenly realized, also the prospect of easy money. Michelle had already told me she knew chefs who wanted pawpaws, this most local, short-lived, and delicate of fruits. If chefs would pay for what was lying on the ground—more of which required only that I shake the trees—I could make some serious cash. I texted her again, asking where I could unload the most at the best price. She gave me the number of the chef she was friends with at Woodberry Kitchen, widely touted as the best restaurant in Baltimore. I called. The guy said he would take all I could supply. I was so excited that I forgot to either ask his price per pound or suggest one of my own.

There was no time to lose. I left the woods, tore back home, and rummaged through the basement until I found the backpack I'd gotten to take elk hunting years earlier. It was an external frame design, built to carry hunks of disassembled elk long distances. Back in the woods, I collected like the possessed man I'd become. I shook trees until it was too dark to see the fruit on the ground. It was a warm September day and I was sweating heavily. I hadn't stopped to eat or drink since breakfast. Abundance mania rounded off with greed for money had an amphetamine-like ability to suppress appetite and thirst. I was still stoned as a rabbit when I stumbled out of the woods at dark with the loaded pack on my back and sagging trash bags in either hand. I hadn't wanted to put too many pawpaws in the pack for fear of crushing the ones on the bottom. As I stumbled up the path, I found a stick, transferred both bags to one hand, and leaned on the stick for support. I didn't know how many pounds I was carrying; I knew only that I couldn't have carried any more. At the short incline up to the bridge over the canal, I had to stop after each step to catch my breath. I moved and felt like an exhausted climber summiting Everest without oxygen.

I drove straight from the woods to Baltimore, where I unloaded sixty pounds of pawpaw to the chef at Woodberry Kitchen. I probably had another twenty pounds left in the car, but I'd weeded out the ones that were overripe or had gotten damaged during transport. I'd settled on five dollars a pound as my asking price and was surprised when the chef wrote me out a check for $300 without haggling. He'd tasted one pawpaw and found it as delicious as I had. Then, in the manner of chefs, he had immediately begun imagining what he would do with it. "I'm thinking it might go well with organ meats," he mused. In my mania—which had diminished only slightly on the two-hour drive to Baltimore—I forgot to warn him against cooking the fruit. I stopped to use the men's room on my way out and, looking in the mirror, saw why he hadn't dickered about the price. It wasn't just that my face was dirty and scratched, with the blood from a cut—I vaguely remembered smacking myself against a prickly branch—dried to a jagged black line across my brow. The striking thing was my eyes. They weren't mine. There was something desperate and wild in them. They were someone else's eyes. I wouldn't have haggled with me, either. (Later, I found out through Michelle that the guy had tried to cook most of them, with the predictable results. I felt guilty. I should have warned him. On the other hand, maybe we'd both been victims of our own greed.)

After I pocketed the check, the greed and mania loosened their hold markedly. They weren't gone, but I suddenly felt how exhausted I was. I got a double cheeseburger and a chocolate shake at a drive-thru—the forager of nutritious wild foods chowing down on junk—and drove back down I-95 with the windows open to help me stay awake. Once home, I sloughed off my pants, shoes, and shirt; left them where they fell; crawled straight into bed; and collapsed.

I rested the next day, and this turned out to be a mistake. When I returned to my pawpaw paradise the day after that, it had been stripped clean. Someone very thorough had helped himself to the rest of it. I shook tree after tree, until there was no question. I cursed the rat bastard thief, whoever he was. This was my spot. Those had been my pawpaws. (That neither of these statements was, strictly speaking, true, never crossed my mind. Foraging activates deep proprietary instincts.) I was suddenly sure it was the "Oriental" Paula had railed about. Jesus, I thought, you're becoming as racist as Paula. This realization had no effect on my ire. Someone had screwed me, pure and simple. There was no way around it and no cure.

Back home, puttering around in my vegetable garden, I calmed down and tried to process what had possessed me. I knew I'd been consumed by greed of a kind and intensity I'd never experienced before. But I couldn't parse it any further. It was, in Rumsfeldian terms, "a known unknown." On the whole, for example, I'd always felt I was less interested in money than most people. And, even if it that weren't true, it wasn't as though I'd made a killing on the pawpaws, especially when I factored in four hours of driving. On the whole, I was just thankful that the episode was over. I was pretty sure that the experience had cured me of the desire to make a quick buck off wild edibles.

As so frequently happens, I was totally wrong about this. I hadn't told Michelle much about my pawpaw incident except the numbers, sixty pounds of fruit at five bucks a pound. I figured she had plenty of time to find out how venal her new boyfriend could be. A few days later, she called to report that she'd just sold seventeen pounds of hen of the woods to a chef at Clementine, another top Baltimore restaurant. "It's been a crazy good year for mushrooms," she said, asking if I'd seen the recent article about mushrooming in the *Post*. I had. We'd had unusual frequent rains at exactly the right time, followed by humid days with warmer than usual temperatures. All of which just happened to be ideal for many species. I asked her what the chefs were paying. "Ten bucks a pound," she said. She sounded happy, as if she'd simply been lucky to find the mushrooms. I didn't hear any desire—expressed or implied—to go back and see if she could cash in by finding more.

Meanwhile, at the words of "ten bucks a pound," the damn switch, the one that I was glad to have turned off for good, got thrown again. I was aware of it happening. I tried to step in, waving my arms at the train already speeding on its way to the amphetamine high that led me to do stupid things. I didn't want to go there again. And if I needed more good reasons not to, there was this: I had decided early on in my foraging career not to mess with mushrooms. There were just too many lethal kinds. Too many of the names—destroying angel, death cap, dead man's fingers, and, my favorite, poison pigskin puffball—sounded as if they'd been earned the hard way. I knew, however, there were two mushrooms that had the advantages of being "choice"—no serious mushroomer would use a word so pedestrian as "tasty"—large, easily recognized, and lacking in poisonous look-alikes. These were hen of the woods (*Grifola frondosa,* also known by its Japanese name, *maitake*) and chicken of the woods (*Laetiporus sulphureus*). Hens and chickens are completely different species, even though their names are similar. But the relevant points, now that the greed switch had been thrown, were that they were big, plentiful, and going for—hold this thought—ten bucks a pound.

Few people, when asked to name the first thing that comes to mind when they think of the word "big," respond with "mushroom." But individual chickens and hens in excess of 100 pounds have been recorded. A thousand-dollar mushroom, I mused, would be a nice find. Further, while many mushrooms require that you travel long distances to find their preferred habitats, I knew that these two grew locally. I also knew that they grew almost exclusively on trees, especially oak. Michelle was an experienced mushroom hunter. She told me that all the hen of the woods she had ever found had been on oak trees, despite the contention of some mushroom books that they also grew on other deciduous species. Chicken of the woods could grow on oak as well as a number of other trees, but—here's the big thing—only on dead or dying trees. (This made it "saprophytic"—the term for an organism that lives on other dead organic matter.) The mushrooms' growth habit plus their gaudy coloration, anything from orange to salmon pink to yellow, meant

I could also find these and not confuse them with anything potentially lethal. In short, the peculiar characteristics of these two mushrooms—big, easily identifiable, growing on trees I could recognize—were such that I easily circumvented my vow not to mess with mushrooms. Ten bucks a pound!

As far as my abundance mania greed went, I felt like a man suffering from a severe hangover who had just received an invitation to a big party. I wanted to go but didn't want to get hurt. I resolved to go about this rationally and with restraint. I began by asking myself where I could find a lot of oak trees.

Though there were oaks sprinkled throughout any of the woods within striking distance of my house, the trees could be few and far between. Then it hit me: cemeteries. I remembered seeing a great number of oaks in a nearby cemetery while prospecting its overgrown edges for edibles. The cemetery in question had nearly thirty-seven acres of manicured lawn, headstones, and ancient oaks. The place was more or less open to the public. I'd seen dog walkers and joggers using it, and a guy on a bicycle wouldn't seem out of place. I biked over and within half an hour had ten pounds of hens in my backpack. A hundred bucks for half an hour's work. I would spot the mushroom, wait until no one could see me, drop my bike, cut the thing from the base of the tree, and shove it into my backpack. I'd needed just three mushrooms to get the ten pounds and feared that putting any more in would crush what I already had. I took the scenic route on my way out, registering at least another ten pounds' worth on other trees. I considered getting these and putting them in bags (a forager never leaves home without bags), but decided against it. It's harder than it looks to ride a bike with bags hanging from the handlebars, especially through rush hour traffic. It throws your balance off significantly. Much better to come back with a bigger backpack.

I wanted to ride home, dump what I'd taken, and return for the others, but realized that it would be dark by the time I got back. I'd need a flashlight to find them again by that time, and it was likely that the cemetery had a night watchman. Looking for mushrooms by flashlight would probably be a good way to make his acquaintance. Then, inspired by greed, I had an idea. I dropped my bike and pack, cut and bagged the additional hens, and stashed the bags in a trash receptacle by a bench near the gate. I didn't know how often or when the trash can was emptied, but it seemed unlikely that anyone would be coming around before morning. I returned by bicycle two hours later. It was dark but I found the trash can with no trouble. And the mushrooms were right where I'd left them. I went home and weighed my haul. My take tipped the scales at twenty-seven and a half pounds. I called the chef at the restaurant Michelle had mentioned, Clementine, and he summoned me to Baltimore. This time, I told him I couldn't make it until the next day. Fine, he said. The next morning I drove up to the restaurant and, unable to find a parking place, left my car running in the alley behind the restaurant. The chef wasn't there but had left instructions. I walked out five minutes later with a check for $275.

Moneywise, mushrooms were to pawpaws as hedge funds were to construction labor. They were faster, easier, and bigger money. On the drive home, I was already thinking about oaks again. And cemeteries. And then it hit me. Arlington National Cemetery, nearly a square mile of rolling hills and home to some of the biggest, oldest oaks in the D.C. area, was just down the road from me. I had taken out-of-town guests to see the Tomb of the Unknowns, as it's now known. I'd ridden through the cemetery occasionally while biking to and from D.C. Bicycles were permitted, but only on a route that led from a gate inside Fort Myer directly to a gate by Memorial Bridge, which spanned the Potomac into D.C. And so, one crisp October day—it really was turning out to be a lovely autumn—I set out. At the gate, I showed my driver's license to the guard and was waved inside. As I entered the cemetery, another guard told me that I had to stay on Megis Drive, the main road. I assented. Within 200 yards, I had seen six oaks with good clusters of mushrooms, both hens and chickens, at their bases. The effect of this, predictable as it was by this time, still hadn't lost its punch. I was flying on dopamine, epinephrine, and a bunch of other neurotransmitters I desperately hope will soon be available in tablet form. Just then a cemetery patrol car, headed the other way, came to an abrupt stop opposite me. The uniformed driver pointed his finger at me. Shit, I thought as the blood drained from my face, I'm busted. My state of mind was such that I completely forgot that I had yet to commit a crime, that I hadn't so much as touched a mushroom. All I knew was that I'd just been caught. "Helmets are required for all riders," the man said sternly. Helmets? It took me a moment to realize what he was talking about. Then I realized my bicycle helmet had been dangling from the handlebars. At the speeds I was riding, slow enough to see everything I could, it hadn't occurred to me to wear the helmet. The important thing, however, was that I wasn't under arrest. I just needed to get with the dress code. I put my helmet on. I even thanked the officer for reminding me. He told me to have a nice day.

A few hundred yards later, I had verified more mushrooms on trees in three directions. Arlington Cemetery is not a public park. You can't drive through in a private car without authorization. You can't jog or picnic. It was, however, legal to walk pretty much anywhere. So that's what I did. Once no one was looking, I dropped my bike and helmet behind a large headstone where they couldn't be seen from the road and began walking.

As I walked, I tried assuming a contemplative look, as if I were meditating upon the sacrifice of the honored dead beneath the ground. Other times I tried walking as if I were in search of a specific grave, some forebear interred here. I made my way down a hill toward an especially promising row of oaks. As I got closer, it looked as if there were hens or chickens on nearly every tree. The problem—and it was a fairly big one—was that there was a funeral under way not seventy yards off. Whoever was being planted must have done well in the military, because there were three large, wheeled cannons near the grave, each manned by a crew of three ramrod-straight soldiers in full dress uniform. There was also someone commanding the gun crews, as well as twenty or so civilians. The first cannon sounded. They were firing blanks, of course, but it was still one hell of a load of powder. The flame coming out of the muzzle alone was eight feet long, the accompanying plume of black smoke at least twice that. The ground shook at each blast. The firing continued. The plumes of smoke quickly turned into dark, ascending clouds as another cannon fired.

I faced the funeral and its guns even as I moved from tree to tree, assessing the mushrooms. I soon identified the moment immediately after each blast as the most opportune moment to drop, cut a mushroom, and shove it into my pack. I noticed that all the civilians winced then and, once they recovered, focused on the practiced, precise motions of the gun crew as they extracted the spent shell and loaded the next. The first bunch of mushrooms I checked was crawling with bugs, well past its prime. But two others looked good. As I crammed those into my pack, I tried to imagine how the people at the grave site stood the noise of what turned out to be a fifteen-gun salute. I knew I couldn't have. (Later, I learned that fifteen guns were what a three-star general or a vice admiral received. A four-star general or an admiral got seventeen. Only presidents merited twenty-one.) The whole spectacle created so much black smoke that you wondered if the EPA knew about it.

An hour after entering, I left the cemetery with what turned out to be eighteen pounds of hens and chickens. I felt guilty about having collected mushrooms in a cemetery devoted to men and women who had honorably served their country. I decided not to compound that shame by selling them. At least not personally. I ended up giving the mushrooms to Michelle, who assured me she had chefs lined up to buy them. Did that lessen my crime? Not really.

And that was it. Only after I'd given Michelle the mushrooms did I realize the full extent of what foraging for profit had done to me. I had desecrated a national shrine, an action that, in addition to being unthinkably rude, carried potential legal consequences. (I have since found out that, according to Title 32, Chapter V, Subchapter D, Part 553, Section 553.22, Definition 7 (e) of the Code of Federal Regulations, "No person shall willfully destroy, damage, mutilate or remove any monument, gravestone, structure, tree, shrub, plant or other property located within the Cemetery grounds." A lawyer might find a fungal loophole somewhere in that language, but the thrust of it is pretty clear. I was fairly sure that "abundance mania greed" was not a recognized disorder, let alone one on which a temporary-insanity defense could be based.) More generally, I simply didn't like what I was willing to do to get sellable wild plants, or how it changed foraging and forager. Foraging for cash brought no lasting joy. The fun of foraging, clichéd as it may sound, really was in the process, the hunt. You found things or you didn't; the stuff you found was ripe or not; you knew what to do with it or didn't. But there were palpable satisfactions in those actions and that process, no matter what the outcome was. Once you injected money into it, the process went out the window. Nothing mattered but the results, measurable in pounds and ounces, dollars and cents.

I knew that Michelle sold edibles fairly regularly. She had chefs who wanted mushrooms, pawpaw, crabapples, cherries, wineberries, black-berries, stinging nettles, pokeweed, and more. As a not-yet-divorced mom who had to pay rent as well as feed and clothe two boys, she needed money a lot more than I did. And yet the money part never got its hooks into her the way it had with me. She kept her perspective. At least that's how it seemed. I never brought the subject up directly, although we touched on it a few times in other conversations. I wondered if it had to do with the fact that Michelle had a lot of other things going on in her life: a wider circle of friends and social life, organizations like Food Makers, volunteering at her sons' schools. I was much more of a loner. I never got a handle on which of us was the exception and which the rule. The truth was that I didn't want to turn that rock over and look too deeply at it. I had a pretty good hunch which one of us had the more balanced life and outlook.

The more I thought about it, the more it seemed that Paula had the sanest attitude toward foraging. From what I know, she seemed to have two categories of foraging. Some edibles were staples, things she collected in quantity, processed, and stored for year-round use. These included black walnuts, chestnuts, hickory nuts, wineberries, apples, figs, pears, and peaches. But there were others—pawpaw, mushrooms, persimmons, sour cherries, most greens—that she didn't preserve. She either collected these to eat that evening or simply grazed on them as she made her rounds about the woods. I still didn't know whether selling foraged edibles simply never occurred to her or whether she avoided it because it went against her own code of ethics. And, as I noted, it was possible that even Paula might have been bought for the right price. But I did come to believe her two basic tenets on wild edibles. One was that once the public heard about something, they fucked it up, tore it down, and otherwise ruined it every time. So you never told where you found things. Second, if you were going to take things from the woods, you took only as much as you could eat, not as much as you could carry. It wasn't really that complicated. It was mostly common sense. Why these lessons were so hard for me to learn is a question for which I have no answer. Except perhaps, as I had more than once overheard Paula telling people, "Heavey does some pretty stupid shit for a smart guy."

KIRK (AND CAMILLA)'S MONKEYFACE EEL

Kirk writes, "I do very little cooking in this place. Except for breakfast and the occasional chili, Fishwife does it all. I'm mainly in charge of catching. Here is the recipe for Monkeyface Eel from the annals of Lombardia:

"Using high-quality American duct tape, affix unfurled wire hanger to the end of a bamboo stick, such that at least 14 inches of it protrude from the end. Make a loop at the tip of the wire, tie 2/0 Octopus hook to loop using 3 inches of 80-lb. test. Skewer small piece of squid on hook. Poke under rocks at low tide. Catch eel. Put in sack. Transport to cleaning station. Put eel out of misery (good luck with this). Fillet eel "off the skin." Or skin first and then fillet. I prefer the former. If the filleted and skull-cracked carcass now crawls across the counter, you can either continue with your vain attempts to put it out of its misery or throw it in the garbage.

"Take your two elongated strips of eel fillet, cut them in half. Then follow these instructions, provided by Fishwife:"

1 cup each: chopped basil leaves and Italian parsley
2 large cloves of garlic, crushed
Zest and juice from half a lemon
¼ cup olive oil
Olive tapenade (or chopped olives)
4 monkeyface fillets (2 large fillets halved)
Asparagus
Summer squash
Salt & pepper

Combine basil, garlic, lemon zest and juice, and olive oil in a bowl and mix well. Whip out a sheet of tinfoil large enough to enclose one of your fillets. Place the fish in the center, smear some basil mixture on it, and wrap into a secure parcel with the foil. Repeat with all the fillets, dividing the mixture evenly. Place on a baking tray, set aside for a sec. (If the fillets crawl across the table at this point, you can attempt to bludgeon them until they are truly, truly dead . . . or you can just go ahead and cook them).

Turn on the broiler. Trim the bottom of your asparagus and chop your summer squash into thick slices. Toss with olive oil, spread out on a baking sheet and sprinkle with salt, pepper, the lemon zest from the second half of your lemon, and squeeze a little juice on there too. Broil until vegetables begin to color, shake the pan a little, toss, then move the veggie pan lower in the oven and reduce heat to 400 degrees.

Pop your fish tray into the oven in the middle rack, bake for 10 minutes (depending on the thickness of your fillets), or until the flesh flakes easily when tested with a fork. Place the opened parcels on serving plates with the veggies, and serve! *Mwah!* Monkeyface never tasted so good.

Chapter Eight:
"You Don't Want to Grab Anything Has Red Eyes"

It was a screwy year for crawfish, Jody reported when I called in January about coming back down. "Water's not there," he said. Most years, the snowmelt from the rest of the country starts raising the water level in the Basin as early as the beginning of the calendar year. So far, that hadn't happened. When I called in February, it still hadn't happened. He'd passed the time "hunting and skinning gators." This was the first I'd heard of this particular sideline. "Oh, yeah," he said. "I do wild, farmed, whatever needs skinning. Usually in the winter. It's piecework. I can do twenty-five farmed gators—they slaughter 'em when they're between four and six feet—an hour. That's faster than anybody I know except the ole boy that taught me, Richard Robin." He pronounced the last name as a Frenchman would, Roh-*ban*. "Richard can do thirty. Watching that boy skin is like poetry, Bill. He doesn't look like he's going fast, you know? But he makes every motion count. That's the secret to it. That and a sharp Dexter-Russell knife—got a white handle on it. And hand strength. You do need that."

Finally, at the end of March, Jody called to say it was time. The water was starting to rise, nature's signal to crawfish to emerge from their winter holes and get busy feeding, molting, and mating. "I'm on the road headed to the processor right now with twenty sacks," Jody said, sounding happy as a kid just freed from school for the summer. I asked how many pounds of crawfish a sack held. About forty, he said. The man had 800 pounds of wild crawfish in his boat. I booked a flight that night. I was hoping to bring Michelle along a few days later, but I wanted to scope things out first.

At Jody's house in Henderson, I happened upon something you don't see every day: swamp people watching *Swamp People*. The History Channel's hit reality show about alligator hunting in the Atchafalaya Basin was playing in the background as Jody, Tracy, and Bryce, their fifteen-year-old, were finishing up a dinner of fried wild turkey tenders and fried potatoes. On the TV, Troy, the show's alpha gator hunter, was driving his boat and talking into the camera about the big gator he was hunting. The Meche family took a clear interest in the show, but Jody wanted to educate me about a few things. "Some of those boys are okay, but a lot of 'em really Cajun it up for the cameras, you know what I'm saying? Troy makes out like he's just a poor swamper. Lemme tell you, he was brought up with money. His father runs a gas station and bait shop and is also a crawfish buyer. He doesn't know what it's like to be out there fishing, having to depend on his prop not breaking if he's gonna make his money."

The other thing was that you had to be rich to even get a gator license in Louisiana. "You have to be a landowner with certified wetland habitat property even to apply," Jody explained. "So you got to suck up to those people if you want to hunt gators. And that's what Troy does." Jody also faulted the way gators were purposely agitated to make them thrash and bite for the cameras. "And those scenes where they show guys sticking their hands in the water with a big gator on the line? Tell you something, podnah. You wouldn't do that unless you tired of having two hands."

There was one other surprise. Rather than go crawfishing, we were to go frogging the next day. In the Basin, just as at home, ripeness was king. And Jody knew a spot where the frogs were plentiful. As it happened, tomorrow was March 31, the last day you could legally take the amphibians. Frog season is open nearly year-round in Louisiana, closing only during April and May so the frogs can mate unmolested. Actually, it had been Richard Robin, Jody's alligator-skinning buddy, who had told Jody of the spot. Last night, he had caught 200 there, which he'd sold to a wholesaler for two dollars each. I asked Jody if taking 200 frogs from an area wouldn't leave slim pickings for us. He exchanged looks with his wife and son before Bryce could no longer keep a straight face. Clearly, I didn't know frogs. Jody was just barely able to keep from laughing. "I wouldn't worry too much about that, Bill," Jody was finally able to say.

While it was possible to catch frogs all year, he continued, late winter and early fall were best. Late winter was good because the water lilies hadn't greened up yet and it was easy to spot the frogs. Late summer and early fall were good because the water in the Atchafalaya Basin usually fell then, concentrating the frogs. Ideally, you wanted days that were warm but not too warm, followed by nights that were cool but not too cool. "Frogs feed on the crawfish under the lilies right after dusk," Jody explained. "If the day's warm, they'll be hungry and active when they start hunting at dusk. Then, when they're full, they float to the surface and kinda lie there. If it's cool, that makes them sluggish and easier to catch." The next day's forecast called for a day-time high in the mid-eighties, dropping to the mid-sixties after dark. Jody reckoned we'd have have excellent frogging.

And so the next night found Jody, Bryce, and me in the drive-thru line at McDonald's for dinner before we headed out. This was consistent with my outings with other serious foragers. Just as the cobbler's children had no shoes, the forager of choice edibles often ate junk food. As we inched forward in the drive-thru, Jody decided that this was as good a time as any to start my frogging education.

I'd already been surprised to learn that most of the Basin's froggers, Jody included, didn't use gigs, spears, or mechanical grabbers of any kind, although many such devices were sold at Hebert's, the local gas-grocery-bait-beer-ice-ammunition quick-stop. Jody grabbed frogs with his hands. For one thing, he said, mechanical grabbers usually killed the frog. A dead frog required ice, and ice required cash. Between all the critters Jody trapped, shot, and caught and then had to keep cold long enough in southern Louisiana to get them where they needed to be before they spoiled, he already spent more on ice per year than he cared to add up. A grabbed frog could be kept alive for days if covered with nothing more than a wet gunny sack. Furthermore, gigs and mechanical grabbers cost money and could be damaged, get left in the truck, or be dropped overboard. Whereas nobody ever forgot their hands. We finally made it to the squawk box and shouted our orders at it.

I knew that you located frogs by shining lights on them, since their eyes reflected the light, but had no idea how this was actually done. Jody kept hard hats with "sealed beams" on the boat for this purpose. Once he spotted a frog, he'd drive the boat over. If possible, he'd try to put the frog on my strong side, my right. My job was to kneel in the front of the boat and be ready to grab the frog. Jody wasn't sure whether the light stunned the frogs or if they simply had too much faith in their natural camouflage. Either way, a frog generally let you get pretty close before it dived.

"Now, Bill," Jody said, and his changed tone of voice indicated that we had come to the crux of the lesson. "You got to remember something when you go to grab that frog tonight." He paused to let me know that what he was telling me was important. "You're not petting that frog," he said. "You're not slapping that frog. You got to . . ." He pressed his lips together, searching for something—an image, a prop—that would illustrate his point. His eye came to rest on an empty Styrofoam coffee cup in the truck's holder. "You got to *grab* that frog." With these words, his right fist shot out like a striking snake, seized the cup, and crushed it so quickly and completely that it basically exploded inside the cab. The noise alone was extraordinary. Even Jody looked surprised, as if he hadn't intended the demonstration to be as violent as this.

"Well, okay then," I said, as bits of suspended Styrofoam whirled slowly down, the cab of the truck transformed into a Louisiana snow-globe. "I think I get it." I couldn't think of anything else to say. It was Bryce who finally rescued us from the awkward silence.

"You got to excuse my dad, Mr. Bill," he said. "He just gets excited about frogging. He really just wants you to have a good time out there." Jody nodded, as if happy to have an interpreter. That was exactly what he wanted, for me to have a good time.

Bryce said there was one other thing. "Mr. Bill, if it seems like my dad's getting impatient or upset with you out there, he's really not. It's just the excitement." I thanked Bryce for telling me that and told him I wasn't worried in the least. This was a total lie.

We got Bryce's order, dropped him at home—frogging is a nighttime deal, and Bryce had school the next day—and headed down the road to the ramp, about eight miles away. I asked if there would be gators where we'd be frogging. "Oh, yeah," Jody says. "Lotta gators. Most of 'em are small, six feet or less, but there are a few big ones around. They'll be out, hunting frogs same as us." He continued talking but I was too busy trying to look unconcerned to take in any more information. I was still trying to process this part and pick a sudden-onset illness—influenza, ptomaine poisoning, acute hypochondria—that would get me off the hook. When I finally checked back in a few minutes later, Jody was still talking. He was saying that frog eyes are white, or sort of greenish, and harder to spot than gator eyes, which were red, as I had already seen while duck hunting. "You don't want to grab anything has red eyes," he said. Right, I thought. No grabbing red eyes.

At a boat ramp fifteen miles east of Henderson along I-10, Jody backed the skiff off the trailer, jumped in, and ran the boat up on the bank, walking the four-inch gunwale forward with a grace you wouldn't expect in a guy built like Jody. Thirty-five feet overhead, trucks rumbled and hummed along the I-10. I'd learned by this time not to be fooled by comfortable temperatures. I bundled up in a hooded slicker for the twenty-five-minute run to our destination, a place named Upper Billy Little Lake. Then, in the rear of the skiff, Jody donned a hard hat and clipped its two wires to a twelve-volt car battery at his feet. Then the night went away. Jody had become a minor god, his headlamp sending out a beam of light you could have hung clothes on. "Jesus, Jody!" I blurted. "You look like the Statue of Liberty. What the hell is that thing?"

"Just a regular sealed beam," he said. "Everybody down here wears 'em at night in the swamp. Comes with a GE 4405."

"What's a GE 4405?" I asked.

"Bulb that comes in the standard unit. It's pretty good. But I put in a TC 7512."

"Which is?"

"The navigation light they use on airplanes." Leave it to a Cajun.

He gunned the engine and we were flying down a canal directly below the highway, a waterway straight as a rifle barrel. Jody's light darted everywhere as he pursued his favorite on-the-water activity— looking for critters. Night just meant that he looked for the reflective eyes of deer, turtles, frogs, and gators, rather than the critters themselves. The light was jumping around so fast I had to look away to keep from getting disoriented.

We turned into a smaller, twistier waterway, then into one smaller and twistier still. Jody called such things "roads" but they reminded me of the four-wheeler trails we'd ridden to get to his duck hole. During the day, he said, this was where he crawfished. He and a few other crawfishermen kept this road open with chain saws and regarded it more or less as theirs. Then the scenery changed. We were slaloming between broad-trunked cypress trees dangling Spanish moss just so, as if both trees and moss had been placed by set designers. It was ridiculously scenic, a living Discovery Channel backdrop. I kept reminding myself that it wasn't a theme park.

Jody throttled down and the boat settled into the water. I put on the helmet and clipped the wires to the battery at my feet the same way Jody had. Now my forehead cast its own godlike light. Meanwhile, Jody had already begun calling out frogs. "Little one over there, two more over there. Little gator by that log." I registered one of the frogs but had trouble seeing the others. Then I made out the glowing red embers of a gator. I remembered the inch-to-the-foot rule—the space between a gator's eyes, in inches, equals its length in feet—from duck hunting. This gator was as big as I was. "They're not afraid of the light, are they?" I tried to say casually. "Not most of 'em," he replied. "Nice frog by that brush there." Jody was clearly unconcerned about gators.

"Ooh, good frog!" Jody called excitedly. "See him?" He illuminated a bush sticking up among lilies. I caught a momentary flicker, then lost it. "Gonna put him on your right side, Bill. Get ready now." I still saw no frog. "He's right in the middle of my light," Jody said. Maybe so, but it was a big circle of light. "He's right there!" Jody said, exasperation creeping into his tone. "*Right next to the boat!*" At last I saw the frog, motionless in the pads, all of eighteen inches away. The damn thing was the size of a rotisserie chicken. I wasn't sure my hand would fit around him far enough to keep him even if I did manage the grab. With no time to waste, I stabbed down at the animal. The frog executed a single, almost languorous kick. I caught a glimpse of his fully extended legs as he dived. They looked as long as the distance from my elbow to my fingertips. The swamp must have been contaminated by some nearby nuclear power plant. There were Godzilla frogs, freaks of nature, breeding in the swamp.

"Aw, Bill, you got to be more aggressive," Jody said sadly. "You're not trying to be his buddy. That's your frog, know what I'm saying? He can't hurt you. And they're tough. You don't have to worry about squeezing him too hard."

"Okay," I said. "Okay." I knew that I'd blown that one. I was nodding my head now, psyching myself up. Jody had been right. You couldn't half-ass this frog grabbing. You had to commit. The truth was that I was more afraid of disappointing Jody than anything else.

Meantime, Jody had already spotted another one. "Good frog," Jody said. "See him? I'm gonna put this one on your left side, Bill."

"I don't see him," I said.

"Right there. Right in the middle of my light." Jody's voice had become patient, as if he were talking to a retarded person. I was thankful for this, since it was what I had become over the past few minutes. "Look in the middle of my light," he said.

"I'm looking, I just don't . . ."

"Right in the middle of my light!" Jody repeated, but his patience had run out, his tone suggesting that Stevie Wonder would have seen the frog by now. And then I did see it. This frog was actually a bit less huge than the last one. I resolved to nail it or die trying. As the boat glided silently forward I leaned until I was halfway out of the boat, feet hooked under the seat for leverage, arm cocked and ready, gauging our speed and the moment to strike. When we were a foot away, I pounced. I grabbed the frog at the narrow point across its back—the waist, if frogs could be said to have such a thing—and plucked it from the water. It was so big that even at its waist I couldn't touch my thumb to any of my other fingers. This was when I discovered that I didn't have the waist after all. I had part of the body and part of one leg. And the rubbery creature was kicking hard to get free. I clutched the frog to my belly with both hands.

"There you go, podnah!" Jody laughed. "Now you froggin'!" I staggered aft and transferred the frog to Jody, who slipped it into a crawfish trap, a rectangular envelope of rubber-coated wire mesh. I looked down at the frog, sitting suddenly motionless save for the fast, faint thrumming of its throat. A pang—guilt, remorse, or both—suddenly coursed through me. I didn't really want to kill this thing. "He looks so . . . cute," I stammered out.

"He'll look even cuter fried up on my plate, podnah!" Jody shot back. "Hoo!"

My grabbing average picked up and I started gaining confidence. Then I grabbed a frog that felt dead, or at least deathly sick. It went limp when I grabbed it and remained so in my hand. "This guy's hurting," I started to say. It was at that moment that the frog, sensing the lessening of hand pressure, made its move, leaping out of my hand and onto the deck, where it continued jumping hard, doing its best to vault over the side of the boat. I was angry at the frog for trying to trick me. I practically fell on the thing, pinning it with both hands. As I struggled, I heard Jody's deep laugh. "That's one of Mr. Frog's best tricks!" he said. "He'll play dead until whatever's got him drops its guard." Well, good for Mr. Frog, I thought. Because Billy Heavey's not dropping his guard again.

We cruised on, the slough opening into a lake. By now, I was thinking of myself as a deadly predator, the John Rambo of frogging. Each frog down there was *my* frog, dammit, something I owned by virtue of having laid eyes on it. Soon I was catching nearly every frog I tried for. Being good at something new was an unusual but not at all disagreeable sensation. "You're doing real good, Bill," Jody said at one point. "You've got an interestin' motion. I sort of smash-grab, you know. I'll push that frog down another six inches when I grab him. But you sorta pluck him out. Almost like an eagle." The degree of relief and pride I felt at these words was shameful. Here I was, a grown man and experienced outdoorsman. I had caught a 150-pound tarpon in Nicaragua, killed a bull elk with a single arrow in Colorado. I had been a father. I had survived an IRS audit. But at that particular moment, there was nothing I wanted more than to be counted a good frogger by Jody Meche.

At a certain moment, Jody brought the boat alongside a four-foot gator floating motionless in the water. He threw the boat into neutral, walked forward, and stared down at it. The gator never moved a muscle. Finally, with a grimace, Jody shook his head. I asked what he was doing. "I wanted to show you how you can pick a gator up. You grab them across the back of the neck and it sorta paralyzes 'em. This gator's just a little too big, though. And if you don't get him just right you got a pissed-off gator in the boat." He seemed genuinely saddened not to be able to demonstrate.

"Oh, that's okay, Jody," I said as airily as I could while contemplating how much I had enjoyed having ten fingers. "I expect we'll find another one."

I didn't know what time it was or how long we'd been out, but I was tired and soaked. Jody reckoned that we'd bagged about thirty-five frogs, averaging a little more than a pound each. It was plenty for a frog fry. And we still had a good run back to the ramp and back to Henderson. He asked if I was ready to go.

"Yeah, I'm ready," I said. "My ass is wet." For some reason this remark cracked Jody up.

The next morning I was back at Jody's house to help butcher, a process I felt obligated to learn if I was going to eat what I'd caught. Jody had

217

covered the trap with a wet tarp, beneath which the frogs sat atop each other listlessly. When he picked up the trap to move it to the cutting board he'd laid across an empty boat trailer, some of the frogs began to mew, like cats, but louder and more plaintively. The sound was unearthly. Frogs have a brain that weighs less than three-tenths of a gram. It's a stretch to think of them as having particularly complex emotions. But those frogs knew this was not going to be a good day.

Jody was set up for business, wearing foul weather bibs and with a garden hose at the ready. He had his Gerber pocketknife, a sharpening steel, a set of pliers designed to pull the skin off catfish, an empty bucket for frog guts, and another bucket filled with water ready to receive the finished frogs.

For my benefit, he narrated as he worked. "You gotta get rough with him first," he said, plucking a frog from the trap. "You grab his front legs, pull 'em back, and kinda push his head flat on the board." He pinned the frog and sawed its head off with a quick push-pull of the knife. The frog cartilage crunched and the head rolled six inches before it stopped and fell over, landing in such a way that it was looking back at its own body with a disinterested gaze.

"Then you cut the legs at that last joint," Jody said, "the one just up from the foot." He started with the right front foot and turned the frog counterclockwise as he cut the other three, his movements deft and precise. "You gotta spin that frog," he said happily. With the legs removed, he inserted two fingers between the loose skin and the frog's back to make room for the pliers, which he then inserted, and stripped the back skin off in a single, long pull. He did the same thing on the frog's other side, then removed the diaphragm and innards with his hands, tossing all this into the gut bucket.

"Your last move is to split the pelvic bone, same as you would a deer. It takes a little strength," he said, pressing until the faint crack came. "And there," he said, tossing it into the water, "is your frog."

I watched him do three or four and then said I needed to try it. I tried to steel myself with the knowledge that a cute bullfrog will eat any animals it can swallow, including rodents, turtles, snakes, birds, and smaller bullfrogs. I closed my eyes for the first beheading. I forced myself not to think as I cut the legs at the first joint.

By my third frog, I found—in a strange mixture of relief and shame —that it hardly bothered me at all to be dispatching frogs. It's extraordinary how quickly humans can become desensitized to barbarism, especially when the stomach is involved. One thing that helped was that the process of butchering required a lot of attention. I really didn't have time to empathize. It took me five times as long to do a frog as it did Jody, which gave me a new appreciation of just how skilled he was.

I knew that it was hard for Jody to watch, although for completely different reasons. He wasn't squeamish. He just couldn't stand to watch somebody do something he could do quicker and better. It was killing him to stand idle and watch my learning curve. Once he had the knife back in his hands, he became his old self. "You got to *spin* that frog!" he'd call cheerfully as the frog's limbs seemed to detach and flee of their own accord. In twenty minutes, the thirty-five frogs were done. He hefted the bucket. "Aw, Bill, we're gonna eat good tonight, podnah!" he said.

We had the meal at the house of Mike Bienvenu, the crawfisherman who had first hooked me up with Jody. We arrived to find that Mike had already cooked up some of the frogs in a rich sauce piquant, which we ate over rice, savoring the light, sweet meat and the sauce and picking out the tiny bones. There were also fried frog legs, which had the same flavor but also a kind of riverine bass note, wild and clean. I was developing a serious taste for frog. I was in the kitchen, tucking into seconds of both kinds—for research purposes, naturally—when I heard laughter out back. Jody was telling the group how tentative I'd been at first and how I'd taken to it as the night went on. "He was leaning so far out the boat I thought he was going in," Jody said. "But he wanted that frog. Yeah, ole Bill was grabbing 'em pretty good. After about an hour and a half, I asked if he was ready to go, and he says—get this—'Yeah, my ass is wet.'" Jody clapped and laughed his big laugh and everybody else laughed, too. I guess having a wet ass comes with the job if you make your living off the swamp. At that moment, however, I felt pretty satisfied. I was soaking up the last bits of frog and sauce piquant on my plate with one hand and had a cold beer in the other. I had a dry ass. And I had acquitted myself honorably as a novice frogger.

A call later that night brought good news. Michelle had found a cheap last-minute flight to Lafayette and would be down the next day. I'd already asked about her coming and Jody said that would be fine, as crawfishing had slacked off a bit since he'd called me and there would be plenty of room. "If it was later in the season and I was catching fifty or sixty sacks a day, it might be a problem. But we'll be fine," he said. "I just want y'all to see it."

Two days later, Michelle and I met Jody at his house at nine a.m., piled into his truck, and headed back to the same ramp we'd used when frogging. We stopped at a bait wholesaler along the way and picked up four 40-pound boxes of frozen fish. The boxes bore the logo of Lund's Fisheries of Cape May, New Jersey. I asked what kind of fish they were and Jody said, "We call 'em 'bunker.' It's a real oily kinda fish." He already had a couple of big yellow bags of a dry crawfish bait—Crusty Chunks, a Purina product. I'd never considered that there might be money to be made manufacturing crawfish bait, but there obviously was. Jody liked to use both kinds in his traps. Fish had the stronger smell, while the Crusty Chunks lasted longer. Jody figured he owned about 1,400 traps in all, enough for four or five "runs," or the number he could handle in an average day. He had only two runs out at the moment. The one we were going to do had been sitting for two days.

Jody was clearly happy to be crawfishing again, singing snatches of songs as he sorted his gear. We launched and twenty minutes later were deep in the same narrow, twisting roads we'd been on two nights earlier. In daylight, I noted bits of pink flagging tape dangling from bushes every twenty yards or so. These marked Jody's traps, each of which was secured to the bush by a string. Jody uses "pillow" traps, which might more properly be called "pillowcase" traps, since they're closed at one end and open at the other and fold almost flat. They're made of vinyl-coated wire mesh and typically measure about two feet wide by three feet long. The traps are dumped and then rebaited through the open end, which is usually then shut with nothing more elaborate than a clothespin. Inset in the other, "closed" end were two inverted mesh funnels. It's through these that crawfish, drawn by the smell of the bait, found their way into the trap. The funnels were constructed in such a way that once a crawfish was inside, it was possible but highly unlikely that it would find its way out again.

Jody wore foul weather bibs against the muck and slime of the traps, even though the temperature was already in the eighties by ten a.m. Before him as he stood in the back of the boat was a squarish metal tray with sides about five inches tall. The edge facing him had no side. It was open and had a sort of throated hole just before the edge. It was down this hole that all the keeper crawfish went, into a plastic mesh sack, just like the kind you buy potatoes in, which tied to the throat. I'd already told Jody that I wanted to help and had been assigned the job of baiter. I sat facing aft on the middle seat, facing the tray. I'd been told to rebait each trap with half a frozen bunker and a handful of Crusty Chunks, which bore an unfortunate resemblance to large dog turds.

At the first flagged bush, Jody threw the boat into neutral and hoisted the trap by its string. As it reached the waterline, he gently pushed away the surface scum so it wouldn't coat the trap's mesh, hoisted the trap, undid the clothespin, put it into his mouth, and dumped the trap onto the tray. Out clattered half a dozen crawfish, their claws spread wide and high and like little gunfighters ready to take on whatever this new world might portend. Each dumping also delivered a fine spritz of swamp water and bait slime into my face. Along with the catch came the partially eaten baitfish and its skeleton, muck, bits of vegetation, a baby catfish, and a few snails. Occasionally, Jody said, he pulled up a water moccasin, but he said this in a way that suggested the foulest-tempered of North American venomous snakes posed no special hazard. Jody projected such confidence and mastery that you felt like such a snake ought to be grateful that Jody didn't bite *it*. He quickly sorted the catch, hurrying the keepers along and down the hole and discarding everything else over the side. Then, in an almost courtly gesture, he dipped the open end of the trap toward me to rebait. I tossed the bait in and he carefully lined the trap back into place. "You always have to set that trap so it's leaning against something," he explained. "If you set it flat on the bottom, the crawfish can't get to the funnels and into the trap. They don't need a lot of room, but they need some."

We moseyed along the twisting road, the sun beating down on us. Michelle sat in the bow and watched. I'd learned after the first few times to turn my face when he dumped the trap and avoid the spritz. After twenty traps, we had less than half a bag of crawfish. Jody admitted that this was uncommonly slow crawfishing, but didn't seem disappointed by it. "It's early," he said. "It'll get better in a few days." At one point, maybe an hour in, Jody complimented me on my work. "You doing real good, Bill," he said. "You're turning into a real master baiter." As soon as he said it, I realized that every person who had ever done the job must have had to endure this pun. I tried to give a good-natured groan, but my heart wasn't in it.

A little later, Jody called my attention to the water. "See how still this water is? All that scum? How low the visibility is? That water should be moving. Current is what keeps this place alive. What you see here is what those spoil ridges do."

The day got hotter. Michelle and I had somehow neglected to have anything but coffee before coming out and had brought neither water nor food. Jody didn't seem to have brought any, either. Unlike us, he didn't seem to mind. He wasn't even sweating, while Michelle and I were both sweating just from being out under the unmitigated sun. We were also hungry, thirsty, and—as much as we hated to admit it—thoroughly bored. We'd both been looking forward to going out with Jody. The unfortunate reality, however, was that the charms of crawfishing were lost on us.

On a really good day, Jody went on, he might get fifty sacks, close to a ton of crawfish. But the wholesale price fluctuated with the supply.

When the crawfish were scarce, the price might go to $1.50 or $1.75 a pound. When the crawfish were running thick, the price might drop to 50 or 75 cents. Like virtually all crawfishermen, Jody had a complicated relationship with Bayou Land Seafood, his regular buyer. "They were paying $1.50 a pound yesterday, but were making noises about dropping it to $1.25 or even a dollar." This was unusual for so early in the season, he said, when the crustaceans weren't especially plentiful. "The price should be higher. They're selling everything they can get, Bill. You can bet your last dollar on that. They always make money. They're not supposed to, but they all talk to each other and set the price. And they know we've got to take it." But if it dropped to a dollar a pound, Jody would sit it out until the price went up or the crawfish started running heavier. "The way it is now, I'm working all day to lose money by the time you figure in your overhead." Jody's overhead—which includes bait for 250 to 400 traps a day, gas for the boat and the truck, depreciation on the truck and boat, and the traps themselves—runs 25 or 30 percent of his total take. Jody says there have been times when no processors would buy his crawfish because he argued with them about the price and tried to organize other crawfishermen to do the same. "But I'm older now. I've learned to keep my mouth shut a little better."

The day wore on, the temperature rising. The water intensified the sun's power and there was nothing tall enough out here to offer any shade. Michelle and I were both working on robust sunburns. I was sweating heavily. And I wasn't even standing up, much less sweltering inside waterproof bibs. How Jody could come out here day after day, on his feet and slinging traps for eight hours in ninety-five-degree heat and 90 percent humidity, was beyond me.

"You get used to it," Jody said when I asked if it didn't wear him out. "You have to." He'd had pain in his shoulder last year, which his doctor diagnosed as a rotator cuff injury. Jody finally traced the problem to the way he was shaking traps over the sorting tray. "I was sorta trying to throw the crawfish out," he said, and demonstrated, shaking the trap as if trying to expel salt from a giant shaker. "When what I should have been doing was just rattling it." He demonstrated again, a motion more like grabbing someone by the lapels and shaking him.

For the life of me, I couldn't understand what Jody loved about this work. He had already told me that he could make better money bending metal tubing on oil and gas lines. He shrugged, saying he did that work when he had to. "But they're not the healthiest places to work, you know what I'm saying? Some of them expose you to a lot of chemicals. And I get bored doing the same thing after a while."

Really? I thought. And what, I asked, did he call lifting and re-baiting 300 traps a day? I winced inwardly when I heard the note of frustration that had crept into my voice. I hadn't intended it to be so obvious. Jody heard it, too. His face didn't change, but he set down the trap he was handling—something he hadn't done all day—and took a moment before answering. It reminded me of the long silence after I'd asked Mike Bienvenu how he kept fighting for crawfishermen's rights when the system was so corrupt.

"We're only five hundred yards or so from where we hunted those ducks in the fall, Bill," he finally said quietly. "You know that?" I said I didn't. I felt suddenly and deservedly chastened. The ramp where we'd launched was twenty miles from the one we'd used when we went duck hunting. I'd have thought we were at least that far from that cypress trunk blind and the narrow lake where Jody had shot the ducks. Everything out here looked pretty much the same to me. To Jody, every inch of it probably distinct. This man had graciously offered to show me the work closest to his heart and I'd all but insulted him. He was too sure of who he was and where he was from to take offense, but I'd clearly shown the limits of my understanding.

"Every day out here's different," he said. "You might hardly make your expenses one day and catch so many crawfish the next that you have to make two runs just to get 'em all back to the truck." Besides, he liked working outdoors, liked being his own boss, liked not having anything but the weather, water, and crawfish telling him what to do. He liked seeing the critters and being attuned to their rhythms and ways, how the birds and mammals would be active one day and not the next. I knew that Jody was counted the best of the thirty or so hunters who belonged to the hunting camp. It wasn't surprising that he was a good hunter. He lived a good part of his waking hours out here. He knew where the deer hid when the season opened and the swamp was suddenly full of rifle fire and men who came only a few days a year to hunt. He knew where the turkeys liked to roost and loaf and feed, when and where the first ducks tended to come in the fall. He'd told me how one member of the hunting club had recently offered $300 for Jody to "guide" him and his son deer hunting. "What they really want is to know my secret spots," Jody explained. "Not for sale, podnah!"

What Jody was all about, I realized, was the act of being hooked up to the swamp, relating to it over the seasons of each year, feeling its rhythms. To me, on this hot day, the swamp seemed a static thing, and hauling crawfish traps was mind-dulling, repetitive work. To Jody, it was a chance to see how the swamp felt on a particular day. And I suppose that once you got tuned in, no two days were exactly alike.

I knew he couldn't get lost out here but wondered if he ever got afraid, working alone so far from help. He frowned, perplexed, as if the very question struck him as odd. He did say that he sometimes worried about being in an aluminum boat when a thunderstorm came up quickly, not an uncommon event in summer. Or about a lightning strike felling a tree onto the boat. But that was really it as far as his personal safety went. His greatest fear was what he might do if he surprised someone else in the act of robbing his traps. It had never happened to Jody, but it did happen. "I'm not near as hotheaded as I used to be," he said. "But something like that, a man stealing my living . . ." he left the thought unfinished as he pulled up another trap. Jody was powerfully built, surprisingly deft in his movements, and exceptionally strong. I'd seen him waltz with perfect ease down the three-inch catwalk from bow to stern with a full ice chest on his shoulder. The thing had to have weighed 150 pounds. I'd never seen him speak to anyone with the slightest edge in his voice. But you also got the sense that you wouldn't want to get on his bad side.

225

By two o'clock we had three and a half sacks of crawfish. "There's still a lot of daylight left, but the fishing's not that good," Jody said. "Besides, y'all look tired." Michelle and I exchanged knowing looks. We'd been ready to go for hours. The spray of swamp water and bait slime seemed to have permeated my clothes, skin, and entire being. Michelle and I couldn't wait to get off the bayou and find food, water, and a shower.

As we stowed gear in preparation for the run home, Michelle looked into the box of now-thawed baitfish. "That's shad, Jody, isn't it?" Jody said he didn't know. He just called it bunker. Then he recalled that he'd heard it called both menhaden and shad somewhere. Michelle looked more closely at one of the fish. She was sure it was a shad, more specifically a hickory shad. She had grown up eating shad, a migratory fish that had once been a major food fish in the country but was now eaten primarily by a dwindling number of old people. She especially liked fried shad roe.

"You eat the eggs?" Jody asked, incredulous. He thought for a moment, then shrugged. "Well, all I know is that it's a trash fish that nobody around here eats," he said. I was trying to square this with the mantra that had led me to Jody, "A Cajun'll eat anything that doesn't eat him first." He'd described every animal we'd seen in the Basin as good to eat. But he was adamant about the inedibility of bunker.

At Bayou Land Seafood, Jody's sacks were placed on a certified scale of indeterminate age. The needle settled at 186 pounds. Bayou Land was paying $1.50 a pound, although the guy running the scales acknowledged that the owner would drop it to $1.25 or even $1 if the crawfish didn't get "nicer," meaning bigger and meatier. The crawfish being brought in evidently had yet to regain their pre-hibernation weight. Jody pocketed a check for $276. As he drove us back to our car, he totaled up his expenses. He had put $48 worth of gas in the boat today and used nearly all of it. He'd gone through four boxes of frozen bunker at $14 each, so that was $56. He'd used up two bags of Crusty Chunks at $13 apiece, so that was $26. And, having driven about fifty miles in a truck that gets fourteen miles to the gallon when towing a boat, that was another $12 in gas. By his count, after expenses, that amounted to $137 for an eight-hour day, not counting taxes, or wear-and-tear on his boat, traps, and ten-year-old truck. "If the price had been a dollar a pound, I'd have made $49," he said. "But that's alright. It'll get better. April's coming."

That evening at the crawfish boil, about a dozen people sat around a table covered with plastic in Mike Bienvenu's house. In the middle was a huge pile of crawfish, bright red from their immersion in the pot outside. They were accompanied by links of smoked sausage, half ears of corn, potatoes, onions, and Zatarain's Crawfish, Shrimp, and Crab Boil seasoning. You ate everything with your hands and threw the crawfish shells to your immediate left. We were eating the freshest possible crawfish. They tasted like the best shrimp, with a similar richness and texture. After a while, you were literally up to your elbows in the food. When the phone rang, there was a general shout for somebody in the backyard—the only place anybody was likely to have clean hands—to come in and answer it. Two men at the table were debating hull styles for crawfish skiffs, a discussion that quickly moved to a level I couldn't follow.

Jody told about taking us out, how I had earned the rank of master baiter and how Bayou Land was going to drop the price to $1.25 a pound even though crawfish were still scarce. "And, listen, we were about to head in when Michelle said the bunker I'm using are shad and how she likes to eat the fish and the eggs, too!" The people around the table went quiet for just a moment and a couple of them shook their heads, as if thinking that a certain level of ignorance was to be expected from outsiders. They were, of course, all too polite to say anything.

I didn't get it. These were Cajuns, after all. But not one of them disagreed with the assessment that bunker were strictly fish bait.

Suddenly, it hit me. The fish we used for bait were shipped down from Cape May, New Jersey. They weren't from here and couldn't be found anywhere near here. And that alone was enough to make them suspect. Because if God had meant for man to eat bunker, or shad, or

227

whatever else you want to call them, He damn sure would have put them in the Basin.

MIKE BIENVENU'S DUCK IN BROWN GRAVY

"First of all you gotta take the feathers off, and then you take the guts out." (Laughs). "You can cut it in pieces or cook it whole, it's easier to brown if it's in pieces. Season it good with red pepper (cayenne) and salt—make it red all over with the pepper. Then you take the point of your knife and you stab it all over the breast and on the legs, because you want that seasoning to get in there good. Get a black iron pot and put little bit of grease in, not a lot of grease but enough to cover the inside where the duck won't stick too much. And then you just put it on medium high heat, about 6 or 7 on an electric stove. Throw him in there and get him good and brown all over, keep turning him til he's nice dark brown. And then you put a little water in there, not much, just enough to keep from sticking, and you put a lid on. And you let it keep on til the duck gets nice and tender. Once he's tender you cut you some onions and bell pepper, and throw that in there with a little bit more water. Then you cover it up again and cook it till it surrenders. The main thing is to season it, and you want to brown it good. And if you got a black iron pot then you shouldn't have a problem.

"It's kind of trial and error. You do it a few times, you start to pick up a few tricks. You get the feel of it, how to add some little bit of water just to keep it from sticking. Not too much.

"A duck to me takes, from the time you start until you finish, about three hours. You want to cook it long because you don't want to fight it when you eat it, you know? You put the cover on it, that's going to smother it and help tenderize. When you cover it, the pot is going to get hotter. And the duck is going to keep browning in the pot till the very end when you add the bell peppers and the onion. I don't know how you all like that, but the reason we put the bell peppers and all in at the end is so they don't cook down to nothing. So when you put the gravy on your rice that you're going to eat it with, you still have some onions and peppers in there. But that's it. And basically that is how we cook everything. Everything we eat, we cook like that. The key to it is to season it and brown it, and then you got it."

Chapter Nine:
People of the Caribou

As the single-engine Caravan floated down toward the gravel runway, black-haired women driving red ATVs appeared, racing over the field, each pulling her own personal dust cloud behind her. Two minutes later, I unfolded myself from the plane and stood squinting in the bright five p.m. sun, thinking that sunglasses would have been a good idea. I'd just landed in Arctic Village Alaska, which lies 100 miles north of the arctic circle. Even in late August, the sunshine lasts fifteen hours a day. The women were dismounted now, having parked the half-dozen ATV's in a semicircle behind the plane. They fell to the task of unloading freight with an economy of movement that bespoke long experience. The plane had held only eight passengers, but it had been carrying a lot of food in its belly. There were dozens of boxes of frozen chicken nuggets, pork chops, hamburger, and bacon. The big boxes that weighed almost nothing held cartons of Marlboro Reds and Doritos. There were even a few boxes of frozen vegetables. All of this was headed for Arctic Village's only store, a two-room affair that also sold snack foods, soda, and the more popular calibers of rifle ammunition.

One of the women, seeing me idle, gave me a nudge with her shoulder. "Get busy," she said. I did, crabbing my way under a wing and passing boxes back. Within five minutes the unloaded plane was nothing but a black mote in the sky and a diminishing mosquito whine. Within seven, only two ATVs remained. And that was only because the two drivers—who resembled each other with a twenty-year age gap, suggesting they might be mother and daughter—were arguing about something in Gwich'in. After a while I realized it was me. The younger, having delivered a final rebuke, secured her baby behind her on the seat and roared away. The older—a short woman with straight black hair—scowled and ignored me as she adjusted the many bungees holding the load of boxes on the vehicle's rear rack. The silence went on forever. The Gwich'in, I was to learn, didn't view silence as a hole to be filled. It was just silence, as natural to them as noise is to us. I could see the village in the distance, a mile or more away down a rough gravel road. It was a long way to hump a twenty-five-pound backpack and a sixty-pound duffel with wheels designed for the polished floors of airports. It dawned on me that maybe they had been arguing over which of them—if either—should give the stranger a ride into town. I stood there, neither smiling nor not smiling, neither looking at nor ignoring my potential ride. With the airplane now gone, there were no sounds at all. No birds, no animals, not even any wind. I wondered what the hell I'd gotten myself into this time.

I'd returned home from the Atchafalaya Basin with a new sense of how deeply the act of getting your own food and livelihood from the land could connect you to that land. Looking back, I realized that the least enjoyable outing of the trip had, in some ways, been the most telling. The hours that Michelle and I had spent catching crawfish with Jody had, for us, been pure tedium. That was because we were outsiders. And, like all outsiders—even those who had decided to come to live in the area and become what Jody and his friends called "pretend Cajuns"—we would never understand the swamp. To Jody Meche and the dwindling number of others who had been born to it, who loved it and understood its rhythms and moods, a day in the swamp was anything but boring.

I hadn't intended my trip to Arctic Village as a counterpoint to the Atchafalaya Basin. I wasn't that smart. But had I been looking for maximum contrast, I couldn't have found two more divergent places. Ecologists considered the Basin the most productive land in the northern hemisphere, while arctic tundra, which started in the hills just above Arctic Village and seemed to roll on forever, was the equivalent of a very cold desert. This was because the subsoil, anything below the first ten inches or so, was permanently frozen, permafrost. The only plants that survived here were low-growing—dwarf shrubs, sedges, grasses, moss, heath, lichen. Like the Basin, the endless tundra did hold some large critters. There was an enormous herd of caribou, as well as moose, wolves, bears, and many smaller animals. But as an elk guide had once told the hunting party I was in as we rode into camp, "Boys, there are a hell of a lot of elk in this country. But there's a hell of a lot of country here, too." In short, the protein density per square mile was a tiny fraction of what it was in the Basin.

I could say that I'd come because, like the Cajuns, the Gwich'in found their traditional way of life under threat from the oil companies. In the Basin, I'd been told repeatedly, the oil companies had made wild crawfishing so difficult that none of the men that I spoke with wanted their children to take up the life. The "inconvenient witnesses"—Mike Bienvenu's description of how oil companies viewed the remaining crawfishermen—were dwindling in number. The Gwich'in were facing an even greater threat from the same people, who were intent on doing whatever it took to get to the billions of gallons of oil thought to lie beneath the coastal shelf of the Arctic National Wildlife Refuge (ANWR). I knew this only because a journalist had told me about a story he'd done on the situation. The Gwich'in, he said, were increasingly finding themselves alone in resisting the oil lobby. Even other Indian tribes, who had already taken oil company money, were pressuring them to give in. So far the Gwich'in had held firm. One reason, he explained, was that they believed they have been following a single herd of migratory caribou for 20,000 years. The Porcupine River herd, numbering about 120,000 animals, was the largest in Alaska. And the place where the oil companies most desperately wanted to drill was the caribou calving grounds along the ANWR coastal shelf. The potential adverse effects of drilling there—even if nothing went wrong—might well mean the end of the Gwich'in way of life. The margin of survival in the Arctic, my journalist friend had explained, is razor-thin. One study estimated that even a 5 percent reduction in caribou births could lead to the demise of the entire herd.

The truth was that I'd been half-listening to the guy for most of this story. The world has never lacked tragedies in the making, and the plight of this particular tribe had no claim on my sympathies. Who were the Gwich'in anyway, and why had I never heard of them? The only Alaskan people I'd ever heard of were the Inuit or Eskimo, and I wasn't entirely sure who they were, or even whether this group subsumed others. The Gwich'in, it turned out, were Indians of the interior. They were an Athabascan tribe, a name given to a large number of indigenous peoples whose languages had common roots. A little later, however, hearing of my project, the guy mentioned that the Gwich'in he'd visited in Arctic Village were among the last subsistence hunting cultures in North America. He suddenly had my full attention. He went on to say that he knew Charlie Swaney, one of the community's best caribou hunters. The caribou's migration to their wintering grounds usually brought them near Arctic Village around the first of September. This happened to be the time of year, before the rut, when the animals were at their healthiest and fattest. It was August when he told me this.

I suddenly become terribly interested in the Gwich'in. Within days, I had called Charlie Swaney. Within a week, I had cultivated him over a number of calls. At last he had given me permission to visit and write about the hunt. And here I was, standing on the edge of the town's airstrip, knowing little more than that I was in a place where I would be, once again, an outsider. Had I known just how much of an outsider, I'm not sure I would have gone.

The woman finally looked at me like a problem she could no longer ignore, sighed as if her troubles would never end, and said, "Okay, get on." I introduced myself. She touched but didn't shake my hand. Her name was Joyce. When she asked, I told her I was staying with Charlie Swaney. I had his name and, as gifts, commodities my journalist friend had said to bring: Marlboro cigarettes, a couple of big red tubs of Folger's coffee, cash, and two boxes of .270 bullets.

I got on behind Joyce, careful to hold onto the ATV's frame rather than any part of her. Five minutes later, she let me off by an unpainted plywood house surrounded by fifty-gallon barrels full of trash and junk. Lying amid the nodding foxtail grass were derelict snowmobiles, scrap lumber, and rusted engine parts. Six or eight dogs, each staked before its own tiny house with just enough chain that it could stand on the house's roof, howled at the intruder's scent. The dogs were smaller, skinnier, and more hostile than I'd expected. Several—particularly the nearest, missing a good chunk of its right ear—looked like it would do anything for the chance to remove my legs.

"Charlie know you're coming?" Joyce asked abruptly. Yes, I said. Of course. Why? "Because his best friend died day before yesterday. Albert Joe. Accidentally electrocuted himself. He was gonna go huntin' with you guys. Now the whole town's getting ready for a funeral." With that she gunned the four-wheeler and was gone. No wonder people hadn't exactly rolled out the red carpet. This was not good. Not good at all. I'd been traveling for two days straight to get to a place where I probably wouldn't have been welcomed with open arms under the best of circumstances. And this was far from that. There was just one problem. It was too late to turn around.

I sat down on a huge wooden spool, the kind commonly seen on construction sites, that was lying on its side in the grass. I had no idea what to do. I waited. I looked at the fox grass that nodded in the wind and at the discarded machinery that didn't. I tried to ignore the dogs. After twenty minutes or so, an ample woman in a brown Columbia Titanium jacket shuffled out and yelled at the dogs. I had gotten Charlie's wife, Marion, on the phone several times when trying to reach him. She hadn't been inclined to talk much to me, but I'd finally persuaded her to tell me her name. "You must be Marion," I said brightly. I was way out of my comfort zone. In my ignorance, I doubled down on what turned out to be the exactly wrong tactic, a sort of desperate extroversion. I introduced myself to Charlie's wife and nearly forced some of my welcome gifts on her—a carton of Marlboro Reds and a tub of coffee. I told her that I was sorry to hear about Albert Joe, who turned out to be Marion's uncle. I later found out that there were basically three families in the town—the Tritts, the Franks, and the Johns.

"Charlie's sleepin'," she said. "He went out hunting Wednesday and got back late last night. Ya bring a tent?" I hadn't. I hadn't planned on camping. "Ya goin' ta stay here then?" Marion asked. Her tone was less than inviting. "If it's convenient," I said, in a tone so cravenly ingratiating that even I found it offensive. Evidently it was not convenient. She pointed at a house nearby rented by her son, Rocky. Rocky had gone upriver to hunt moose. They were going to need meat for all the people coming in for Albert Joe's funeral from Gwich'in villages scattered across northeast Alaska and the western Yukon. She told me to put my stuff there and come back in a couple of hours.

The house was one big, dusty room, with a mattress on the floor, a card table and three stools by the window, and a central woodstove but no wood. Pop-Tarts wrappers and Rockstar drink bottles littered the plywood floor. On the far side of the room was a Nintendo Wii connected to a small monitor. I unrolled my sleeping bag on the mattress and lay down. I was exhausted but hyper. I had thought this would be an adventure. I suddenly had no idea what I thought I was doing here.

If nowhere had a middle, this was a contender. Arctic Village is one of the most isolated communities in North America, well above the Arctic Circle on a bend of the east fork of the Chandalar River. The nearest hospital was in Fairbanks, 290 miles south. Fort Yukon, another Gwich'in town and the only settlement of note, was 120 river miles away. To the north lay the first ridges of the Brooks Range, the 700-mile chain of mountains that runs across northern Alaska and into the Yukon Territory. The town sat on land whose status was—and still is—in dispute, but was run largely by and for the Gwich'in. A town council governed. The residents didn't buy hunting licenses or tag the game they killed. They hunted according to traditional seasons. There were no roads leading here, thus few cars or trucks. In the summer, the river was navigable by shallow-draft motorized skiff, but only locally knowledgeable people attempted it and it was no cakewalk for them. Basically, everything came by charter plane, and this effectively tripled the price of goods. Gas, at the time, was ten dollars a gallon. A pound of ground beef was six dollars. There was no alcohol, and no running water except at the Washeteria near the school, where residents could get treated water, wash clothes, and bathe. There were no motels, restaurants, or theaters. The one store carried little. Unsponsored outsiders weren't allowed. And, as I was discovering, just because they let you visit didn't mean they had to like you.

It was a tough place to make a living, and nearly half the population lived below the poverty line. The only work was seasonal—mostly firefighting and construction. Nobody could afford "store food" year-round. The state's own website, the Community Information Series, characterized the local economy as "subsistence-based." Two-thirds of the meat eaten here was bush meat, primarily caribou, at least in good years, when the herd's migration route brought it close to town. People also ate ground squirrel, hare, ptarmigan, porcupine, muskrat, beaver, lynx, Dall sheep, waterfowl, fish from the Chandalar and Old John Lake, and the occasional moose found farther upriver by hunting parties like the one Rocky had gone on.

Gwich'in people would later tell me they felt weak and got sick if they didn't get wild meat regularly. At first, I didn't understand this. I was from the "a calorie is a calorie" school of thought. But the Gwich'in, as they themselves said, lived in two worlds. Yes, they had satellite TV, Oprah, and the CBS *Evening News*. The boys in low-slung jeans who hung around the one-room "youth center" had the same sullen look as the kids in Fairbanks, or in Arlington for that matter. At the same time—and this was what so often made them impenetrable to me—they were also only a generation or two removed from nomads who lived in skin tents and maintained miles-long "caribou fences" to drive the migrating animals into corrals built at intervals along the fence, where they could be more easily killed with spears. Some of the fences were believed by archaeologists and cultural anthropologists to have been maintained over countless generations. As for their craving for wild food, there were many reports dating back to the nineteenth century of Gwich'in men and women in missionary hospitals sending word back to their families, pleading with them to bring their native foods so the patients under the white man's care could regain strength.

While I understood this intellectually, I never really got it at—the pun is inescapable—a gut level. It was more than simple preference or custom. It was as if caribou combined both communion wafer and daily bread. As a modern American, I simply had no cultural correspondent. I did come to a new understnding of the word "caribou." In addition to the animal itself, caribou was also that for which there was no substitute.

In the eleven days I would spend here, I would come to see that for the Gwich'in the physical act of hunting was everything. In its simplest form, it meant getting out on the tundra; observing a few caribou twenty-five miles away through a spotting scope; trying to guess, from their heading and their manner of travel, where they were going and whether you could beat them to an ambush point along that route in the next day or two; and then killing them. The meat itself was just the hunt's most obvious product. But at another level, it was hunting—the mustering of knowledge and skill that had no end, more of which had been forgotten than was known by anyone alive—wherein they discovered, defined, and affirmed themselves as Gwich'in. This, I would come to believe, was at least as essential as the meat.

I was told by several people that if you overlaid a map of the range of the Porcupine River caribou herd on a map of Gwich'in traditional homelands, you'd note their congruence, except for one place. That was the caribou birthing grounds, where the oil companies promised their exploration and drilling would have no ill effects. The Gwich'in called it Izhik Gwats'an Gwandaii Goodlit, "the sacred place where life begins." It was and had always been off-limits to the Gwich'in. No Gwich'in was thought ever to have seen it, let alone entered it. Certainly no one in Arctic Village had seen it. Charlie Swaney would tell me, "That place belongs to the caribou. It's where they take their first breath, first step, first bite of food. The forage there is better. There are few bears or wolves. The winds keep the flies away."

The Gwich'in refused to take part in the Alaska Native Claims Settlement Act of 1971, under which the United States paid nearly $1 billion for Alaska Native lands that had been taken over the years. As a woman told me one night, "We're not conquered. They never conquered us. They think they bought us, and they didn't even do that. Now they want to buy us again. Money, it goes away as soon as it comes. That land is what has always kept us alive. We can't sell that."

I finally met Charlie that evening at his house. Five people were cutting up caribou on a plywood board at a table and sorting it into piles, which were then bagged and taken away. On a tarp on the floor lay whole legs, some with the fur still on, as well as other hunks of caribou waiting their turn beneath the knife. A TV blared from a ceiling mount, but no one seemed to be watching. Charlie shuffled into the room from a back bedroom, looking as if he'd just woken up. He was forty-five, with the black hair and high cheekbones common among Gwich'in, but taller and lankier than most. He touched my hand and accepted a box of Winchester .270 Ballistic Silvertip bullets from me with a slight smile. "I like these 130-grain bullets," he said quietly. "Flat-shooting." He said that he had meant to call and tell me not to come on account of the funeral but that he had lost my number. He'd been out hunting and had gotten the news himself only upon returning last night. The hunters had taken six bulls on the first trip and one bull two days ago. There had been two bulls traveling together, but fog rolled in before they could get the second. With navigation impossible, they had to spend the night up on the tundra. But Charlie had forgotten the tent poles and—since there were no trees "on top," as the tundra above the village was called—they'd spent the night inside the collapsed tent and ended up getting almost as wet as if they'd had no tent at all.

"You can feel the whole mood in the village change when they see that meat come in," Charlie said. "People know they're gonna eat good."

I said that I was sorry for his loss and that I wanted to be the least of his worries. We would talk about hunting after the funeral. "He was looking forward to meeting you," Charlie said of Albert Joe. "He just got careless." His voice was empty. He shook his head and looked away.

The death of Albert Joe—a public, profane, silly, and beloved man with a weakness for Spam, a habit he'd picked up during his time in the U.S. Navy—had rocked the village. But it hadn't hit anyone else as hard as it did Charlie. Albert Joe was twenty years older and had been everything one man can be to another: best friend, best man at Charlie's wedding, father figure, hunting buddy. Lately, I learned, Albert Joe had been spending most of his time trying to wean the village boys off video games. He wanted to get them up into the country to learn what Gwich'in boys had always learned—to hunt, fish, and run a trapline; to read the weather in the clouds; to triangulate their location by distant peaks on the endless steppe of tundra; to see a caribou and, by noting how it moved, know what it was thinking and where it was going. The thread that tied the Gwich'in and the land together for millennia was coming unwound here as surely and inexorably as it did anywhere else when ancient ways contended with modern ones.

In the last decade or so, Charlie told me, times had been hard in the village because the Porcupine River herd had changed its route. The animals hadn't showed up in any significant numbers since 1999. That was the last year villagers set up their traditional September camps on the ridge four miles away, just below the tundra. Many children had never experienced those camps, formerly a highlight of the year. Charlie blamed the bad hunting on changed weather. "The winters have been getting colder, the summers are hotter and wetter. There's something wrong with the earth, and it's telling us the only way it can." In the mouth of anyone from my world, these words would have sounded pretentious. Charlie made them sound like common sense. The good news was that this year was looking better. Meat had already been brought into town. There had been numerous sightings, by hunters with spotting scopes up on the tundra, of more caribou on the mountains. Already there were tents being erected on the ridge.

I asked what people did when the caribou didn't show up. "There are moose upriver sometimes, which they didn't have in the old days," said Charlie. "We eat more store food, more noodles. We set nets under the ice on Old John Lake for whitefish, pike, and lake trout. Sometimes you can catch grayling upriver. But it's not the same without caribou. Fish is better than store food, but it doesn't make you strong like caribou."

"The land is turning into a bowl of water," said a woman at the table. "We've had so much rain that the river's eroding the banks. It's getting wider."

"The willow is growing tall," added a man who had not spoken until now. "Twenty years ago, it never grew above your knees, and now it's over your head some places!"

"Tell him about the polar bear," said another woman.

Polar bear? Polar bears were coastal animals. Arctic Village is a good 100 miles from the sea, with a mountain range in between. The bear had first been sighted up on the ridge two weeks ago. Since then it had been seen three more times outside town. Charlie had seen it through the spotting scope he kept by the window. He'd watched as it ran down a long slope and up another, a distance of six miles, all of it at a run. He thought it was probably trying to escape the same insects that sometimes drove the caribou mad. But he'd never seen a caribou run that far without stopping. "If it can run like that, it can run down a caribou easy." These people were accustomed to large predators, having lived with brown bears and wolves for millennia. The bears encountered around town were usually the young, curious males, and could be dangerous, especially if they smelled meat. It was understood that no one left the village without a rifle. (Indeed, when I walked up to the ridge camp one afternoon a few days later, mostly for the exercise, I encountered three teenagers—two girls and a boy—just outside the village on their way down from the ridge. "Oh, good," said the boy, unslinging the rifle on his shoulder and handing it to me. "You can give this back to my mom. She was worried about not having a gun in the tent tonight." He handed me a bolt-action .30/06 with open sights. "Chamber's empty but the magazine's full. You know how to shoot one of these things?" I told him that I did. With that the three resumed walking and chatting. (I found out later that children are taught to shoot well before they write their age in two digits.)

People were fearful, both of this particular bear and of what its presence implied. Not even any of the elders could remember ever having heard of a polar bear near town. Several people at the table vowed to shoot it if it came any closer. To Charlie, the explanation was obvious. "They're having trouble finding seals, and they've gotta eat. So they're following the caribou now." He left unsaid a far bleaker possibility that I felt sure was on everyone's mind—that this might be the start of a whole shift in the natural order of things.

Charlie said he had to take care of a few things but that I should follow everyone else down to Albert's house, where members of his family were hosting dinner. (In fact, for the three days leading up to the funeral, nearly every breakfast and dinner I ate was held at one of two houses: Albert's or that of Gideon, his brother.) I walked down and took my place in one of the lines passing by outdoor tables loaded with Gwich'in and store food: fried caribou, caribou stew, and caribou soup. A roasted caribou head—teeth and all—sat in a tinfoil roasting pan. The older people seemed especially fond of it and took their time picking the choice bits of meat from the bones. I helped myself to a tiny piece. Nearby were platters of caribou ribs and salmon casserole with macaroni noodles. There were cases of Pepsi and 7-Up, bowls of Doritos and pretzels, a jar full of red licorice strings, a plastic cup full of cigarettes, a pork roast, doughy store-bought rolls, and heavily iced cakes, most of which were still encased in plastic, as if the wrapping were an important part of the presentation. There was a plate of sliced grilled Spam, which sat untouched, a sort of memorial to Albert Joe. As the line moved, I ate the little piece of meat from the head, which prompted a smile from the woman next to me. "You like caribou eye?" she asked. I smiled and nodded. The meat was surprisingly chewy and satisfying. Upon further discussion, it turned out that I was eating not the eyeball itself, but the "membrane behind the eye." Another woman, obviously mistaking me for a sophisticate, pointed to a bowl full of blueberries suspended in white goo and proudly said, "That's Eskimo ice cream." Then, as if spilling a dinner party hostess's secret, she whispered, "It's supposed to be blueberries and whipped caribou fat. But we usually don't have that much fat to spare. Especially now, so early in the season. So we use Crisco." I smiled and plopped a spoonful onto my plate to be polite. The blueberries were small and flavorful. But no fruit could disguise the unctuousness of good old Crisco. Another woman, Lorraine Trimble, told me that she had picked the berries. I told her how good they were and asked how much she had picked this year. "Nineteen gallons," she said proudly. "I'm down to nine gallons now. My kids like to eat them with milk and sugar. And we give them to the elders. Cissy and I"—she inclined her head toward another woman— "we go out and pick all day, all night. We stay near town, but at night it's spooky, especially with that polar bear around. People get mad at us for going. They come out with guns and guard us."

While I had been standing in line, a young mother carrying a toddler in her lap drove up on an ATV. The boy clutched a toy assault rifle with both hands and took it with him. Now, ten minutes later, I saw one of the elders, a little peanut of a man in blue coveralls and a baseball cap, emerge from the house. I'd seen him several times around the village. He radiated some kind of self-possession and humility. Whereas most adults passed the town's young men—the alienated ones in shades and baggy jeans—without a glance, this man always spoke to them. They couldn't maintain their masks around him, couldn't help smiling and joking back when he raised his arm as if to hit them. He was carrying the child's toy gun, which he bungeed to the ATV frame, then went back inside. It was never too early to teach a boy that you didn't enter someone else's house with a rifle.

The next morning I encountered Charlie carrying a gas can. "Go down to the river," he said. The hunting party had evidently gotten two moose and had radioed that they were coming in. He was getting gas for his Argo, an eight-wheel ATV and the only vehicle in town that could handle the tundra. Charlie owned the only one here, but it seemed to be quasi-public property. People contributed toward its gas and upkeep.

The east fork of the Chandalar ran wide, shallow, and muddy past the opposite end of town. I walked to a bank above the river and sat among the others, all of whom were smoking. A man checking a twenty-foot net strung across the mouth of feeder creek let out a whoop when he discovered a whitefish caught in it. He retrieved the large, wriggling fish and banged its head against a boat gunwale. A clutch of women appeared as if by magic, talking excitedly. One cleaned the fish deftly with a small knife on a board laid across an oil drum. The roe, liver, fat, and intestines were set aside. The women crowded around, each wanting a taste of the roe. There was enough for a spoonful each, and they giggled and joked with one another while waiting. One offered me a taste from the communal spoon. It tasted pretty much as I'd expected—mild, fishy, oily, granular, and still cold from the water. It could have done with a bit of salt and lemon juice, but it packed a lot of calories. I guessed it would be a welcome change if you'd been eating only caribou. The woman who had cleaned it wrapped the fish in foil, wrapped the liver separately, and pushed the fat to one side. Then she carefully slit open the intestines, wiped them clean, and wrapped them up. "We call this chiksoo," she said, and I couldn't tell if she meant the intestines or the whole fish. I was about to ask when one women shushed us. In the distance we caught the mosquito hum of outboards.

The Chandalar is full of oxbows and Arctic Village had zero ambient noise, all of which meant that despite the sound the boats were still far away and wouldn't arrive for another two hours. When the first skiff finally came into view, carrying one man and two moose—quartered and wrapped in their own hides—it barely managed four inches of freeboard under the load. Just behind came a boat carrying three more hunters with their rifles, tents, kitchen gear, and close to a dozen big jugs of outboard gas. All of the men's clothing and hands were brown with dried blood. Only their faces were unmarked. Although they were gaunt and tired, there was no disguising the hunters' pride. Friends called out and they answered laconically. There were hands touching the boats before they touched shore. The hunters off-loaded nothing, not even their own guns. They simply stepped off and the crowd split before them as they walked up from the landing. Charlie had brought a plate of sandwiches. Others had brought trays of Pepsi. The men collected sandwiches and drinks almost without breaking stride. They looked as if they wanted nothing in the world so much as to lie down and sleep.

The town's young men formed a bucket brigade to off-load the meat, grunting as they lifted big pieces of dismantled moose and passed them from shoulder to shoulder, heedless of the blood, and onto the tarp-lined back of the Argo. In less than five minutes the landing was empty of people. The only sign of what had just happened was the dirty red tint of the bilgewater in the skiffs.

In the fifteen minutes it took me to walk back to Charlie's, ten women had already received the Argo and its load and were breaking down moose quarters on two makeshift plywood tables outside the house. There were more women at the table inside. Alice Smoke, seventy-five, opened a bone the size of a baseball bat with a saw, scooping out marrow with her knife. It quivered, ivory-colored against the knife's almost black, pitted blade. "Better than Chinese food," she said happily, and ate from the knife. Then she offered me a sliver. It was surprisingly mild. I'd expected the fatty richness of beef or veal marrow, but this was astonishingly light and smooth. There was an unexpectedly pristine quality to it, not unlike an oyster.

In the meantime, a joint that had been making its way around the table reached us. "You smoke?" one of the women asked, something in her tone suggesting that she feared I might disapprove. "Sure, why not?" I said breezily and took a ceremonial toke from what had become a finger-burning roach. It tasted like crummy pot, but I inhaled and passed the roach to Alice, mostly as a courtesy. I couldn't quite picture her smoking dope. And even if she did, the roach was little more than a burning cinder. I thought these things primarily because she had the lined face and cheerful attitude of the babushka in *Thunder Cake,* one of my daughter's favorite picture books. Alice, it turned out, had obviously not read *Thunder Cake,* because she took the roach nimbly and proceeded to suck every last bit of smoke from it. Like nearly everyone else here, Alice could probably have kept up with any rapper working today, dopewise. I suddenly realized that the spindly plant by the window, which was the only houseplant plant I'd seen, was marijuana. I knew that many villagers visited Fairbanks regularly. That must be where the dope came from. I was later told that you could count the people in town who didn't smoke—Charlie was among them—on one hand. Virtually all of these same people were adamant that alcohol remain illegal. "All the guns around here, a small town where you have to get along with people you may not like," one man said to me later. He shook his head. "If people got drunk, there'd be a lot of fighting."

Nearby, another elder, Maggie Roberts, was busily chewing something. She cut and offered me a piece of leg tendon. "Babiche, we call it," she said, still chewing away happily. "Good for constipation." The taste was meaty but faded quickly, leaving me with tendon that I chewed for twenty minutes without appreciably altering its structure. Finally, I discreetly palmed it and dropped it into a trash can. The babiche must have brought back memories, because Maggie began talking of how when she was little, her parents still traveled seasonally, following caribou, moose, Dall sheep, small game, and fish. Her father hadn't wanted to live in Arctic Village or any settlement, she said. Once alcohol came, there was trouble too often. Mostly they were living in seasonal cabins by then rather than traditional wooden-frame skin huts. "If we found a place with a lot of caribou, we'd stay there," she recalled. "You'd make a rack of dry willow and hang meat on it. We'd make a fire underneath it and smoke it. We didn't have tarps in those days. We'd make a roof of spruce bark so it wouldn't get wet when it rained." When they'd smoked the meat enough to preserve it, they'd move again, the family's dogs carrying everything: food, blankets, tents, the various parts of their stove, the caribou skins the family slept on. Dogs were seldom used to pull sleds. "That didn't happen until after the white people came. The Russians,

I think, were the first ones here. We traded furs with them. Before that we didn't have pots and cups." She said this the way someone in my world might mention having run out of eggs or hot sauce. I checked myself again, aware that these people and I lived in the same world but had arrived here by very different paths.

Sometimes, she continued, the men would go up in the mountains to hunt. "The dogs carried the meat down, maybe forty pounds each, in leather packs on their sides. The men would send them down from the mountain. 'Go to grandma,' they'd say. And they'd come to us. And the women would send them back with tea or tobacco if we had any. 'Go to grandpa,' they'd say. Just those words. And the dogs, they knew what it meant, they'd do it." I checked myself again. What could it have been like to be people so closely attuned to the animals we keep as pets, to set one a task like that and know it would do it? I knew only that I didn't, couldn't, know. She worked as she talked, guiding her knife through a haunch, the haunch growing ever smaller as the pile of boneless meat in the middle of the table grew bigger. I was hoping she would tell me more. She did. It was as if the babiche had unlocked her memory. One time her mother made new boots for her father. He had been wading waist-deep out in the river, tending his fish traps. The water had been cold and he'd had to come out frequently to dry off and warm himself before going back in again. Her mother decided that she needed to make him better boots. "We didn't have rubber in those days," she said. "I mean that we knew what it was, but we didn't have any rubber ourselves. So my mother, she took skins she'd tanned. It was the skin from the caribou's lower leg, which is the strongest part, you see. She sewed them good, real tight, with babiche. And then melted the moose fat, you know, and just worked that in for a long, long time to waterproof them. After that, he didn't get wet." My mind reeled a bit. I knew that I was very tired. I couldn't quite believe that I was hearing this, that a tiny woman was telling me of hunter-gatherer life when she was a child; of dogs that carried heavy loads miles up or down mountains at a word; of a woman who tanned leather, sewed watertight boots of caribou skin, and waterproofed them with moose fat.

And there was more. She just vaguely remembered going hungry once or twice when game was scarce. It wasn't famine-hungry, she said. They hadn't had to eat their dogs or anything like that. But she remembered that she and the other children got only a bite or two of ground squirrel each and some broth. Their mother kept the cabin warm, told them to drink water, and not move around too much. Maggie said she herself must have been very small because she could barely remember it. "But my father, oh, he was always talking to us about the famines in the old days. About coming across a tepee and there being no sound and of the whole family lying inside like they were asleep. But dead. 'So you have to learn to do things for yourself, to hunt and fish and trap,' he'd say. In famines, you know, people would try to eat anything. They'd even boil old hides. Usually they couldn't eat that, but they would try. My parents, when they'd butcher a caribou, they'd throw the hooves with some of the leg attached over a branch or a tree. That way it could be found, even in the snow, if there wasn't anything else to eat. You could make soup from that and it would keep you alive."

She described her favorite dish when she was a child. "We'd get some caribou bone marrow, some ground meat, and bone grease. That's the stuff that floats to the top after you boil the pounded-up bone joints for a long time. You skim that off and set it aside. First you whip up the raw marrow. It starts out red, then turns pink, and finally white. You have to whip it a long time, you know. Then you add the bone grease. You keep stirring that, whipping it up over the fire. After a while it looks almost like whipped cream. And then you add in the cooked ground meat until it's all mixed up real good. Then you let it cool off, just like a cake, and cut it up into slices. That was a real treat."

I stood watching this small woman quietly chewing moose sinew as she cut meat. She was tiny not only physically—maybe five feet tall—but also in her aspect. She had no need to call attention to herself or to be counted. I thought of the men I'd met who had large egos and taught "survival skills" and could scarcely disguise their hunger for recognition. And then I looked at this tiny woman who knew more about animals, plants, privation, survival, hunting, fishing, trapping, and dogs than they or I ever would.

The only male fool enough to hang around a group of busy women, I was soon pressed into service loading cardboard boxes—which fell apart under the meat's weight—and helping deliver them to houses around the village. I didn't know the name of the woman I was following and knew by now not to ask if she didn't say. I rode behind her on her ATV and carried boxes into houses and put them in the chest freezers most people in Arctic Village had. Some people were home, some weren't. I had no idea who got meat, who didn't, what kind, or why. And I never saw the matter discussed. There was obviously a system that everyone knew and understood, for I never saw any hint of discussion or dissent. It was known, just not to me.

I was slowly waking up to how completely I'd misread these people. I'd been trying to break the ice rather than warm it. My eager handshakes and attempts at engagement had been intrusive, uncouth. Direct questions were proof of my crassness. Direct questions about sensitive topics like what the Gwich'in "believed in"—questions I'd actually asked—were proof that whatever advantages "Englishmen" had over Indians, such as firearms, matches, and immunity to disease, we had the manners of wolves. And when my gregarious bluster hadn't worked, I had doubled down on the only tactic I had, which was the very thing working against me. Listening to Maggie Roberts, I realized that what I should have been doing all along was trying to make myself small.

The Gwich'in believed that there was a time when men and animals lived in peaceful intimacy. It took me a while to realize that this was not a folktale or metaphor. To the Gwich'in, this was historical fact. Only after the communion between people and animals was severed had the human race sorted itself into different groups—some fished, some farmed, some traded. The Gwich'in, it was agreed, were the ones who followed and hunted the caribou. Gwich'in people and the caribou had a special connection, a partial knowledge of each other's innermost thoughts and feelings. Every caribou was thought to have a bit of human heart in it. And every Gwich'in had a bit of caribou heart. Although the original bond had been broken, that sense of relationship—to animals generally and to caribou specifically—was still operative in these people in a way it hadn't been for me and mine for so long that I couldn't begin to grasp what had been lost.

Charlie told me at one point that it was bad luck to shoot a raven, which could bring bad weather—or worse. It could cause sickness to come. It could make game to go away. While ravens might steal food from you, they were fundamentally on your side. "They're very smart birds," he said. "They'll tell you sometimes if the weather's changing. They'll squawk in a way that means that caribou or other animals are coming." Likewise, Marion, up on the ridge smoking caribou meat on a rack of dry willow sticks loosely covered with a blue tarp to trap the smoke, told me that she didn't shoo the birds known as camp robbers away from the meat. (The bird, the gray jay, aka "Whiskey Jack," is a "scatterhoarder." It chews its food into a ball coated with sticky saliva, causing it to adhere to the place where it is stored, often a fissure of bark or the underside of a tuft of lichen.) "There's a story about them we tell. This man was out in the bush and he got lost and was starving. So these two camp robbers come to him and start singing nearby. And so he goes to them and they fly to the next bush and sing some more. And that's how they led him back to his village. So we don't mind sharing food with them because they helped us." I had no idea how deeply Marion, who repeatedly tried to sell me matchstick-sized joints of pot for ten dollars, believed this. My few attempts to inquire more deeply were invariably deflected, as if such things shouldn't be subjected to the blunt instrument of everyday conversation.

Maybe that deflection was necessary because, in the broad sense, engagement with the natural world was the heart of what it meant to be Gwich'in. In my world, love of the outdoors was channelized. One developed an "interest": birding or kayaking or backpacking. For these people, the daily act of securing your own food—and the wide awareness of every part of the natural world that task required—were what it was to be alive. There was no division of "work" and "play." There was only living. One of the men I was to meet later, Jonathan John, would come the closest to describing this full-on engagement. "My grandma said we used to live just like animals, because animals were all that was in our brain."

Four days later, one day after the funeral, we were finally going hunting. I rode up to the camp in the back of the Argo with Charlie and two other men, Jonathan John and Roy Henry. The plan was to go out "on top" the next day. "Up until a couple of days ago, the bulls' antlers were still in velvet, still soft," Charlie had told me. "Until their antlers are completely hard, their big concern is protecting them from injury. You understand? They know they're gonna need those antlers to fight with other males during the rut and to fend off predators. They'll go off by themselves in the densest cover they can find." Now their antlers had fully hardened. I didn't know how he knew this, but there was no doubt in his voice. "Oh, now they'll go anywhere," he said, sounding as excited by their sudden mobility as if it were he whose antlers had suddenly hardened. Right now, Charlie said, was the time to hunt—while the bulls were fattening up for the rut, traveling widely in search of the best grazing. This weeks-long mating season wouldn't start for more than a month. By then the bulls would be so focused on mating that they would cease to feed, their flesh becoming so stringy and rank with hormones that not even the dogs would eat it. By the end of the rut, just as winter was closing in, the average bull would have lost 30 percent of his body weight.

At camp that night, I fell in love with ground squirrel, much to the consternation of my hosts. I had approached the fire, where I saw more cooks than usual tending to something there. Seeing me, Marion had said, "You want to try ground squirrel, eh, Bill?" It was a breezy challenge and she all but winked at the others. I didn't know what ground squirrel was but I knew that I'd better accept. Sure, I said. She reached down to the ground beside her and produced a recently gutted rodent.

It was lacking a tail but considerably larger than the squirrels at home. She tossed it unceremoniously into the fire. The air instantly reeked of burned hair. She rolled the thing from side to side using two sticks, then flipped it out onto the ground, evidently to cool. When it finally stopped giving off smoke, she picked up the blackened, hairless lump in one hand and, using the back of a knife, gingerly scraped the singed fur from the warm carcass. That was it for prep work. I flashed on Martha Stewart dressed in a crisply ironed chef apron holding a singed ground squirrel in her hand, wondering how the hell she was going to fill up the rest of the show. Marion dropped the squirrel into a pot of boiling water with a handful of salt. "Takes about an hour," she said.

Ground squirrels were like Ball Park Franks—they plumped when you cooked 'em. Though unlike hot dogs, this thing had a head. The only unblackened parts of the head were its yellow incisors, which became more prominent as flesh burned away and the head and body became bigger. The squirrel looked angry in death, as if ready to inflict one final bite.

After an hour, Marion poured off the water, twisted off a leg, and plopped it onto my plate. The fat alone was extraordinary, nearly half an inch thick. The squirrel looked as evil as ever but the smell was appetizing. I put a forkful of the dark meat in my mouth. I couldn't believe how sweet and rich it was. It really didn't need anything but salt. I ate some more. It was unlike anything I'd ever had, but great barbecue was the closest correlate. "Marion, this is great!" I said. She exchanged looks with the women. This was not what they had expected. One woman joked, "He's becoming Indianized." Another teased me. "You're like the elders," she said. "They love ground squirrel, so we usually take them some." I protested that I, too, was an elder, but evidently they were not entirely happy that the joke had backfired. Despite my pleas, I was offered no more of the delicious meat.

We did not go hunting the next day. Nothing up here happened in a hurry—the Gwich'in themselves joked about "Indian time." Morning coffee and cigarettes gave way to more coffee and more cigarettes. Charlie went back into town to fetch someone who had radioed up

251

wanting a ride to camp. Just before leaving, he saw the look on my face. "When you hurry is when you make mistakes," he explained. I nodded, indicating that I got it. Mistakes in this world, even small ones, could be fatal.

The next morning, after pancakes with syrup, fried caribou, and coffee, it was time for . . . more cigarettes. Nearly every adult smoked, and when the village ran short of tobacco it became the chief topic of conversation. Then another pot of coffee. Finally, just after noon, Charlie, Jonathan John, Roy Henry, and I loaded up. We each had a sleeping bag, rain gear, and extra layers. It was clear and in the fifties, but the weather "up top"—the treeless tundra that rose only a few hundred feet higher than the village but was an entirely different world—could change especially fast. Everyone but me had a rifle. Charlie had the tent and had remembered the poles. We had food in a cooler and some logs. "Not much to make a fire with on top," he explained.

We finally started up toward the tundra, passing caribou antlers, some half sunk into the soft ground, which was carpeted with moss, sedge, and lichen. Caribou antlers were proudly displayed by hunters in my world, but I'd seen none on display anywhere in Arctic Village. "We don't pick them up," Charlie said over the Argo's growl. I asked why—wincing when I heard the bluntness of my own words—and Charlie shrugged. "That's just how we do," he said. "Some of these antlers," he flicked his head at a set turning the color of old grass, "are older than I am." A few years ago, he told me, there had been a woman from the outside who, despite the objection of her hosts, collected antlers and brought them into camp. Then, still ignoring the Gwich'in, she took them to town. They told her she had been unwise and would be even more unwise if she took them away. She flew home with them. "Last year, I heard that she took sick," he said. "And then she died." He shrugged. "Some people don't believe it when we say not to take them." I was almost sorry I'd asked. I'd spent time in remote areas of foreign countries, including Iran, Mongolia, and Nicaragua. None of them had felt anywhere near so alien. None of those landscapes had the power and presence I was feeling here. I wasn't just in another culture. I was in another world, one governed by forces I was ignorant of. I did know that these forces scared me. I tried to sound casual when I said, "Charlie, just so you know: I'm not messing with any antlers." I couldn't tell whether he nodded in reply or was just jolted by the particularly hard bump we hit at that instant.

After half an hour, we had reached the ridgetop and descended into the tundra, passing a small lake on our right. We stopped and climbed to the saddle between two hills and then up the taller one, stopping just below its summit. We found a windbreak there, hundreds of carefully piled stones. There was no telling whether it was recent or ancient. We sat in the lee of the structure and looked out over the endless steppe of tundra. It was the largest swath of earth I'd ever seen, literally hundreds of square miles of land rolling gently away until it rose to the first of three or four waves, each taller than the last, of the Philip Smith Mountains, part of the Brooks range. The tundra was luminous with the fall yellows and reds of berry bushes—blueberry, cranberry, salmonberry, bearberry—along with the variegated greens of willow, sedge, and grass. These plants topped out at three feet. It had probably looked like this 5,000 years ago. Land that had never felt the blade of a bulldozer or plow, never been broken by roads or roofs, never cut by wire or pipe. I could see three distinct weather fronts battling for dominance: on my left, rain, a gray curtain that blocked the horizon; in front, a netherworld of fog; on my right, shafts of bright sunshine from an unseen source. Between the fog and sun, fifteen to twenty-five miles away by my eye, was a short, wide rainbow more vivid than I'd ever seen. It rose from the ground like the blade of a sword someone had stuck there. It felt like God's workshop, a place where He tinkered with the weather. I could have drunk it in all day.

Charlie sat, anchoring his elbows on his knees, and raised his sixteen-power binocs, while Jonathan manned the spotting scope I recognized from Charlie's kitchen table. Wordlessly, they clamped down on the scenery, squeezing it with their eyes for caribou. I had tried the binoculars in camp and found that I couldn't hold them steady enough to use. I couldn't fathom how Jonathan could free-hand the sixty-power spotting scope. No one spoke for long minutes. I exchanged shrugs of shared uselessness with Roy, an old friend of Albert's who had come for the funeral. Neither of us had optics. It wasn't likely either of us would see something these guys didn't.

At last Charlie grunted softly and asked Jonathan what he made of the group on the second mountain range, up where the gray of the rock face met the uppermost yellow band of willow. I hadn't given much thought to Jonathan until now. He was a taciturn man in a navy ball cape with scraggly facial hair and a voice like Oscar the Grouch. Turning the scope to the indicated spot, he finally deigned to use the scope's tripod. "Yah, some nice bulls in that group," he murmured. "Two real big ones on the right. Had them in silhouette for a moment. They're moving pretty good." Charlie and Jonathan both tried to show me through their respective optics, but I couldn't see anything that might have been caribou. "It helps if you already know the country," Charlie said. "That way, you know when you're seeing something that wasn't there before." He said the trick was to look for little black dots, specks. If the specks moved they were caribou. Although this was the shortest glassing lesson I'd ever received, it was also comprehensive. I asked how many and how far off the bulls they'd seen were. Charlie thought and said, "There's about nine in that group. And, oh, twenty-five miles or so." Jonathan nodded in agreement. "Yah, about that."

"So they'll be here in . . ." I asked, letting my voice trail off.

"Two days," Charlie answered. "If they keep coming this way." He turned back to glassing. In the next few minutes Charlie identified four additional groups of bulls, none of them numerous. Each of the bulls that were traveling together amicably now in the various bachelor groups would go its own way when the rut kicked into high gear. "Then some of them will kill each other with their horns," he said.

He and Jonathan spotted another clutch of bulls they estimated at forty miles away. He had sighted one group that he thought was coming our way. If animals in this group kept coming, they'd probably pass a rock dome twelve miles away. We'd be able to see them better and ambush them from there. With no more discussion, the decision to try for these bulls had been made. We got back into the Argo for the four-hour ride. Several times, crossing the streams that invariably ran in the seam between hills, we had to get out while Charlie used the Argo's winch to cross. The Argo never went fast, but it always went. It took us the full four hours to reach the dome.

When we arrived, we climbed the rounded outcropping to glass again. Charlie handed me his rifle and had me follow two steps behind him as we walked quietly up the hill. "Be ready," he said. "Caribou like high places like this. The wind keeps the flies away." I had told Charlie I was a lousy offhand shot, but I was happy to be holding the rifle and honored to be thought of as more than a passenger. I had decided not to take any shot over 100 yards unless I could get into a sitting position. I stayed close, ready to hand the rifle back to Charlie quickly if an animal beyond my self-imposed limit presented itself. It wasn't easy. Charlie never looked like he was working at it, but the guy could cover ground.

We didn't jump any caribou, but we glassed until ten o'clock, when the light finally started to go. Charlie hadn't seen the group he was after. This was good, however. He explained that the terrain was such that they'd drop below our line of sight if they were headed our way. That we couldn't see them wasn't proof, of course, that they were still headed our way. But Charlie seemed encouraged and that was enough for me. I thought of what Jonathan had told me earlier, "My grandma said we used to live just like animals, because animals were all what was in their brain." Charlie's brain worked like that. He didn't talk a great deal about caribou, which surprised me at first. The hunters I knew speculated endlessly about the habits of deer or ducks. I wondered whether, paradoxically, it was the very primacy of caribou that meant there was no great need to discuss them, or whether there was an ongoing but nonverbal conversation about them that was beyond my ken. I noted that when Charlie did speak of caribou, his observations were always framed in terms of what the animals required at a certain moment and why.

We set up camp below the dome, collecting drinking water from pools in the moss here and there. I helped start a fire with the wood we'd brought while Roy Henry put up the small tent. Dinner was simple and quick: coffee, instant macaroni, and fried caribou. Salt was the only condiment. We hadn't walked much, but riding in the Argo was like riding a slow-motion mechanical bull. I didn't know about the others, but I was exhausted. The tent was absurdly small, designed for two men with minimal gear. We laid our sleeping bags out and essentially fell into them fully clothed. There wasn't room to roll over or change position. How you landed was how you slept. Each man laid his rifle between him and the next man in what I'd come to think of as "Alaska ready" condition—the bolt closed, the chamber empty, but the magazine full. All that was needed to be ready to shoot was to work the bolt once and pull the trigger. There was a rock under my back when I landed. For the only time in my life, I was so tired that it made no difference.

I awoke the next morning to find Charlie gone and Jonathan and Roy still asleep. I crawled out of the tent and walked quietly up to the top of the dome, trying to keep downwind of where Charlie might be in case he had animals in sight. After nearly an hour, I saw him walking my way with his rifle. He had killed a cow for camp meat and needed the Argo to haul it. After that, he'd seen the group of bulls. So far, his hunch had held. They looked as if they would pass by here in a couple of hours. Jonathan and Charlie quickly dressed and quartered the cow, a task as familiar to them as opening the mail was to me. At one point, Jonathan had removed the lacy membrane of fat covering the stomach in one piece, almost like a doily, and hung it on a bush to dry. "Icha'ats'a chu, we call it,'" he said. "Old-timers used to use the stomach as a cooking pot," he continued, rolling the carcass so the guts spilled downhill. "They'd clean it out and put pieces of meat in it. Then they'd dig a hole and put hot rocks in, some dirt, and then that folded-over stomach. In an hour or so, it'd be ready. That was before we had pots." This was a veritable torrent of language for Jonathan, as many or more words as I'd heard him say in my days here. We loaded the cow and went back to camp, and Jonathan began frying up some of the fresh meat. Charlie stood atop the Argo to keep tabs on the bulls.

They must have changed course or moved faster than he thought, because the next time I looked over Charlie was gone, already jogging across the tundra with the .270 in one hand. That he had said nothing—merely grabbed the gun and gone—told me how urgent the situation was. I took off after him. By this time he had slowed to a brisk walk, which was good, because I couldn't run in this terrain. At every step I sank four inches into the ground. It was like running in cement. I saw the spot he was headed for, a rock mound atop a slight rise about a mile off. Within 200 yards, I'd removed my parka, vest, hat, and fleece jacket. Meanwhile Charlie scissored away on his long legs.

A few hundred yards from the mound, he dropped to a crawl. I'd closed the distance a bit, but he was still about 300 yards ahead of me. A moment later, he looked back and made an emphatic "down" motion with his arm. I hit the spongy ground as if struck by lightning. The last thing I wanted was to be responsible for a busted stalk. After a minute, he looked back again, seemed relieved that I'd obeyed, and, with a sweep of his arm, indicated that I should stay low and approach from farther downwind. I doglegged to the right, in a low Groucho Marx walk. When I finally got to the rocks he was calmly smoking a cigarette. "You shouldn't have done that," he said quietly. "You'll get tired." In a whisper, I asked how far the bulls were. "About a hundred yards," he said. Then he stubbed out the cigarette and stood. From a mid-crouch I could just see three bulls placidly walking along. They stopped when they saw Charlie, as if unsure what this two-legged creature was. All three were large and fat, with dried scraggly strips of velvet still clinging to their antlers. A few hundred yards behind them were some cows with calves.

Charlie dropped the first bull with a neck shot, then shot again when it tried to rise. He put two shots into the next caribou, which staggered, stood still for a long moment, and toppled over. It looked dead before it hit the ground. The third bull, farther off, took a bullet and stood, seemingly unperturbed by the lead insect bite, as if it was trying to remember something. I heard the click-clack of Charlie pushing shells into the rifle's empty magazine, and the snick as he shoved the magazine back into the rifle, then another shot. The bull rocked slightly as it absorbed another bullet. Then it turned and began slowly walking directly away from us. I remember being struck by the deliberate way it did things. There was no lethal shot at this angle and neither of us spoke as we prayed for it to turn. After another forty yards, it finally did, offering a 175-yard quartering-away shot. Charlie's shot was high, splintering a piece of antler above the animal's head. The next shot appeared as a red blossom just behind its ear. The bull fell into a heap.

Charlie showed no elation. If anything, he seemed strangely subdued, almost down. I imagined it was regret at not having killed as cleanly as he expected of himself. Maybe it was that, as for many hunters, the final act of the hunt—the killing—was, while necessary, the part he liked least. Maybe it was both. In any case, he was suddenly all business. He handed me the rifle and a handful of shells. "I'm going back to get the Argo," he said. His voice was firm and flat. "I don't want any crows or bears on that meat." With that, he was gone, walking in that same ground-covering stride. I loaded four bullets in the magazine and one in the chamber, closed the bolt, and engaged the safety. Only then did I look around. The cows and calves had altered course and were heading away from me. In the distance I saw another group of caribou behind the cows, though they were too far to distinguish bulls and cows. I must have sat for half an hour or more. There was no sound, only the occasional pulse of a breeze. No birds or bears came. I marked and memorized where each downed caribou lay. It was easy to lose them against the tundra. The way to find them was to look for the only things that didn't sway at all in the wind.

We spent about two hours gutting and cutting the caribou. Charlie said that we had too much weight on our hands to wrap the meat in its own hide, that we needed to skin it all out. Roy and I worked together silently, skinning the caribou, then using the skin to stack the meat on, then tossing the pieces into the tarp lining the back of the Argo. By the time we loaded everything, Jonathan and I, riding in the back atop meat, gear, and guns, were sitting noticeably higher than Charlie and Roy in front. We rode for four or five hours, stopping only for water at the seams between hills. It was eight o'clock by the time we reached the ridge camp, still bright as afternoon. I suddenly realized how tired and bloody I was. My hands were covered with the dark caribou ink. My shirt, pants, and boots were stained with it. It was strange to be covered in blood but not to feel dirty. I realized that it almost felt the opposite.

I was also ravenous. I attacked a plate of fried meat and rice without washing. When I hit a tough piece of meat, I grabbed the nearest thing, which happened to be my hunting knife, the same one I'd been using to butcher. After dinner, awaiting the cup of coffee that I hoped would keep me awake long enough to dig my sleeping bag out and find a place to unroll it, I washed and rinsed my plate and utensils in the tubs of soapy and clean water by the kitchen. Back at the fire, Jonathan looked at me and shook his head. "Shouldn't wash your knife like that," he said. "Soap and hot water, they're bad for a hunting knife."

Charlie nodded in agreement. "Rolls the edge." In practical terms, this made no sense whatsoever. The important thing was that they thought enough of me to instruct me in the basics of knife care. I felt grateful, even honored, for this. I thanked the both of them for telling me about soap and hot water.

We drank our coffee in silence for a few minutes. "When it's all over, your trip," said Jonathan, "you gotta make a conclusion about it, right?" I told him he was correct. I asked what he thought it should be. "Well, . . ." he mused, the tip of his cigarette glowing as he took a puff. "This world, this country, it's rough, you know? You see it. So you got to be tough. Not just in your body but also in your mind. That's what I'd say."

I bade everyone good night, found an empty tent, and was almost instantly asleep. When I woke the next morning, Charlie had already gone. He had taken some other guys out up top. There were still a lot of people in the village who needed meat.

BOILED GROUND SQUIRREL

Take one freshly trapped and deceased ground squirrel.

Gut it using your knife and fingers.

Throw the carcass into a medium-to-large fire with a good bed of coals and active flames. It's best if the fire is made outdoors. When all the animal's hair has been singed black—you'll be able to tell by looking and by a smell that makes you think you will never again be hungry—remove the carcass. Roll from side to side with sticks until it stops smoking.

When the animal has cooled to the point that it can be picked up in your hands, do so. Using the spine (back edge) of a knife, scrape the singed hair off the animal, throw it in a pot of boiling water, and add a small handful of salt. Cook at a slow boil for one hour.

Remove squirrel. Drain. Eat.

Epilogue:
Don't Ever Let that Man Near a Stove

I had blood on my hands. And boots, one pants leg, and even my forehead, thanks to a reflexive swat at a late-season mosquito biting there. It was October and I was up to my wrists in the body of a doe I'd shot minutes earlier as she nosed for acorns twenty-five yards from my stand. She had run for forty yards, white flag of tail tracing those leaping arcs through the air only whitetails seem capable of. On the fourth or fifth, she'd landed unsteadily, taken a wobbly step, and collapsed. One moment she had been feeding calmly. Thirty seconds later she was dead, never having known of my existence or what had happened. She'd died as almost all deer do, eyes wide open. I remember hoping that my own death would be as swift and tidy. I thought of Charlie Swaney's face after he'd dropped those three bull caribou. How there had been no elation or euphoria at bringing down so much meat. If anything, he'd looked subdued, almost unhappy. As if killing was his least favorite part of hunting.

Returning home after visiting the Gwich'in had been like returning from another world, and I was still processing the experience. As I field-dressed the deer, I kept replaying an encounter I'd witnessed in Charlie's house. Like Albert Joe, Charlie had been trying to wean the village boys from video games and get them up into the woods and tundra. I had been in the house, pretending to be absorbed in the blare of the TV, when Charlie had summoned his twelve-year-old nephew for a rare dressing-down. The week before he had taken the boy up to the camp along the ridge to trap ground squirrels and practice shooting.

After a while, the boy, saying he needed to go back to camp for more bullets, had left. But he hadn't gone to camp. He'd hitched a ride all the way back to the village to play on his computer.

"We're worried about you and your friends," Charlie said. His voice wasn't loud but his words sounded formal, rehearsed. "We're worried that you're not gonna be ready when hard times come. You're not gonna know how to get around up on the tundra or feed yourself." He told the boy that he wasn't going to find the knowledge he needed to survive in his video games. It was waiting for him in the woods and "up on top," meaning the tundra. "God gave you that land up there," Charlie said, his voice rising slightly. "He put it there for you to learn and to use. But if you don't learn it and use it, you won't love it. And if you don't love it, you won't fight for it. You won't keep it. And then you'll end up like those Indians living in apartments in Fairbanks."

I'd at first thought he meant the last line as a kind of joke. There were worse fates, after all. But then I saw. To Charlie, an apartment wasn't about where you slept. It was about renouncing who you were. The way a man defined himself as Gwich'in was by engaging in the act of subsistence—by hunting and eating caribou and the other wild foods that gave a man strength. To turn your back on that, to go to a city and live in a box, was to become deracinated. To Charlie it was the supreme self-betrayal, the ultimate fall. For what was such a man? He was no longer Gwich'in. He was nobody. He was a walking ghost.

I felt as if I were some strange reverse image of those alienated boys. They hungered for the pleasures of the big world outside Arctic Village while I, frequently feeling lost in the wider world, hungered to be more deeply connected to the natural world they'd been born into. I could never become an Indian, just as I would never be a Cajun like Jody Meche or even an urban sea forager like Kirk Lombard. I was a modern man still trying to find out where I belonged. Why I hungered for that when so few of my peers did was something I still didn't understand. ("Why seems it so particular with thee?" as Gertrude asks her melancholy boy.) But, in hindsight, I could see that the desire to know that other world had always been there. Playing cowboys and

Indians, I'd always wanted to be the Indian. It wasn't until much later that I could put a name to what I craved. And this was why I was so drawn to hunting, fishing, and foraging.

I stood up from field-dressing to stretch my back. Michelle and I figured that to get through the year, we'd need to freeze at least three deer, of which this was the second. I was proud of having succeeded on this day's hunt. I was likewise proud of having killed cleanly. Or so I thought at first. The more I explored it, however, the less pride I found. Instead, something a baseball player had said to a sportswriter after losing a game came to mind: "Losing hurts worse than winning feels good." Killing cleanly, I realized, didn't feel like winning. It meant rather that I had escaped the guilt and remorse that come from causing unnecessary pain to an innocent being. Hunting is a primal drama that has a cast of one—you. It has an audience of one—also you. In fact you are everything: judge, jury, prosecutor, bailiff, defendant, and witness in the case of What You Just Did. There's no way you come out of that mess with completely unsullied hands or unmixed emotions. And yet hunting keeps pulling me back.

Having cut free the viscera, I lifted one of the deer's hind legs and the innards slid out in one big mass. I found the heart and cut it free. Eating organ meat of any kind was a threshold I'd only recently crossed. The previous season Brian, one of Michelle's friends at Food Makers, who was into home charcuterie, had asked for the heart from one of the deer we'd taken. He told Michelle that he'd used the idea of a Philly cheese steak for inspiration, pounding the raw meat flat, grilling it with onions, and serving it under melted provolone on some good bread. He claimed it had been fantastic. We tried the same technique. It *was* fantastic, surprisingly chewy, lean, and meaty—I'd read somewhere that there was no fat on a deer's heart—yet satisfyingly rich. The heart had quickly become one of our favorite parts of the deer.

By the shed in my backyard, we'd hoisted the deer on a gambrel fitted through the hind legs just behind the knee, upside down, and let it hang for a couple of days to age. The weather had been perfect, daytime highs of forty-five to fifty and nights that hovered just above freezing. I decided to wrap the deer in a tarp to avoid offending the neighbors. The sight of a dead animal, I had to remind myself, can be a shock and seem like a deliberate affront to many people. Arctic Village kept pulling at my notions of normal.

It had been a banner year for edible fungi and Michelle and I had been making the most of it. As we exhausted the familiar places, I bought a road atlas of the District to help find new grounds. One day, we found ourselves prospecting in a gritty and unfamiliar area of Northeast. But the atlas showed skinny green fingers of Rock Creek Park in the ravines between strip malls and storage facilities, so that's where we went. Behind a place that sold swimming pool chemicals to contractors, we parked and peered down a slope so steep that there was no way of knowing who or what might be down there. We held onto vines where we could and slid on our butts where we couldn't. I loved that I'd found a woman who enjoyed doing crazy stuff like this. Nobody else I'd ever been with would have gotten out of the car in this part of town, let alone for the purpose of disappearing down a ravine so steep it felt more like spelunking than hiking.

In any case, if there was a possibility of mushrooms someplace, we were going. As soon as we got to the bottom, we encountered a tremendous downed beech tree. Michelle began eagerly climbing through the jungle gym of its branches. Thirty seconds later she let out a whoop. "Oh my God!" she called. "A lion's mane!" I was still climbing through the limbs. I found her sniffing a round ivory-colored fungus that looked more like an oversize bleached goatee than a mushroom. "It's so fresh!" she cried, almost delirious at the find. She came over and kissed me full on the lips. "You did it, Billy! You *found* this place."

"Of course I did," I said. "I knew there'd be a—what'd you call that thing?" Lion's mane, she repeated. It was apparently a jackpot mushroom in the mid-Atlantic.

"*Hericium erinaceus*," she said. "In the tooth fungus group. The 'hairs' on this—see how nicely they hang down—are actually 'teeth' to 'shroomers. But this is one of my all-time favorite mushrooms. Pretty rare and extremely delicious. They taste like lobster." She had me take a picture of her with it, which she texted to Hue. He was a fairly serious mushroomer himself. They had been corresponding about their recent finds. I sensed some rivalry at work.

A little later, I heard a three-syllable yell that sounded like something you'd yell when delivering a karate chop. I hustled over and found her holding up a particularly nice hen of the woods, maybe a six-pounder. I asked her if it wasn't a hen. "Right," she said.

"So what was that word you yelled?"

"Maitake," she said. "The Japanese name for it. It means 'dancing mushroom.' Apparently, if you found one in the old days, you'd be so happy you'd dance." Michelle was a babe in all circumstances, but never looked so alive and alluring as when she was excited by a prize fungus. I maitake'd my way up to her and kissed her.

"I knew there'd be mushrooms here," I told her, feeling joyously goofy. "Babe, I'm telling you. I have the gift. It's like I'm, I don't know, bulimic or something." This was one of our private jokes, from a scene in *Zoolander*, a terrible movie that Michelle's older son, for reasons I never quite got, was overly fond of.

"You're full of it," she said, slipping away. "But this is one mad spot for the fungus. Keep looking." I did. In the meantime, Michelle had received a text back from Hue. He was stuck at the Pentagon, as usual, working late. It wasn't the mushrooms he was jealous of, he wrote, so much as the fact that we were in the woods and looking. Michelle wrote back that he should skip out and join us. "Can't today but how about tomorrow?" he replied. "It's my birthday, so you guys better show me something good."

Disclosing his birthday was unusually forthcoming for Hue. His wife, he'd mentioned in one of his earlier texts, was out of town at a conference. That meant he'd be alone. We decided to invite him for dinner and to ask Paula and Gordon, too. I wasn't sure how my two most influential foraging teachers would hit it off, but I had wanted them to meet for some time. "We should do it up," I told Michelle. "Make it an occasion. It's his birthday after all. Plus I owe the guy."

"How so?" she asked.

"Well, he introduced me to this totally hot foraging chick," I said. "Who initially thought I was too old and too vanilla. But she seems to have come around. And now I was sort of hoping we'd spend, you know, a good bit of the rest of our lives together."

I was nearly as shocked at what I'd just said as Michelle obviously was. We'd become a unit so effortlessly that each of us had talked about how this was it for both of us. We'd also marveled at our luck, at how improbable it was, given the geography alone. But we hadn't mentioned the "m" word. Michelle had been out of her marriage for only nine months when we met. I'd been out of mine for six years but hadn't gone through with the divorce. There hadn't been any particular need to until now. The truth was that I'd been thinking about asking her to marry me for some time. But only in the abstract. I had not gotten as far as when and how. But evidently I'd just decided, because I'd done it. I'd spoken the words. Standing about six feet away from her, I realized that I'd just popped the question. And what I remember from that moment is that suddenly I didn't know what to do with my hands. They had become useless and strange, like a seal's flippers at the end of my wrists. I looked at the two of us, our muddy boots, the long smears of dirt on our jeans from sliding down the side of the ravine in this no-man's-land. It wasn't the ideal setting by most standards. But Michelle had looked especially beautiful in the dim light; her eyes alight with the "flow" of being completely absorbed in the task and pleased with the growing weight of mushrooms in our bags. That, I decided, must have been what reached in and pulled the words out of me.

"Bill Heavey," she said. "Are you asking me to marry you in this trash-filled corner of Rock Creek Park?"

"Yes," I said. "I mean I'm asking you here. But I think the ceremony should be someplace else." I was joking because I was overcome and didn't want to start crying. She buried her head in my shoulder and we held each other. I felt warm tears on my neck. Tears, I thought. Tears are a good sign. And I welcomed them because hers preempted my own. Her tears gave me a job to do, which was to tend to them.

"Yes," she said, lifting her head. "Of course I'll marry you." She was blinking back her tears and smiling in a way I'd never seen before. It was a big smile. One I'd never seen on her. On anyone else I knew, it would have looked fake, a put-on smile. On her it wasn't. It was the smile that she'd kept hidden until now. But now something in her had dissolved, fallen away. One of my first impressions of Michelle was that she let you in only so far and no further, but did so with such skill that you hardly knew that you'd gotten as deep as you were ever going to get. And even when I saw that in action, saw the curtain dropping, I couldn't have said how deep I'd been let in or how much more there was to see. But now the curtain was gone. Leaving her, the little girl and adult woman and mom who stood before me now. We'd already said everything. We just stood there for a while. And then I took a deep breath and led her to some mushrooms I'd found earlier, to see if they were edible. They were slippery jacks, she said, a kind of bolete. And very good to eat. We bagged them up.

The next afternoon, I thawed the backstrap of the doe I'd killed a week earlier. Paula and Gordon were coming at six and always showed up on the dot. Hue, who was leaving work early so that he and I would have time for a brief mushroom walk, showed up, as usual, fifteen minutes early. He was in his office clothes but carrying a bag with his woods duds and boots. Michelle started to recount our finds from the previous day but Hue waved her off. "Enough talk," he said, heading for the bathroom to change. Then, to me, "You ready?"

Ten minutes later, Hue and I were walking down a path toward the Potomac. It was a warm day for October, the woods damp from recent rains and very still. Hue was favoring one leg a bit. That could mean only one thing. "How's jujitsu these days?" I asked breezily. He just smiled and shook his head, conveying either a refusal to discuss it or a kind of resignation. Hue just couldn't bring himself to tap out when an opponent had the upper hand. It was dumb to sustain an injury you could easily avoid. And yet I couldn't help admiring the warrior in him, the refusal to surrender. I told him I was having my own problems, an increasing stiffness in my back along with some pain. It seemed as if the floor got farther away each morning as I bent to put on my undershorts. The orthopedist I'd seen had told me to do as little as possible for six weeks and then come see him again.

"Those guys are full of crap," Hue said. "You gotta keep moving. Even if it hurts a little. In the long run it'll hurt worse if you stop." This was about as long as I'd ever heard Hue go on about something. I had a feeling he was right. I resolved to find another doctor and to keep exercising in the meantime. We walked on. I spotted a large mushroom halfway up the hill above the path and hiked up to find a chicken of the woods. Alas, it was bleached out and falling apart. "Too bad," Hue said. "Would have been a beaut in its prime."

We pressed on, crossing and recrossing the stream on well-placed stones. The dense canopy opened only at the edge of the river, the water running high from the rains. It was mesmerizing to watch that much power—the sheer physics of a river, all that mass and momentum. My phone vibrated in my pocket. It was a text from Michelle. "Glad you boys are getting some bonding time but I need someone back here to get a fire going."

"Time to boogie?" Hue asked. It was. We headed up the trail and were about halfway out when Hue let out of grunt of surprise and reached under a downed tree by his feet. The mushroom he pulled out was about the size of a softball, yellow-gray, and looked more like a piece of sea coral or a cauliflower. "*Sparassis*," he said, pronouncing the Latin name. "We call it the cauliflower mushroom." He was smiling, a good sign that it was not only edible but tasty. "They're parasitic and saprobic, usually grow on hardwoods or conifers." He saw the look on my face. "Saprobic just means that they live on decaying organisms," he said. "They're hard to clean because of all the folds and the way they sort of envelop whatever they're growing on, but they're worth the trouble." He looked happy to be bringing back something he had foraged to the meal. A little farther on, I spotted a splotch of white in the crotch of a beech. Bingo. Another lion's mane, just two or three ounces, much smaller than Michelle's. But a lion's mane nonetheless. And in prime condition, according to Hue. "Good eye," he said. I was pleased. To see something a guy like Hue misses takes a pretty good eye. I just hoped he hadn't seen it first and said nothing, in order to test me.

Michelle had been busy while we were gone. I had left the house in its usual state, which Michelle once characterized as "hostile neglect." I just figured that anyone I knew well enough to invite for dinner already knew my view that life's too short to do housework. My pre-party cleaning consisted of sweeping the floor and clearing enough space on the table to eat. Michelle, however, operated differently. Although we had decided not to share the news about getting hitched until our divorces came through, we were a unit. She may have felt it reflected badly on her to just accept the fact of my barbaric sloth, at least in the domestic arts. In any case, she had tidied the hell out of the place. It was like somebody else's house. We'd decided to punt on the notion of a completely wild dinner and had gone to Trader Joe's for a flourless chocolate birthday cake, a loaf of bread, and three bottles of wine. She had dry-rubbed the venison with coarse salt, cracked pepper, juniper berries she had foraged, and rosemary from the transplant by the front steps that was turning into an herbal Godzilla, outcompeting even the bull thistles around it. She said she also "threw together a sorbet" to serve with the cake, using serviceberries we'd picked and frozen in June. I asked how one "threw together" a sorbet. "It's just ice, fruit, a little sugar. You puree it in the food processor and then put it in the freezer."

"You mean the blender?" I asked. "I don't own a food processor."

"Of course you do," she said. And showed it to me. It was a KitchenAid, complete with three blades. It had been sitting silently in the deep, two-shelved cabinet above the fridge for years, the Buddha of kitchen appliances, use and nonuse being one and the same to it. I couldn't even have told you who gave it to me. I sure as hell didn't buy it.

On the stove was also a pot of the wild rice I'd brought back from a trip to Wisconsin, where I'd been the guest of Sam Thayer, author of two authoritative books on wild foods. We'd spent a couple of days "knocking" wild rice on lakes where the plants still grew in clean water. And then there was a sautéed mix of the four or five kinds of mushrooms from the day before, including the prized lion's mane. She greeted the one I'd found with a little cry of joy, quickly cleaning it, slicing it, and adding it to the mix. She had even gathered up the last of the garden tomatoes—they were running pretty small by October—and some basil, and chopped them up with some salt, garlic, and a drizzle of olive oil to make the bruschetta that Paula and Gordon so loved since she'd introduced them to the dish the first time they'd come for dinner to meet her.

I poured drinks for everyone, and went outside to attack the charcoal. It has always struck me how food that men aren't allowed within ten feet of in the kitchen suddenly falls under our purview once it's no longer under a roof. Equally surprising is how we somehow rise to the occasion, cooking it with a skill we were powerless to muster indoors. My dad, who couldn't make a piece of toast in the kitchen, was a skilled griller of meats in the open air, able to deliver steaks rare, medium-rare, and even the challenging rare-side-of-medium-rare some people occasionally requested. The mechanism of the phenomenon confounds me, but I've seen it happen many times. My father was a charcoal griller and passed the gene on to me. Propane is easier and faster, but you might as well be cooking inside—propane is to charcoal as digital music is to analog. I'm also intimidated by the idea of an open flame near a canister of compressed flammable gas. It's as if, having set out to make a car bomb and having it 99 percent assembled, you decided to pause and cook dinner over it.

Gordon came out to watch the fire with me. He was telling me about a walleye hole he has fished for—he stopped to do the math—sixty-five years. It's about twenty miles upstream, a place where he deems the water clean enough to eat the fish. "Only thing is they don't show up until we've had a few days of cold weather," he said. "I mean in the twenties. Some years we don't get that anymore." He studied his glass. Despite the fact that Gordon and I have known each other for well over a decade, he remains the most diffident of men. I knew he was about ready for another drink but that he would say he was just fine if asked. Instead, I wordlessly passed him the tongs as if I needed his help for a moment and took his glass from him as he reached to help me. "You got me," he muttered, but there was a smile in his voice.

Inside, Paula was inhaling the last of the bruschetta. "Man, this shit is good," she said, her mouth full. Hue looked mildly askance. I shrugged. I'd told him about Paula's inability to edit her speech. Here were my two chief tutors, as knowledgeable in their own ways about the woods as any two people I knew. But they came at it from different angles.

I threw the tenderloin onto the fire and closed the lid. Venison is a bitch to cook correctly. Being so lean makes it the most unforgiving of meats. A minute too long on the grill and it comes out gray and dry instead of red and juicy. I like it just past carnivore-red. Not so rare that it's cold inside, but not much past that, either. I'm anything but a laid-back cook. I hover, poke, and prod. I worry. I don't trust clocks. I use my fingers. After the meat began to feel more solid, I flipped it. Three minutes later, after squeezing it everywhere, I decided it was done. I had tried, as usual, to err on the rare side, since you can always throw it back on. By the time I'd let it rest and cut into it, I saw that I'd come closer to the cliff than I thought. It was on the rare side of medium-rare, but I'd just missed overcooking it. Cooking well afforded me a slightly more positive experience than killing well. But a large part of my brain insists on viewing success as having merely escaped failure.

We sat down to a table loaded with food and dug in. Hue mentioned that lion's mane was one of his favorites. Paula then offered up her opinion that lion's mane was overrated as a mushroom and that she preferred oyster mushrooms, particularly with venison. I thought the lion's mane fantastic, the taste closer to lobster than any other flavor I could think of. That a mushroom could do that was a kind of revelation. And Michelle and I exchanged knowing looks as Paula, helping herself to the mushroom sauté for the third time, took the remaining pieces of the lion for herself.

At a certain moment, Michelle leaned over and whispered, "Look around you." I did.

"Yeah?" I said.

"You did this," she said. "Think of where you were two years ago. You knew Paula and Gordon, but now they're like family." This was true. In fact, I'd insisted they come for Christmas dinner at my mom's in Bethesda. "You found and became friends with Hue. You found me through Hue. You got this deer. You grew the tomatoes and basil and garlic we're eating. You knocked wild rice in Wisconsin and brought it home. You and I picked the serviceberries. We found the mushrooms we're eating." I looked around the table. The thought hadn't occurred to me, but it was true. I'd had a direct hand in more than half of what we were all eating. I looked around the room. We were an unlikely group, but these, I realized, were my closest friends.

Paula, always the soul of discretion, said, "What are you two talking about over there?" She was trying to be her belligerent self, only by this time she was too well fed. As if she were happy in spite of her best efforts.

"Who wants to know?" I shot back. Hue held up his empty wineglass, signaling that all the bottles on the table were dead. I gathered them up and repaired to the kitchen to open more. Michelle's words kept hitting deeper. I had found the love of my life while learning to forage. I'd eaten things I'd never dreamed of, from my lawn salad and caribou eyeball to the heart of a deer to frogs to herring I'd caught and smoked myself. I'd been to the arctic and the Pacific and the Atchafalaya Basin. I don't know how long I stood there turning it all over. I do know what broke my reverie. It was Paula, leaning over to tap Michelle on the arm.

"I ever tell you about teaching this goofball to make a pie? Jesus Christ, honey, whatever you do, don't ever let that man near a stove."

Acknowledgments

This book would never have been written without the cooperation and support of many people. Everyone mentioned in these pages helped. So did many who aren't mentioned. I apologize in advance to anyone I've left out.

Special thanks are due to Chris Parris-Lamb, my agent. If you are a print journalist for any length of time, you develop an rat-like tolerance to all stimulants, except an absolute deadline of the kind not often found in the world of book publishing. Chris went above and beyond what any agent owes an author and held me to the deadlines I couldn't impose on myself. For which I am ever grateful.

Special thanks also to Michelle Gienow, who unstintingly gave her encouragement, support, and advice. Paula Smith knew Michelle was smarter than I was instantly. It took me longer to realize this.

Jack Unruh, who did the illustrations on the jacket, is actually an incredibly sweet man and stalwart friend. He just can't bring himself to make me look pretty. Jack, we need to talk about this. Thanks to Morgan Entrekin at Grove/Atlantic for not pulling the plug when others would have. To Sid Evans, who helped me conceive and organize much of the book. To Jamison Stoltz and Deb Seager. To Paula Smith, Gordon Leisch, Dickie Tehaan, Ray and Joe Fletcher, Danny Ward. To Charlie Castaldi, Gioconda Belli, Heather Josyln. Rich "Hue" Huston. Greg Hannan. Samuel Thayer. Steve Adams. Mike and Alice Bienvenu. Jody, Tracy and Bryce Meche. Toni DeBoisier. Casey Bedouin. T. Eward Nickens. Kirk and Camilla Lombard, who put up with my snoring in their spare room for a week. Factual errors in Chapter Seven attributed to Kirk are, without exception, mine. Dr. Milton Love, thank you for your marvelous books. (And please note that Kirk is worried you'll blame him for my errors.) Jordan Grosser. Feral Kevin. The Gwich'in Tribal Council and the residents of Arctic Village, Alaska. Especially Charlie and Marion Swaney. Alice Smoke, Maggie Roberts, Jonathan John and Roy Henry. To Scott Wallace. To my editors at *Field & Stream,* including Anthony Licata, Joan McKenna, Mike Toth, Nate Matthews, David E. Petzal, and Slaton White.

To Emma and Olivia Heavey. And to my mom, Elizabeth R. Heavey, who gave me *The Joy of Cooking* in the hope that I would learn to cook. No one can say you didn't try.